A NEW HISTORY OF THE ORGAN

The west-end organ of the *Grote Kerk, Alkmaar*, built in 1639–45 and drawn by Pieter Saenredam in 1661. For a similar design, see Plate 15. The protusion in the left foreground is the tester of the pulpit. See also pp. 141–2.

A NEW HISTORY OF THE
ORGAN

From the Greeks to the Present Day

Peter Williams

INDIANA UNIVERSITY PRESS
Bloomington and London

Manufactured in Great Britain

Library of Congress Cataloging in Publication Data

Williams, Peter F
  A new history of the organ from the Greeks to the present day.

  Includes indexes and bibliographical references.
  1 Organ—History. I. Title.
ML550.W38   786.6'2   79–2176
ISBN 0–253–15704–8   1 2 3 4 5 84 83 82 81 80

Contents

Contents

Illustrations

Acknowledgements

Line drawings have been prepared for this book from sketches made by the author. Photographs, unless acknowledged below, come from the author's private collection.

Frontispiece Bildarchiv der Oest. Nationalbibliothek, Vienna (ALB 42040)

1 Studio Camera (Régis de Roten), Sion

2, 10 J. L. Coignet, Chateauncuf-Val-de-Bargis

3 Photo Mas, Barcelona

4 Foto Villani, Bologna

6 Photo-Commissie, Rijksmuseum, Amsterdam

13, 19, 20, 21, 22 Jürgen Ahrend, Leer

15 Lichtbeelden Institut, Amsterdam

16 Bundesdenkmalamt Oesterreich, Vienna

17 Caisse Nationale des Monuments Historiques, Paris

19, 27 Lala Aufsberg (Bildarchiv Foto Marburg), Marburg

23, 26 Deutsche Fotothek, Dresden

37, 45 Marcussen, Aabenraa

38 Rijksdienst (Monumentenzord), Utrecht

49 Koenig, Sarre-Union

Preface

By 1977, the centenary year of the third and best-known edition of that remarkable book, Hopkins and Rimbault's *The Organ*, many of the facts and conjectures behind its section on organ history—the best published organ history before the twentieth century—had been confirmed, denied or refined. Much progress has taken place even in the last few years, and the most recent English organ histories are scarcely more up to date. The present book, therefore, is both a belated salute to the third edition of Hopkins and Rimbault and an attempt in its own right to bring the history of organs up to date, or at least to trace that history as I understand it.

There are several reasons for writing a new history of organs. Firstly, like all complex subjects, it is a history that needs to be looked at afresh each generation. Written sources need to be reinterpreted; old organs need to be re-heard and their authenticity assessed; the music needs to be studied in relation to very specific types of organ; and the trends in new organs need to be compared and evaluated. Secondly, too many histories have been attempted in which scholarship is not matched with personal experience, or *vice-versa*; the tendency today is to see these two as indispensable to each other, and in that respect this new history is mirroring current tendencies. Thirdly, the histories still in print are all confined within certain boundaries—of time, period, scope, national emphasis or inbred traditionalism, their length reflecting not so much comprehensiveness as what material was available to their authors. Most histories suffer from provincialism, and the chief differences between them have been only that the province itself has varied from author to author.

This book attempts to trace the history of organs briefly but comprehensively, striking a balance between the structural detail of importance to the technically minded and the archival or theoretical matter of interest to other readers. I have tried to strike a balance also between one period and another, not describing a disproportionate number of nineteenth- and twentieth-century apparatuses, for example. The simple reference system includes most of the key sources of information listed at the end of each section; these lists have been kept brief and may therefore serve as select bibliographies, relying particularly on the most recent sources which, in addition to containing the latest research, will also be found to give longer and more complete bibliographies. The translations into

English have all been newly made by me for this book, unless the reference note shows otherwise. The illustrations serve two purposes: while the line drawings show crucial principles of construction and so stand for many periods and areas, the photographs represent a more personal choice of organ cases and other details. So many of the famous organ cases have already been reproduced so often that this collection of photographs concentrates rather on organs typical of their kind and less splendidly exceptional.

Finally, I would like to assure those organists who pick up books on organs in order to see if their favourite instrument is described, that should they be disappointed on that score they can nevertheless consider themselves participants in an instrument with the longest history of all, with a repertory larger than that of any other instrument and with a magnificence beyond any other musical invention from the Greeks to the present day.

Edinburgh, June 1978 PETER WILLIAMS

Note on Pitch-names and Compass

In this book, octave-pitches are shown as follows:

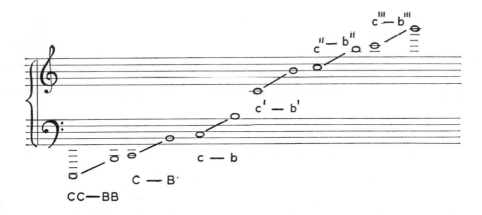

Compass-indications show the compass either for manual and pedal alone, e.g. manual C–d''', pedal C–d', or for both together, e.g. C–d'–d'''. Incomplete compass is shown by specifying those notes between which the appropriate accidentals were omitted, e.g. CDE–c'''d''' shows that C♯, D♯ and c♯''' were left out.

Abbreviated stop-lists show firstly flue-stops (mixtures expressed as Roman numerals), and secondly reed-stops (trumpet-type followed by others). Thus

8.4.2⅔.2.IV.II.16.8.4.8

indicates principals or flutes 8', 4', 2⅔' and 2'; mixtures of IV and II ranks (such as Mixtur and Zimbel); trumpets 16', 8' and 4'; regal etc. 8'.

European Organs

Ar	Arnstadt
Fr	Frederiksborg
Gr	Grosshartmannsdorf
	(Nr. Freiberg)
Po	Potsdam (Nr. Berlin)
Ch	Chirk
NS	Nieuw Scheemda
	and Scheemda
Do	Doetinghem
My	Malmesbury (Nr. Bristol)
Fd	Frauenfeld (Nr. Zürich)
Ei	Einsiedeln (Nr. Zürich)
Mu	Muri (Nr. Zürich)
Gn	Gröningen (Nr. Halberstadt)
K.L.	Kloster Lüne (Nr. Luneburg)
Ne	Netstal (Nr. Zürich)
Hi	Hirsau (Nr. Stuttgart)
ML	Maria Langegg (Nr. Melk)
Ma	Marienhafe and
	Westerhusen
Me	Merseburg and
	Naumburg
Hu	Hagenau (Nr. Strasbourg)
Kl	Klosterneuburg (Nr. Vienna)
Ol	Oliwa (Nr. Danzig)
Ot	Ottobeuren and
	Rot-an-der-Rot
Ro	Roskilde (Nr. Copenhagen)
S.M.	St Maximin
S.F.	St Florian (Nr. Linz)
S.D.	St-Denis (Nr. Paris)
S.J.	St Juan de las Abadesas
Tr	Treviso (Nr. Venice)
O.R.	Old Radnor

I   The Word 'Organ'

In its earliest known appearances, the term *organon* (ὄργανον) was used by such writers as Plato (*Laws*) and Aristotle (*Politics*) to denote not a musical instrument as such but a tool or 'instrument' in the more general sense: *organon* is a tool with which to do a job of work or *ergon*. Both *ergon* and *organon* are traced to the root ս̯erǧ-, leading to two branches *uerg-ergon-Werk-work* and *uerg-ergon-organon-organ*. This is a curious coincidence that makes the once common German term *ein Orgelwerck* a tautology not noticed by Praetorius or any other classically educated theorist.* In Plato's *Republic* and in the work of later writers, *organon* denotes any kind or all kinds of musical instrument, tool or contrivance; to none of them does it mean 'pipe organ' of any particular kind. Even Hero of Alexandria's famous first-century term 'hydraulic organ' (ὄργανον ὑδραυλικόν) should not be understood as necessarily meaning a musical instrument in modern parlance. Rather, 'hydraulic organ' should be seen as indicating 'a tool or device making use of an *aulos* operated by water', in which phrase even *aulos* probably denotes not a musical wind instrument, either reed or fipple, but merely a 'pipe' in the more general sense of tube or conduit. Thus, the adjective 'hydraulic' refers to the use of water and air conduits, and the device 'hydraulic organ' has no specifically musical function, at least by definition.

In the later periods of classical and early patristic Latin, the various terms *organum*, *organa* and *organis* gradually move from the general usages found in classical Greek to something more specific in which the context shows there to have been a musical connection of some sort. Using the term *organum* to refer to a kind of polyphony is of course post-classical and has led to many speculations on one side or the other ever since; it should be noted that Arabic sources contemporary with early polyphony of the organum kind also had their own versions of the Greek for referring to the instrument itself (*hedhrula* for *hydraulis*, *urghanon* for *organon*), and there is no ambiguity there between an instrument and a musical *genre*. In medieval Latin further ambiguity arises about whether the term should be singular or plural.

* To the etymologist of today, however, tautological or repetitive nouns are familiar (e.g. 'greyhound' is constructed from two words of similar meaning).

In his commentary on Psalm 150, St. Augustine correctly explains the Vulgate Latin *organum* as derived from 'a Greek term' and was quite scholar enough to realize that the Vulgate was wrong to use the word in this psalm. According to John de Trevisa's translation of St. Augustine in 1398, the definition reads (Carter 1961):

> Organum is a generall name of all Instrumentes of Musyk: and is nethelesse specyally apropryte to the Instrument that is made of many pypes: and blowe[n] with belowes.

That simple sentence amounts to a complete history of the organ. Elsewhere, St. Augustine uses both singular *organon* and plural *organa* in the same sentence to refer to the same object, as do later writers in various languages—old High German (Notker's *orglun* and *organâ*, 10–11th century) and middle English (e.g. 'money paied to the organe maker for the orgonis', 14th century). The singular–plural usage no doubt also bears on the reason why present-day Slav languages still use the plural form (*orgány*, *varhany*) and how it is that in French the gender changes between singular and plural (*petit orgue*, *petites orgues*). Presumably *organa* looked like a feminine singular word, as was the case with other neuter plurals in French and Norman.

In English, such derivations from *organ* as 'organic' and 'organize' are usually found only much later and are in general characteristic of the living vocabulary of the renaissance. Sometimes they are found first in a musical sense (e.g. *organic*, 'like an organ'), sometimes not. Thus *organize*, 'to give an orderly structure to', appears in the seventeenth century, while *organize*, 'to apply one or more sets of organ-pipes to' other instruments, appears only in the eighteenth century, no doubt a peculiar usage derived from French *organiser* made familiar for hybrid instruments by theorists of Dom Bedos's period (1770s). The English plural *organs*, like its French and German equivalents, seems to have belonged exclusively to the musical use of the term, and in some languages the singular form appears to have been much the later of the two. In seventeenth-century England, a 'pair of organs' denoted an organ with two manuals or, more precisely, with two cases ('A Double Organ, vizt. a Great Organ and a Chaire Organ' at Canterbury Cathedral, 1662); but during the sixteenth century, particularly in documents prepared by non-musical scribes— i.e. sources far less useful than the frequent reference to them now suggests—the phrases 'a pair of organs' or 'a pair of virginals or regals' may sometimes have indicated something now unknown, but in most instances meant merely 'an instrument of many pipes or strings'. Rarely will it be certain what precisely the term meant to an English scribe, not least since he very likely took over that very phrase 'a pair of' from French or Flemish usage (e.g. *une peres d'orgues* at Beaune, Burgundy, 1447). Similar points could be made about such phrases as 'a pair of stairs' found in fifteenth-century French and English,* because as in contemporary German, 'pair' (*paar*, *ein Paar*) indicated not only 'two' components but 'any number more than one'.

A further conclusion to be drawn from the origins of the word 'organ' is that all appearances of that word in any English translation of the Bible are unreliable. Old Testament Hebrew uses the word *ûgab* on four occasions, apparently to indicate some kind of wind instrument, perhaps a (vertical) flute; but there is no justification for translating it as 'organ' in any sense. Septuagint Greek uses *organon* most often in its general sense of 'tool', while Vulgate Latin seems to use *organum* in both specific and general senses. Obviously it was the mistranslation that caused at least one medieval illuminator to depict the unspecified instruments (*organa nostra*) hanging on willows in Psalm 137 as little organs slung on the branches (Stuttgart Psalter, 10th century); and very likely we should see any harps hanging there as equally unreliable, charm notwithstanding. However, some Hebrew scholars have thought not only that *ûgab* means 'organ' but that ' "Organ" in the original is derived from a Root which signifies to *Love with ardency and vehemence*', in the words of the Revd. Mr. John Newte (*Lawfulness and Use of Organs*, London, 1696). He is referring to the verb *âgab* from which *ûgab* (and Greek *agape*, 'brotherly love') may ultimately be derived. If this were so, then 'organ' was so called because it had a lovely or sweet tone, rather like the medieval wind instrument *douçaine* or *dulzian*, from *dulcis*, 'sweet'; but alas it is not so.

Bibliography

CARTER, H. H., *A Dictionary of Middle English Musical Terms* (Bloomington, 1961)
LÖSCHHORN, B., 'Die Bedeutungsentwicklung von lat. *organum* bis Isidor von Sevilla', *Museum Helveticum*, 28 (1971), 193–226
Oxford English Dictionary
RECKOW, F., 'Organum', *Handwörterbuch der musikalischen Terminologie*, ed. H. H. Eggebrecht (Wiesbaden, 1972–)

* Such etymologies also suggest that in the case of virginals and regals, the plural form is the most correct today, since the singular form is not contemporary with the instruments themselves and dates only from after their obsolescence. We should say 'virginals' and 'regals', but 'organ'.

For some 2,200 years now it has been possible to define the organ as an instrument with four basic components: 1 a wind-raising mechanism worked by lever or pulley, sending air under pressure to 2 a 'chest' storing that wind until it is admitted by 3 a mechanism worked by some kind of 'keyboard' to 4 one or more rows or 'ranks' of pipes. If any one of these components is absent, the instrument is not properly an organ—for example, if during the eighth century it was a question of a group of Arab slaves blowing into the airchest or if during the twentieth it is more a question of electronic sound-producers replacing true pipes. To what extent other instruments known in east Mediterranean cultures influenced the hydraulic or bellows organ—particularly the syrinx, the synagogue magrephah and the bagpipes—can only be conjectured, and no history of the organ can usefully be diverted by such conjectures. In the case of the Chinese *shêng* the relationship is even more conjectural, despite assertions of previous historians.

There is no evidence of any kind, archaeological, literary or even mythological, that can be interpreted with certainty as suggesting pipe organs to have been known before the Hellenistic period or to have originated elsewhere than in the areas under Hellenistic influence. Later authors such as Philo of Byzantium (3rd century B.C.), Athenaeus (*Deipnosophistes*, 2nd century A.D.) and Vitruvius (*De Architectura*, early 1st century A.D.?) claim the organ to have been the invention of one man, Ctesibius (Ktesibios) of Alexandria, a third-century B.C. engineer who applied air under pressure to the working of the pump, the water clock, the catapult and the hydraulis. For him the hydraulis or hydraulic organ served more as a model or demonstration of the principles of hydraulics, i.e. the science of water harnessed for power, than as a musical instrument of new and vast potential. Thus when Pliny the Elder refers to Ctesibius's *hydraulis organis*, he should be understood as referring to 'hydraulic machines or contrivances', although Vitruvius himself suggests that Ctesibius first observed how sound was generated from his pressurized air ('wind', in modern parlance) and then 'made use of that principle in devising hydraulic organs'. It is not surprising that some later commentators such as Tertullian (160–225) accredit the invention of the hydraulis not to Ctesibius but to his illustrious contemporary Archimedes; but whoever invented it, all later sources including modern histories that assume it to have had a musical purpose are making assumptions difficult to justify.

The general principles and some of the details of Ctesibius's hydraulis were described in two particular sources: Hero of Alexandria (probably 1st century A.D.), who may have worked from Ctesibius's own *Commentaries*, now lost; and the Roman Vitruvius, who had very likely seen an organ of some sophistication and could expand his source with further details of interest to himself. Hero does not mention Ctesibius by name and his description covers an instrument less developed than Vitruvius's. Fig. 1 outlines the blowing mechanism Hero describes. On its upward stroke, the plunger in a cylinder, operated by a pump handle, pushes air firstly to close the inlet valve on the right and secondly to pass through

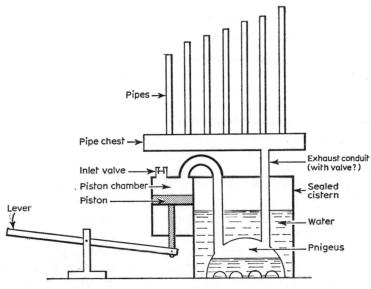

Figure 1

the conduit on the left to a *pnigeus*, a hemispherical chamber held in a cistern containing water. The air under pressure ('wind') forces the water out through the openings at the bottom of the *pnigeus*, thus raising the water level in the cistern; the weight of the displaced water gives pressure to the wind thus forced along the exhaust conduit to the pipe chest. When the plunger is pulled out to prepare for the next stroke, the weight of the water also maintains pressure in the *pnigeus*. Presumably a valve, not shown by Hero, prevented air from escaping along the first conduit back into the piston chamber. When in the chest, the wind is prevented from blowing the pipes by the mechanism shown in Fig. 2. When the key is depressed, a perforated strip running between the top of the chest and the foot of the pipe is moved into position, and the wind passes through to the pipe; when the hand releases the key, a horn spring pulls the strip back to its original position, and the wind is blocked.

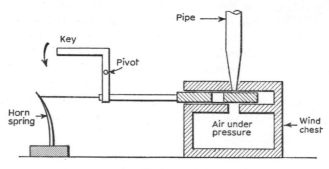

Figure 2

Vitruvius describes how wind for the pipes in his organ was provided by two cylinders operating in alternation, many examples of which, judging from late Roman depictions of various kinds, required two blowers. Since Hero's sketch is merely diagrammatic, one can not know that the hydraulis described by him did not also have two blowers. But another element recorded by Vitruvius certainly did represent a major advance in organ design: his ranks were separable, i.e. each rank of pipes had a valve which could be closed to cut off its wind. The chest had a channel which ran lengthways under each rank of pipes, and wind was admitted to this channel by a valve operated by an iron handle. The key spring was made of iron, very likely inferior to Hero's horn. As Vitruvius's keys seem to have been placed immediately below their pipes, either the keys were unequally spaced or the spacing between them must have been wide enough to accommodate the largest pipes, which were still modest in size.

In the hydraulis, the water cistern is effectively a reservoir of wind or air under pressure; the wind itself could be raised by means other than piston and cylinder. Forge bellows were already well known and their potential was described in the *Iliad*, so that at least in theory the water of a hydraulic organ could be compressed by wind raised by bellows as well as by a piston and cylinder. The cistern merely stored and stabilized pressure. There is no evidence that wind was raised by bellows before the second century A.D., however, when Julius Pollux describes what seems to be a bellows organ as something smaller and less powerful than the hydraulis. Nor does Hero's account give any indication of what kind of pipes were involved (flue or reed, open or stopped) or what their material, size, compass, tuning, pitch or voicing were. The term 'hydraulic' does not of itself imply that the water organ sounded like a set of *auloi*, which themselves had as varying a nature as they have a dubious etymology; nor can the reports of the loudness of outdoor organs of the late Roman Empire be regarded as unequivocal, since notions of loudness change. Nevertheless, everything points to the hydraulis having a strong sound and its wind pressure being higher and more constant than that produced by forge bellows.

That Ctesibius was also said by Vitruvius and others to have invented a water clock offers an interesting parallel to the makers of organs and clocks in the medieval cathedrals of western Europe and may also suggest how traditional are the linking of, and even obsession with, various kinds of mechanical gadgetry. Either way, specific musical references to the playing of organs date only from some century and a half after Ctesibius. Perhaps between those periods it remained 'a museum piece, a mechanical curiosity in a show-case to be exhibited to scholars passing through Alexandria' (Perrot 1971, p. 43). The Delphic inscription of *c*. 90 B.C. tells of one Antipatros competing at Delphi on the hydraulic organ (ὕδραυλος), playing for two days and 'covering himself with glory'. Cicero, Lucretius, Petronius and others wrote of the instrument's powers, and at least one emperor (Nero) had it as his favourite instrument: like Caligula's antics, Nero's organ was an emblem of his foibles, a sensual epicureanism of the kind ridiculed by Cicero. Not the least interesting element in the whole history of the organ is a persistent tradition of puritan criticism of it, writers from Cicero to Milton and beyond seeing it as a temptation away from Reason or from Right. No doubt one cause for this was that by the second century A.D. at the latest the Roman organ was to be heard at some of the more important theatres, games, amphitheatres, circuses, banquets and even perhaps processions; one third-century source (a Greek inscription at Rhodes) also suggests it to have been played in Dionysian festivals.

But whatever their musical use, water organs had several costly requirements—precision engineering, good materials, intricacy—and were difficult to maintain, move from place to place and keep from corrosion. It is not difficult to imagine bellows gradually replacing the piston, cylinders and water cistern, but when, where, by whom and how is not known. Such references as that by Julian the Apostate (332–63) may refer to a bag of bull-hide feeding the pipes; but it is not clear from this whether the bellows replaced the pump or cistern or both, nor even whether a 'bag' is the same as a bellows. Nevertheless, inscriptions found in several provinces far from Rome (Arles, Colchester, Budapest, Asia Minor) show the organ to have been played in gladiator contests, though how—as prelude, interlude, background music, postlude—can only be conjectured. In the Nenning mosaic, the player seems to be poised during a gladiator fight, apparently to play at a suitable moment—perhaps a death signal, or to rouse the spectators in some way. Organs were still to be heard in the later Roman Empire, and such late poets as Claudian (*c.* 400) describe organ playing as making a major contribution to the celebrations attending weddings, the swearing-in of new consuls, and various kinds of banquets during a period in which 'the singer has thrust out the philosopher' (Ammianus Marcellinus, *c.* 350).

The few references of the fifth and sixth centuries include some by the early Church Fathers, particularly those living on the south and eastern coasts of the Mediterranean, who may have seen provincial equivalents of the outdoor organs played in the various public shows held in Rome itself. But whether it was from personal experience that such writers as Boethius wrote of hydraulic organs, or Cassiodorus of a bellows organ with wooden keys, will never be certain. The general picture seems to be that bellows organs were known in the Eastern Empire to a greater extent or at an earlier point than in the Western, where the hydraulis disappears with the Decline during the fifth and sixth centuries. While much can be conjectured from iconography, little if anything is certain; thus in the Nenning mosaic only the context (some kind of gladiatorial contest), the position of the organist (standing or seated high) and the organ's approximate elevation size (one by two metres) are at all certain. Even the number of pipes is unclear, as is the reason for the faint decrease in the length of the pipes (for enharmonic tuning? because of pictorial licence?). Mosaics, bas-reliefs, terracottas, coins and other objects provide nearly 40 extant representations of the Greek-Roman organ; often it is alone, at other times it is playing with one or more instruments, particularly brass. Some representations suggest the instrument, perhaps in smaller sizes, to have been known in the houses of the well-to-do, where girls or women played it; other sources show the organ to have been present in theatres or at plays, though for what purpose is unknown. It is probably out of the question that such Christian writers as Cassiodorus (6th century) heard even the most hesitant, primitive polyphony or organum, either in or out of church. That the nature of the hydraulis was soon forgotten or misunderstood is suggested by the eleventh-century MS Berne Anonymous (a good source in its own right), where it is stated that organ pipes can be made hydraulic by placing them in water, which is sucked through the pipes and causes them to sound—a fancy still infecting the imagination of Jesuit amateur physicists of the seventeenth century.

Parts of two Roman organs are said to exist: fragments from Pompeii (now in the Museo Nazionale, Naples) and major remnants of a small organ found in Aquincum, Hungary (now in the Aquincum Museum, Budapest). But the Pompeii fragments, perhaps from two different instruments, are not certainly part of any organ, although their pipes are cast, probably not unlike those of some Roman organs. The Aquincum organ is more nearly complete, but it was so 'reconstructed' in 1958 that even further work done since 1969 has not quite elucidated some of the questions. Its dedicatory plaque has the date 228; there are four rows of 13 bronze pipes each, one row open and three rows stopped with oak stoppers; all pipes were cast, not rolled. The chest is made of wood, lined inside and out with thin bronze sheets. The whole organ is very small, about 60 cm high, 38 cm wide and 25 cm deep. Within the chest below each rank of pipes runs a channel to which wind is admitted by slotted metal slides pierced with one central hole; the wooden keys operate lateral sliders. The pipes show a complex form and structure at the mouth, whereby the air stream is directed by the shape of the pipe foot itself ('pinched' in towards the flue) on to the upper lip. The open and stopped pipes differ in detail but not in principle.

Two crucial questions remain about the Aquincum organ and its type. First, how was the wind raised? No trace of this part of the mechanism exists, and it can only be guessed whether the organ was a small hydraulis of the kind described some time earlier by Vitruvius (as the inscription 'hydra' on the instrument suggests) or a bellows organ without water cistern, with wood-and-leather bellows liable to perish quickly or to leave behind only fragments misunderstood by the inexperienced archaeologists of a later period. It seems clear enough that the Byzantine organ of the Dark Ages was blown by a bellows-blower who arrived with his bellows and attached it to the organ before he began work; the notion of an organ with its own forge bellows is probably medieval, not classical or Byzantine, and builders learnt to produce constant wind only by providing numbers of such bellows (26 at Winchester Cathedral, for example).

The second question for the Aquincum organ is, were the four ranks played together at will or does the small and apparently non-proportional variation in pipe length between the ranks—which can be modified by the stoppers or, in the case of the open pipes, by the bronze tuning-slides—indicate that each rank played 13 notes of one particular mode and was not meant to combine with any other? This last was shown by Walcker-Mayer in 1970 to be quite plausible, for the result is that one rank has a Pythagorean diatonic scale c'–g''' while the three stopped ranks represent similar segments of the Hyperiastian, Lydian and Phrygian modes or *tonoi*. The little organ would then have been able to produce treble flute-like sounds in four different *tonoi*, like a little portative organ of one rank in later medieval ensembles. Some late sources suggest that different wind and string instruments had different *tonoi*, so perhaps the Aquincum organ was designed to play in varying ensembles.

Modern attempts at reconstructing water organs suggest that they might have had a wind pressure anywhere between 7·5 and 30 cm, but it is not known if the pipework was always flue and, if so, whether the diameters were constant. Literary sources often refer to fingers playing the keys, but there can hardly have been anything of the finger technique familiar from the later fifteenth century. Written sources give little evidence on several of the most important factors, but inconography suggests that the pipes were usually flue, their diameter constant, their tuning not necessarily diatonic, chromatic or even enharmonic, and that chests with more than one rank may have produced different timbres and perhaps fifth-sounding ranks. None of these details is certain, however, and while the Aquincum organ confirms one or two of them, it is only knowledge of the later organ that encourages us to read some of the other details into the evidence for the various kinds of classical hydraulis.

Bibliography

APEL, W., 'Early History of the Organ', *Speculum*, 23 (1948), 191f

DEGERING, H., *Die Orgel, ihre Erfindung und ihre Geschichte bis zur Karolingerzeit* (Münster, 1905)

KABA, M., *Die römische Orgel von Aquincum* (Budapest, 1976)

PERROT, J., *L'Orgue de ses origines hellénistiques à la fin du XIIIe siècle* (Paris, 1965; Eng. trans., adapted, London, 1971)

WALCKER-MAYER, W., *Die römische Orgel von Aquincum* (Stuttgart, 1970; Eng. trans., Ludwigsburg, 1972)

The Byzantine and Arabic Organ

The new Roman Empire of the East, based on Constantinople, had already made its own mark by the fifth century, and its scholarship and theology had become far removed from the practical technology of Alexandria or Rome. The old Greek treatises were preserved in Byzantine copies: Philo of Byzantium, author of engineering works and perhaps a younger contemporary of Ctesibius, is himself witness to the interchange between his native city and Alexandria. But although it was on Byzantine sources that the Arabs later based their own treatises, in Byzantium itself practical engineering projects like the making of organs remained undeveloped. At the same time, it is probable that by the eighth century western Europe itself had forgotten such Roman masterpieces as the Vitruvian hydraulis, for no extant literary or iconographical source makes any reference to organs in Italy or in the lands of the Franks, the Goths or the Lombards. In the absence of other information it does seem that the revival of the organ in western Europe during the ninth and tenth centuries came about because the instrument was introduced—or a few examples of it were introduced—from the Eastern Empire.

Although some Byzantine sources seem to hint otherwise, it is certain that the organ was not used in the church itself; however flourishing an architectural school there might have been for the early churches of Anatolia or Old Georgia, the organ was not one of its interests. Nor did the Orthodox Churches ever change their position on this issue, though certain churches in the sixteenth and seventeenth centuries may have had organs. In the Eastern Empire the organ remained part of a secular tradition, in particular for the courtly pomp of the capital city itself. It was no doubt from their use at banquets, weddings, processions and circus events such as chariot races that organs were in part made of or plated in gold and given costly decoration of the kind described so enthusiastically by the scribes of that and later periods. Both the Blue and Green factions at court had their organs, but it is difficult to believe that the instrument was common or ever became an object of less than wonder and surprise. In his palace the Emperor had automata, in particular the famous 'golden tree' with moving, whistling birds activated by wind produced by pressure of water—presumably not unlike the sixteenth- and seventeenth-century garden organs built for some of the stately homes of Europe, from the Villa d'Este at Tivoli to the Duke of Devonshire's house at Chatsworth. But in the Emperor's palace could also have been heard true organs, in which the ninth-century Emperor Theophilus took an active interest, and which his son had melted down and handed over to the mint. Nothing is known of the sound, pipework or function of the organ in the Great Reception Room, nor how isolated it remained; but one ninth-century source refers to '60 copper pipes' in what appears to have been a large table-organ. 'Copper' no doubt means bronze, and it may well have been that the instrument, wherever it was, was blown by bellows without water cistern; an Arabic source of the following century describes bellows feeding air into an organ of some kind (Farmer 1931, pp. 58–60):

> It is made of three large bags of buffalo skins, one being joined to another. And there is mounted upon the head of the middle bag a large skin. Then there are mounted upon this skin brass pipes, having holes [i.e. open pipes with changing diameters] upon recognized ratios, from which proceed beautiful sounds, pleasing or melancholy, according to what the player desires.

Unfortunately, but typically, it is not as clear from this as a first reading might suggest, whether there are two bellows or three (see also Fig. 4) and whether there is a reservoir or not. But the Emperor Theophilus was said to have had 'two very large organs, entirely of gold', and it is significant that his architect should be anxious that they should rival those of the Caliphs of Baghdad. Such details confirm the prestige attached to organs received as gifts in the courts of western Europe or the East; but the technical details of them will never be known, and little should be read into the phrase 'very large'.

Evidence is better on organs being sent and received as special gifts or serving as a sign of regal power. Thus organs were sent to Spain on a diplomatic mission from Byzantium, and in 757 the Emperor Constantine Copronymus sent the most famous organ-gift of all, to Pepin, King of the Franks at Compiègne, a gesture much commented on by the scribes of the period. Later, a Benedictine scribe of St. Gall (probably Notker) reported that the 'King of Constantinople' also sent an organ to Charlemagne himself in 812, with bronze pipes, 'bellows of bull leather' and three specific sound-effects (the rumbling of thunder, the trembling of a lyre, the tinkling of *cymbala*). In far later sources these would indicate the *pleno*, the flutes and the mixtures. But the source is isolated and therefore doubtful, the language hyperbolic and perhaps intentionally psalmodic in flavour, and the whole story looks like a gloss on the Pepin episode. Thus it is idle to speculate on whether the *cymbala* were little bells activated by the bellows or high-pitched mixtures for each note. What is clear is that such instruments were not church organs but extravagant gifts, not unlike the thirteenth-century organ of 90 pipes sent from one Arab court (probably the Caliph of Baghdad's) to the Emperor of China or the sixteenth-century automaton sent by Elizabeth I to the Sultan.

Several ninth-century chronicles refer to the arrival at Aachen in 826 of the Venetian priest Georgius as an event of importance: his undertaking to build a hydraulic organ may have seemed to bring to the west the fruits of eastern technological labours and as such to have been more than the simple contract of an organ-builder. A poem glorifying Charlemagne's son Louis speaks of Georgius's *organum* as a national or royal symbol of power (Perrot 1965, p. 397; Perrot 1971, p. 213):

Organa quin etiam, quae numquam Francia crevit,
Even organs, which the Kingdom of the Franks had not yet seen,

unde Pelasga tument regna superba nimis,
wherein the pride of the Greeks swelled inordinately,

et quis te solis, Caesar, superasse putabat
and was the only reason they felt superior to you, Ceasar,

Constantinopolis, nunc Aquis aula tenet
in Constantinople—now [such organs] are at the court of Aachen

Another source calls it a *hydraulicon*; if it had musical purposes, as distinct from scientific–didactic, it too would have been used on occasions of courtly pomp rather than in the chapel services. One contemporary pictorial source, the early ninth-century Utrecht Psalter, made in France (perhaps at the Abbey of Hautvillers, near Rheims), shows a hydraulis taking part in an ensemble illustrating Psalm 149; it is drawn with a better understanding of instrument and playing method than was once thought, probably deriving from iconographical sources of an earlier period, sixth- or even fifth-century Byzantium. The two hydraulic chambers and the two sets of pipes—with a common diameter but with lengths in the proportions $1 : 2 : 3 : 4$—are plausible enough (Hardouin 1966, p. 36–9), offering some parallel to the signalling purposes of *cymbala* in the early medieval church, i.e. as sets of four hand-bells or *quadrillon* (*carillon*). There was no question of this organ producing a melody as such, nor does such psalter illustration provide evidence of how or even whether instruments were indeed used in church, particularly in the church services of either Mass or Office.

That literary or pictorial sources, particularly in the centuries before printing made exchange of knowledge easier, tend to create their own tradition irrespective of the technical data that are supposed to be their basis, is even clearer from the Arabic documents. By the time Arabic or Islamic culture had reached its high level during the eighth to tenth centuries, scribes knew of organs with both pumps and bellows but rarely seem actually to have seen one. In copying an earlier source with an explanatory diagram, for example, a scribe would make it more elegant and thus lose some or all of the character of the original: it would become less accurate and even ultimately unintelligible. This process has so affected the source material concerning the famous Muristos that it is difficult to be certain what he is describing.

Muristos appears to have been a Greek or Byzantine, probably copying, compiling, editing or glossing—it is not clear which—the works of Ctesibius, perhaps for the Muslim centre at Baghdad. The Arabic sources give little hint as to his period or origins, an issue somewhat complicated by Farmer's observation in 1931 that in Arabic script *Qatasibiyus* (Ctesibius) has a graphic similarity to *Muristos*. A tenth-century manuscript refers to his treatises on 'Flue-pipe Organ and the Reed-pipe Organ' (Perrot 1971, p. 190), but the contents are not known, nor is the reliability of these terms at all certain. But the copies that do exist talk of two instruments, neither of which is a true organ but both of which no doubt derive from Ctesibius's lost *Commentaries* and are there-fore important. The first 'organ' had a chest of 12 pipes fed with air under pressure from a regulator into which four men blew gently. How is not clear, but the weight of the pipes compresses the wind which is admitted to each pipe through a valve or stopper, presumably worked by some kind of key not described. The pipes themselves may have been reeds, looking from the diagrams to have been of varying length but similar diameter; but the texts suggest the length to be the same and the diameter to vary. The loudness could be made to vary too, and Muristos's account is governed by the familiar classical claims that such simple sounds produced by twelve pipes can have various effects on the listener, softening his spirit or rousing him to activity as the case may be; ap-parently the 'organ' could do that so effectively that it was better for the blowers to stop their ears lest they be affected by the sounds they were helping to produce. Muristos is probably not speaking of melodies as such or even of the *tonoi* vividly and persistently described by Greek and Byzantine writers, but of the sounds produced by different combinations of his few pipes played with peaceful or violent wind-production.

Muristos's second or 'Great Organ' was a signal instrument perhaps like the Jewish *magrephah* and serving as a siren: the single pipe could be blown at great pressure (hence the lengthy account describing the pneumatic technique making that possible) and was used in battle by the Greeks, according to Muristos. The travelling distance of the sound has been interpreted as some 12 km (Hardouin 1966, p. 27). The wind was produced on the same principle as the hydraulis, except that four pumps were involved. The tradition for signal organs has still not been fully explored, but it could well be that the difference between a siren and an organ is finer than has been supposed and that even the early Benedictine organs—which were after all contemporary with the oldest known sources of Muristos's writings—were used more for signal purposes than for music as such.

Although there is no evidence that the Arab caliphate of Córdoba in Spain was responsible for any kind of organ being reintroduced into Europe by this route, it is certainly possible that this was so and that further work undertaken on this period in Iberian musical history may lead to a link being discovered between Spanish Arab instrument-making and ninth-century Benedictine muscial life. Whether it will ever throw light on the big questions—when were reeds first made? when did compass increase beyond an octave? when did mixtures replace one-pipe-per-note? when did the pallet replace the Vitruvian key-slider?—is very doubtful.

Bibliography

FARMER, H., *The Organ of the Ancients from Eastern Sources* (London, 1931)

HARDOUIN, P., 'De l'orgue de Pépin à l'orgue médiéval', *Revue de musicologie*, 52 (1966), 21–54

PERROT, J., *L'Orgue de ses origines hellénistiques à la fin du XIIIe siècle* (Paris, 1965; Eng. trans., adapted, London, 1971)

4   The Early Church Organ in the West

One of the greatest unsolved puzzles of music history is how and why the
organ came to be a church instrument in western Europe from about the
year 900. It would be safe to assume that before that date, and in many
cases after it, any reference to an organ, whether blown by bellows or by
piston and cylinder, whether with or without a water cistern, however
large or loud it was reported to be, was to an organ built for secular
purposes, musical, scientific, didactic or ceremonial. Probably the nearest
any organ came to being a 'church instrument' was if it was used as a
signal or siren summoning the people to a procession or perhaps to a
service.

Sources of information on organs for the period A.D. 500–1000 are so
meagre as to leave any summary potentially misleading. Thus no one
knows how typical was the gift of a Byzantine organ to King Pepin;
perhaps the Venetian priest Georgius, sent to Aachen in 826, had been
trained in an Arab or Byzantine centre; perhaps any instrument referred
to in the sources of the period was no more than a noise-machine; or
perhaps it was no more than a hydraulic engineer's model. None of these
speculations take the historian very far, but one can certainly assume that
Georgius's organ was not made for church but was taken from one
Merovingian or Carolingian residence to another (Hardouin 1966, p. 23).
Similarly, how well the hydraulis was understood in the tenth century
or whether it was ever effectively copied by craftsmen is unknown;
whether the presence of two players on the hydraulis in the Utrecht
Psalter reflects anything more than the artist's misunderstanding of
literary sources and whether the position of their hands was more than
guesswork by somebody who had never seen even the most elementary
keyboard played, are also unknown. The hyperbolic terms in which
medieval writers describe organs helps to blur further even the outlines
of organ history. There were references to organs with 1,000 breaths, like
that of St. Aldhelm of Malmesbury (translated in Mc Kinnon 1974, p. 8):

> *Si vero quisquam chordarum respuit odas,*
> but if anyone despises the songs of strings,
>
> *et potiora cupit, quam pulset pectine chordas,*
> and desires other things, than that one pluck strings with
>   plectrum,

quis Psalmista pius psallebat cantibus olim,
by which the devout psalmist once accompanied his songs,

ac mentem magno gestit modulamine pasci,
and desires to feed his mind with loud music,

et cantu gracili refugit contentus adesse,
and refuses to be content with graceful song,

maxima millenis auscultans organa flabris,
hearing the great organs with a thousand breaths,

mulceat auditum ventosis follibus iste
let him please his hearing with windy bellows

Such references were at least part of a literary tradition—'a thousand' is a frequent hyperbolic in such verse—and allusive or punning: *hydra*, an abbreviation for the hydraulis already found on the inscription at Aquincum, was the hundred-headed monster of mythology. But it does seem that Aldhelm, whatever the details of his figurative purpose, is contrasting lyrical string music with the loud sound of organs.

A hint that organs were beginning to have another purpose is clear in the commission given by Pope John VIII (872–82) to Bishop Anno of Freising (Perrot 1965, p. 399):

> *precamur autem ut optimum organum cum artifice, qui hoc moderari et facere ad omnem modulationis efficaciam possit, ad instructionem musice discipline nobis aut deferas . . . aut transmittas*
> moreover, I ask you to bring or send us an excellent organ for the teaching of the science of music, together with a performer who can play it and produce the total efficacy of modulation

Although the last phrase is difficult to paraphrase—it cannot mean 'modulation' in the modern sense and may denote merely the basic understanding of scale, pitch, proportions, tuning and the *tonoi* (Vitruvius's phrase for 'playing an organ' was *in organo modulari*)—the evidence that organs ('devices'?) were known as teaching aids for the science of music is most instructive. It is from much the same period as Pope John's commission that the oldest known treatises on pipe making date, and they too existed mostly by virtue of their didactic function: they applied the theories of proportion to pipe making rather than gave directions for building church organs as such.

The early church was governed by two particular attitudes towards instruments in general and especially in the liturgy, attitudes which worked against a quick or easy acceptance of organs in church. Firstly, much of the liturgy originated in the practices of the Jewish synagogue, which had no true organ; and secondly, the church in the patristic

c

period tended to resist anything profane or of luxurious association. Obviously the Roman circus organ offended both of these background conditions. But by the ninth century the intellectual and liturgical style of the church had changed. Since the church of Charlemagne showed in its liturgy many elements from imperial ceremonies as a whole—the vestments, processions, incense, candles, apse with throne, choirs, the Dismissal—it would indeed be strange if instruments were not included; their absence would suggest some very specific and strongly felt rejection. But there is no evidence that this was the case. Organs were not forbidden, and by the tenth century even bells—quite as open to abuse as organs— were sometimes specified in Benedictine directives. Their ringing accompanied the arrival of a king, bishop, duke or other dignitaries. When, for example, they were specified for the following purpose at the Benedictine Abbey of Einsiedeln (Schuberth 1968, p. 107):

> *in summis festivitatibus*
> on the highest feastdays
>
> *ad Te deum laudamus omnia*
> to the Te deum [sound] all
>
> *signa*
> bells

they were very likely following out one of the traditional rôles of the organ. By then, presumably the organ was no longer a mere signal or siren. Indeed, by the eleventh century at least one theoretician, John of Afflighem, defined *organum* as polyphony (*diaphonia*), so called because the effect resembled that of organs (Schuberth 1968, p. 118):

> *eo quod vox humana apte dissonans similitudinem exprimat instrumenti, quod organum vocatur*
> because the human voice, suitably changing its tone [or, 'combining different tones fittingly'] produces something similar to the instrument called organum

Nevertheless, whether the earlier sources referring to the sounds of organs at a burial or wedding or during a procession justify the view that they were producing such music as organum, is very uncertain.

No doubt a key to the puzzle of how and why organs became church instruments lies in the development of the Benedictine order. Not only were its new abbeys cultural centres but its large churches themselves gave opportunities to the advancement of music in general. Even before the so-called Monastic Revival of the tenth century, the Benedictines helped to develop musical polyphony, musical notation and presumably musical performance, particularly through their literacy and scholarship, which ensured a scribal tradition. It could well be that the Benedictines were the great exception: amongst *all* branches of the Christian church they were perhaps the only community to develop organs and polyphony, fitfully at first, and to do so for one or other kind of church service. The instrument was never officially approved or even acknowledged as a church instrument in any known papal or pontifical document, despite one fifteenth-century historian's claim that Pope Vitalian (656–72) introduced or sanctioned it (Perrot 1965, p. 285). The Benedictine link occurs time and again before and during the tenth century: such abbeys as St. Gall, where the theorist Notker Labeo (d. 1022) was in orders, Fleury (S.-Benoît-sur-Loire) where pipe proportions were studied, the big churches of Winchester or Halberstadt where there were famous organs. It is even possible that it was the Benedictines' regard for organs that led such Cistercian authors as St. Aelred, Abbot of Rievaulx, Yorkshire, to refer disparagingly in 1166 to the sound of the bellows, the tinkling of bells and the 'harmony' of organ pipes. The new reformed Cistercian order also took against church bells and other visual or aural distractions of the spirit.

One detail in St. Aelred's complaint, however, is particularly signifi-cant: he deplored a crowd of people watching the organ display as if 'in a theatre not a place of worship' (*non ad oratorium, sed ad theatrum*; Perrot 1965, p. 402). This certainly suggests that some or all organs were placed inside buildings; but whether it suggests that such instruments were used before, during or after the service is less certain. Perhaps the organ was rather an object of curiosity, like a cathedral almanac clock, without liturgical function as such. But St. Aelred was writing in the twelfth century when sources begin to imply that an organ was indeed used in some way during services, perhaps again for signalling purposes like bells at the Elevation or like the organs said in some sources to sound at the exclamation 'Thrice Holy' in old Byzantine ceremonial. The ninth- and tenth-century references are all more ambiguous. For example, the Benedictine Abbey of Bages, Spain, was consecrated in 972 to the sound of voices and organs (Perrot 1965, p. 403):

> *vociferabant enim sacerdotes et levitae laudem Dei in jubilo, organumque*
> *procul diffundebat sonus ab atrio laudantes et benedicentes Dominum*
> for the priests and deacons exclaimed the praise of God in jubilation,
> and at a distance the organ poured forth its sound from the forecourt,
> praising and blessing the Lord

The *atrium* may have been a forecourt or narthex of some kind, and it certainly looks as if the organ was playing at a distance (*procul*), pre-sumably outside the nave of the church. In that case, it can hardly have had a liturgical function other than adding clamour at moments in the consecration service. Similar points may be made about other references

to organs at that period; but those concerning organs used in memory of
—or perhaps as a votive offering by—the great abbots and barons are
even vaguer. The Benedictine Abbot Gerbert, Archbishop of Rheims
(991–5) was said by William of Malmesbury to have had a hydraulic
organ put into the cathedral. No doubt it was an object of mechanical
ingenuity, like the *horologium arte mechanica compositum* ('clock made on
mechanical principles') that accompanied it as *doctrinae ipsius documenta*
('documents of this learning'; Perrot 1965, p. 401) for which such cathedrals were becoming vital centres long before their illustrious gothic
successors were built. Integral to the activities of its church seems to have
been the tenth-century organ commissioned by another Benedictine, St.
Oswald (Perrot 1965, p. 399):

> *et diebus festis follium spiramento fortiore pulsati, praedulcem melodiam
> et clangorem longius resonantem ediderunt*
> and on feast days, blown by the strong wind of bellows [the organs]
> produced a very sweet melody and a long-resounding noise

Perhaps this resounding was to the credit of the saint, as that presented
during the same century by St. Dunstan to the Benedictine Abbey of
Malmesbury was said to be at the time; but the fact that Oswald's organ
played 'on feast days' rather suggests its clamour to have been additional
and thus ultimately incidental.

What kind of organs these were is not known. The report of St.
Oswald's refers to copper pipes and bellows, that of St. Dunstan's only
to bellows. Nor is anything certain of other tenth-century organs known
about from later sources, such as that in Halberstadt Cathedral built
under its Benedictine Bishop Hildeward and reported on by Praetorius
six or seven centuries later. Perhaps Abbot Gerbert learnt about water
organs from Benedictine sources based directly or indirectly on Hero or
Vitruvius; or perhaps he learnt about them from the Arabs in Córdoba,
where he lived for a time. If the Bages organ poured forth its sound at a
distance, it presumably had a strong sound, though it is clear from
Aldhelm's poem that notions of loudness were based on simple comparison with soft-sounding string instruments. Fortunately for our understanding of this period of organ history, several of these key issues—the
importance of the Benedictines, the size and type of organ, its function,
its location—arise in connection with one of the most celebrated of all
organs, the tenth-century organ of Winchester.

Several misunderstandings have arisen over this organ and there is
little point in repeating them. The organ was made in or by *c.* 990, some
decades after the Benedictines were fully established at Winchester and
later than modern organ histories suggest. Shortly after 990, the monk
Wulfstan composed a hyperbolic and conventionalized verse-letter about
it (translated in Mc Kinnon 1974):

talia et auxistis hic organa, qualia nusquam
and you enlarged the organs, such as are nowhere

cernuntur, gemino constabilita solo.
seen, fixed on a double floor.

bisseni supra sociantur in ordine folles,
twice six bellows are joined above in order

inferiusque jacent quatuor atque decem.
and below lie four and ten.

flatibus alternis spiracula maxima reddunt,
with alternating breaths they render a great amount of air,

quos agitant validi septuagenta viri,
which 70 strong men stir up,

brachia versantes, multo et sudore madentes,
moving their arms and dripping with much sweat,

certatimque suos quique monent socios,
each eagerly encouraging his companions,

viribus ut totis impellant flamina sursum,
to drive the air upward with all strength

et rugiat pleno kapsa referta sinu,
and cause to roar the full chest of ample curve,

sola quadringentas quae sustinet ordine musas,
which alone supports 400 muses in order,

quas manus organici temperat ingenii:
which the hand controls with organistic skill:

has aperit clausas, iterumque has claudit apertas,
it opens the closed and in turn closes the opened,

exigit ut varii certa Camena soni.
as the fixed song of various notes requires.

considuntque duo concordi pectore fratres,
and two brothers of harmonious spirit sit,

et regit alphabetum rector uterque suum,
and each, a guide, rules his own alphabet,

suntque quaterdenis occulta foramina linguis,
and there are hidden holes in four times ten tongues,

inque suo retinet ordine quaeque decem,
and each holds ten in its own order.

huc aliae currunt, illuc aliaeque recurrunt,
here some tongues run, there some return,

servantes modulis singula puncta suis.
maintaining the individual holes for the proper pitches.

et feriunt jubilum septem discrimina vocum,
and they strike the seven separate joyful tones,

permixto lyrici carmine semitoni,
mixed with the song of the lyric semitone.

inque modum tonitrus vox ferrea verberat aures
and in the manner of thunder the iron voice beats upon the ears

preter ut hunc solum nil capiant sonitum,
that they may receive no sound but this alone,

concrepat in tantum sonus hinc illincque resultans,
the sound so clamours—echoing here and there—

quisque manu patulas claudat ut auriculas,
that one closes with his hand the openings of his ears,

haudquaquam sufferre valens propriando rugitum,
hardly able to bear the roar in drawing near,

quem reddunt varii concrepitando soni,
which the various sounds render in their clamour,

musarumque melos auditur ubique per urbem,
and the melody of the muses is heard everywhere in the city,

et peragrat totam fama volans patriam.
and flying fame goes through the whole country.

Wulfstan is therefore speaking of an organ with 26 bellows, placed in two tiers and blown by 70 (7?) men phased in alternation; 400 pipes (*musae*—does this term imply reeds?); ten ranks (does the 'curved chest' refer merely to the line of pipe-tops?); 40 notes arranged as two sets of 20 keys, each set played by an organist; a diatonic scale with B flat ('lyric semitone'), each note with its part in the melody ('fixed song'—cf. *canto fermo*) and the overall sound very strong ('iron voice'); the keys taking the form of perforated sliders ('tongues' with 'hidden holes'—see also Fig. 3), pushed in and presumably pulled out.

Obviously there was indeed an organ at Winchester, but Wulfstan's account is not convincing in its detail. There is little corroborating evidence for such large instruments: the numbers given for pipes, bellows, ranks and keys are scarcely plausible, whatever the size of the pipes and however the wind was raised. The number of players smacks more of literary or iconographical tradition than of likely practice. For example, the illustration of the hydraulis in the Utrecht Psalter (see p. 31) may even have been known to Wulfstan personally, since it is possible that the manuscript was once in Winchester. The general style of the poem is that of a layman not concerned with technical accuracy and very likely puzzled by the contrivance, as perhaps he was meant to be. Nor is it easy to see how such an instrument could have had a liturgical part to play, not only since 70 men (?) were required for its full effect each time but because the church itself was partitioned into several small rooms of which only the nave seems to have been large enough (*c.* 50 ft. by 24 ft.). But services are not certainly known to have been held there, and if the organ were on either the floor of the church or in any gallery there may have been at the east end of the church, there would not have been room for 70 (?) blowers. If the organ were placed near the west or south door it is difficult to see how it could have been used except as a signal-organ ('heard everywhere in the city') or as a wonder, offering some musical parallel to a clock or moving statuary.

As to the general kind of instrument involved, 'the tenth-century organ at Winchester must certainly have been an organ of the type described by Theophilus' (Mc Kinnon 1974, p. 16), many details of which are unclear but which still gives the best evidence we have of the early medieval organ. Theophilus, probably a German monk, worked during the first half of the eleventh century on a large encyclopedia (for circulation in Benedictine centres?) and described techniques used in making objects for the church and its rite—painting, gilding, glass-blowing, metal-forging, bell-casting, organ-making. Copies of his treatise do not entirely settle the question of authenticity, and at least the final part of it is probably the result of a later compilation of different treatises. But the general picture is clear and genuine enough for one to gain some idea of instruments in this crucial epoch. Figure 3 shows how the wind, raised by two or more bellows which the body weight of the blowers

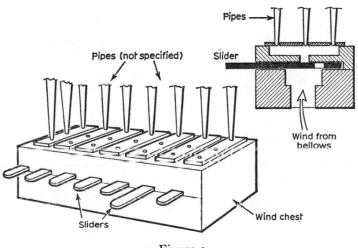

Figure 3

closes, passes to the ranks of pipes when a perforated hand-slider is pulled out far enough for its hole to align with the vertical channel drilled (?) through the board between wind chest and pipe foot. To stop the sound, the slider is pushed back. The chest could be made of wood or moulded in metal, and the whole organ could be placed within the wall (presumably at gallery level), showing only the pipes to the church and having these covered by a hanging textile of some kind when not in use.

A second eleventh-century treatise is the anonymous Berne Codex, a manuscript probably originating in the Benedictine Abbey of Fleury and describing a chest type in which wind did not pass to the two ranks of pipes from one channel but from two. Each pipe had its own duct from the wind chest, so that the slider needed as many holes as there were ranks. Like Hero's, the Berne key was a pivoted square which pushed the slider into the sounding position, while a horn spring pulled it back afterwards. Very likely several kinds of positive and portative organs of this and later centuries had their keys working from some such system.

Theophilus described bellows in the section of his encyclopedia concerned with forging, and from several sources of that period it seems that organ bellows were often made large and capacious—presumably in order to compensate for leaks and pressure drop between feeder and pipe. Theophilus has three such feeders propelling wind through channels into a *conflatorium* or receiver. Before the interior channels meet, the wind passes through a copper valve which flaps open as wind is pushed through and flaps closed as soon as the bellows are exhausted; in the Berne Codex this valve is placed at the entrance to the receiver. The

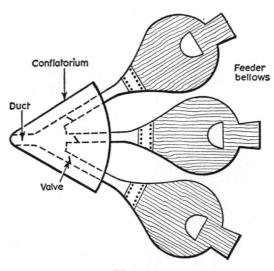

Figure 4

wind is then conveyed along the trunk, which can be curved or straight, to the pipe chest. An organ may be fed by more than one *conflatorium*, and several eleventh- and twelfth-century illustrations of the period show such equipment, for example the Harding Bible and the Cambridge Psalter. Somewhat later illuminations, such as the thirteenth-century Belvoir Castle Psalter, show the organists using their fingers separately, which suggests that however broad the keys might be, their spring-loaded weight was becoming trimmed.

A third part of the construction is the pipe making, described in the section *sicut fistulae* of Aribo's *Musica*, in the treatise by Theophilus and in the Berne Codex, which together create a consortium of knowledge on this vital subject. Theophilus first advised his reader to equip himself with a treatise on pipe proportions (*lectio mensurae*), which either gave him an idea of Pythagorean ratios or provided him with a table of actual pipe-scales: it is not clear which. The copper (or copper alloy?) for the pipes was to be beaten very thin, soldered and shaped on a conical mandrel, which would therefore make the whole pipe and not merely its foot conical; the Berne Codex seems to suggest the more familiar pipe-foot shape, and it is difficult to know whether the treatise accredited to Theophilus is authentic at this point. But his implication that pipes have the same diameter is not unreasonable for an organ of less than two octaves, as is the case here. The sounding length of the longest pipe is given by the Berne Codex as 'almost 4″, but it is not clear what the foot-standard was or whether actual pipes could be made to the given scale, since no allowance was made for end-correction. The compass itself resembles that of those theoretical texts which discuss musical proportions in general and which circulated widely in central Europe. Theophilus also referred to the voicing of the pipes carried out at the mouth in such a way that it was possible to produce a tone 'fat' (*grossam*) or 'more thin' (*graciliorem*); it seems from his description that these mouths had pressed-in apertures of the kind known from late Roman iconography.

In addition to Theophilus, the Berne Codex and Aribo's *Musica*, each of which was no doubt copied and used as a basis for more treatises than now exist, there is a body of medieval theory on organ pipes which deserves consideration in view of the misleading statements often made about it. The many manuscript sources dealing with this subject have been seen as 'treatises on organ-building' (e.g. Mahrenholz 1938) or as 'treatises on pipe measurement' (Perrot 1965), but recent research into the by now completely collated texts has led to their reappraisal (Sachs 1970). The largest group of texts—30 accounts or references in 155 different sources or copies from the tenth century onwards—describes the length of organ pipes calculated by proportions or ratios from an initial pipe of no specific length. Most measurements of this pipe length take the end-correction into account, a constant factor when a row of pipes has the same width and mouth shape. A smaller group of texts—11 accounts in 11 sources—concerns the width or diameter of pipes; these are later sources, from the fourteenth century onwards, and describe the sophisticated relationship between mouth width, cut-up and foothole to the diameter of the pipe. There is bound to be some limit to the practical or even theoretical usefulness of any such texts, since variable pipe widths and a quasi-Pythagorean demonstration of end-correction are mutually exclusive. What, then, do these medieval treatises try to do?

In general, the treatises so resemble the many texts concerned with the calculating of bells and monochords that they should all be seen together in this light: hollow tubes blown by wind (pipes), solid metal hit with hammers (bells) and thin wires made to reverberate (strings) could all be cited as examples of Pythagorean ratios or proportions according to which e.g. a pipe half the length of another will sound its octave, one two-thirds its length will sound its fifth, and so on. Theorists since Boethius had applied number theory to music, and works covering pipe propor-tions by Notker Labeo, Aribo, Engelbert of Admont, Jerome of Moravia, Walter Odington, Georgius Anselmi and the compiler of the late ninth-century treatise *Scolia enchiriadis*—each of whom probably inaugurated a school of theorists—can perhaps best be seen in the same tradition. Most copies of a text ascribed to Wilhelm of Hirsau provide drawings showing the size of the initial pipe not unlike the margin-rule or line given by Schlick in his *Spiegel* five or six centuries later (see p. 75); but this is the nearest any theorist came to hinting that no mere proportional calcula-tion but real practical experience of organ-building lay behind the theorizing.

Calculating constant end-correction as a value of the diameter leads to the frequently repeated conclusion that the medieval organ-builder gave his ranks of pipes the same diameter throughout. Iconography has also been used to support this idea. But the less siren-like the organ had become over the centuries, and the less dependent on written sources were the craftsmen themselves—how many of them could read?—the less likely it is that a constant diameter could have been accepted for a rank of pipes longer than two octaves, or even one. Only Theophilus and the Berne Codex discuss organ-building as such, and even when the Berne Codex gives practical hints such as that pipes follow the modern diatonic *genus* or mode, he was not necessarily referring to an actual instrument used for any musical–liturgical purpose. On the other hand, when the Sélestat manuscript of the eleventh century and the Berne Codex describe a pipe chest of seven notes, sounding (according to Sélestat) unison-octave-unison pipes, it is possible that they are speaking only of a sample diatonic heptachord as a part standing for the whole: a one-octave model from which something larger could be designed, like such illustrations as that in the twelfth-century Harding Bible where a set of eight keys shows one each of the known notes. But it can never be known whether such treatises and iconography conveyed anything more practical than a corpus of knowledge passed along a literate stratum far removed from the world of illiterate craftsmen. It is obviously possible to make an organ without understanding, much less being able to reason about, the acoustical phenomenon of pipes, and it is not only during the medieval period that traditions and customs would make it unlikely for the development of any craft to have to hang on written-down accounts. Only print technology could have brought craftsmen to depend on verbal or even visual models, and five hundred years after Gutenberg printed his first book this is still not the case in many crafts.

Bibliography

HARDOUIN, P., 'De l'orgue de Pépin à l'orgue médiéval', *Revue de musicologie*, 52 (1966), 21–54

MC KINNON, J., 'The 10th-Century Organ at Winchester', *The Organ Year-book*, 5 (1974), 4–19

MAHRENHOLZ, C., *Die Berechnung der Orgelpfeifenmensuren vom Mittelalter bis zur Mitte des 19. Jahrhunderts* (Kassel, 1938; Eng. trans., Oxford, 1975)

PERROT, J., *L'Orgue de ses origines hellénistiques à la fin du XIIIe siècle* (Paris, 1965; Eng. trans., adapted, London, 1971)

RECKOW, F., 'Organum', *Handwörterbuch der musikalischen Terminologie*, ed. H. H. Eggebrecht (Wiesbaden, 1972–)

SACHS, K.-J., *Mensura fistularum: Die Mensurierung der Orgelpfeifen im Mittel-alter*, I (Stuttgart, 1970)

SACHS, K.-J., 'Remarks on the Relationship between Pipe-measurements and Organ-building in the Middle Ages', *The Organ Yearbook*, 4 (1973), 87–100

SCHUBERTH, D., *Kaiserliche Liturgie* (Göttingen, 1968)

WILLIAMS, P., 'How did the Organ become a Church Instrument? Questions towards an understanding of Benedictine and Carolingian cultures' (*Fest-schrift M. A. Vente*) (Utrecht, 1980)

5 The Medieval Church Organ

The kind of organ described by Theophilus suggests how the instrument
had developed halfway between the Roman organ of Aquincum and the
late medieval remnants at Sion, Norrlanda, Kiedrich and elsewhere;
even if Theophilus's treatise were discovered to be merely a compilation
of other sources, it can give some idea of at least one kind of organ that
must have been known. Similarly, much can be assumed with some
degree of certainty about the organ traditions that lay behind the fifteenth-
century treatise of Henri Arnaut de Zwolle. But the whole period from
the eleventh to the fifteenth century is far less clearly understood today
than is commonly suggested. Rarely in the history of music does conjecture masquerade more confidently as fact than in the two chief
questions concerning organs during this period: firstly, what kind of
organ is indicated by such-and-such a source? and secondly, what was
this organ used for? Despite bold assertions that the ninth-century
organist played in 4ths and 5ths, that *alternatim* chants were heard in the
Mass before the twelfth century, or that organs played *organa* or polyphony of the kind developed in the thirteenth-century cathedrals of the
Île-de-France—an idea encouraged by the theorists' terms *puncti
organici* for held notes or *voces organales* for the quick upper parts—there
is no evidence for any of them that can be taken as irrefutable proof.
Reasonable though it may be to assume that organs of the Theophilus
type served to play in polyphony or to aid troping of the plainchant in
the new motets heard in such large Benedictine churches as St. Gall,
Metz, Benevento and Winchester, the evidence is ambiguous. Nor indeed
is it as obvious as it may be thought at first why organs should begin to
take a more integral part in the Mass or Office than did other ingenious
and expensive machinery found in such cathedrals, such as bells and
clocks.

Technical details of the medieval organ are equally conjectural.
Despite claims by many a modern writer, it cannot be shown that 8ths
and 5th ranks were used in abundance during the centuries around
Theophilus, or that reeds and stopped pipes were known. Iconography
by no means proves that organists had to use all of the hand to thump the
keys, and far too much has been read into the common phrase *pulsator
organorum* ('striker of the organs'): *pulsator* is common in classical and

late Latin for the player of any instrument, e.g. lyre. Church archives do not prove that the 'little organs' sometimes mentioned from about 1390 onwards in northern France or the Netherlands were second manuals of large organs; even if they did, it can not be assumed that the two keyboards were placed together in any way; and even if it could, it would be a mere casting back of later knowledge to assume that those manuals had the same pitch and were playable together. In short, a circumspect interpretation of the evidence as it exists will lead only to new doubts about how the organ developed.

Yet it is certain that from the eleventh century onwards organs became more and more familiar. Monastic churches continued to play a major part in their development, though whether the ceremonies at which they played were strictly liturgical is not yet established. Either way, organs often succumbed to the fires that swept medieval cathedrals—Canterbury in 1114, Freising 1158, Merseburg 1199—which may well suggest that they were fixed in place, very likely near (above?) the inflammable wooden stalls of the monks, canons or priests. Large tracts of Europe were still without organs, however, and it should not be expected that areas such as Schleswig or Poland would show much sign of them before the thirteenth century, or that Arab-dominated Spain and Turk-endangered Austria would develop an organ until even later, despite the pockets of high culture in or near those lands (e.g. the diocese of Salzburg or court of Granada). Where organs were known, sources of several kinds suggest that they were popular. Some imply that they were heard during Mass, for example the twelfth-century Norman *Roman de Brut* (Perrot 1965, p. 299):

quant li messe fu commensie	when Mass was begun,
qui durement fu essaucie	which was executed rigorously,
mout oïssiés orgues sonner	the organ could be heard playing,
et clercs chanter et orguener	and clergy singing and performing organum.

But such references are not reliable; poets' sources of information were too often other poets. More convincing is the reference in Chrétien de Troyes's *Lancelot*, a Breton cycle of *c.* 1170 (*ibid.*):

qu'aussi con por oïr les ogres	just as, for hearing the organs, people
vont au mostier a feste anuel	are used to going to the monastery
u Pentecoste ou a Noel les	on the annual feast of Whit or
janz acostumeement	Christmas

Here the context of time and place is clearer: it is a question of organs in monasteries or minsters, heard only on special or certain occasions, and then not necessarily in any liturgy as such. It is interesting that it was sequences and the Te Deum which good sources of the ninth and tenth centuries show to have been suitable for polyphonic treatment by choirs, because these movements were exactly those most closely associated later with the organ, like the *Magnificat* for both Protestant and Catholic organists of the seventeenth century.

It cannot be proved from manuscript illumination that other instruments including the little portatives were used for such music, and in any case by the thirteenth century various regional churches of Spain, Italy and France had banned all instruments other than organs. Even at this date, 'large organs'—a term found in archives of such major churches as the Petrikirche, Erfurt in 1291—may have had a signalling function, and when the bishop of Mende (who died in 1296) referred to the organ sounding five times during Sanctus (Perrot 1965, p. 301), he was probably not referring to a genuinely musical interpolation. But while the reformed monastic orders of Cistercian and Carthusian (Charterhouse) ruled in turn against any kind of instrument, major organs were as likely to be found in the thirteenth-century secular cathedrals across Europe, from Exeter to Prague, from Barcelona to Lübeck, as in the abbey churches themselves. Whether erected on screens or hanging on an upper wall of nave or quire, organs were usually placed near the *cantores* and no longer by or above the west or south entrances. It was not until the fifteenth century that specially bequeathed chapels in large churches had their own organs, and not until the seventeenth that the west wall began to be a prime site for the organ. It is obvious that when the organ was placed near the *cantores*, it could perform from time to time in alternation with them, i.e. priest or precentor would sing one verse of the text, organ would play the next in varying degrees of embellishment. When this began to happen is still not clear but can be supposed to be during the late thirteenth century.

Presumably there is no question of the congregation as such taking part when a theorist like Johannes de Florentia (*c.* 1350) describes the technique as *partim organo partim modulatis per concentum vocibus* ('partly with the organ, partly with the voices singing in consort'; Perrot 1965, p. 360). Several fourteenth-century documents suggest that whatever it was the organ played, it did so on certain feast days, local or universal as the case may be. At Halberstadt Cathedral, for example, the organ played on Christmas Day, during the week after Easter Day, Finding of the Holy Cross, Reliques of St. Stephen, Ascension, SS. Peter and Paul, Dispersal of the Apostles, Mary Magdalen, SS. Stephen and Sixtus, Assumption, Patron Saint, Nativity of Mary, St. Michael, St. Gall, All Saints and twelve other feast-days including Trinity and Annunciation. For three centuries organs seem to have been used only on feast days, and it is probable that they always remained silent during Lent, Advent and in some churches at other seasons such as Corpus Christi. By the end of the thirteenth century other instruments were often banned (Milan, 1287), presumably, as one Spanish document noted, on account of potential abuse when other instruments played together (Williams 1966, p. 269); by the fourteenth, *alternatim* performance was common, particularly in the Offices such as Vespers; by the early fifteenth, many areas such as the Upper Rhineland, north-central Germany, cities of northern Italy and the countries between Normandy and Brabant, had organs in most of their larger churches; and from the mid-fifteenth the organ's development is clear in outline as too its position in the western church was assured, with the exception of some reformed churches.

Although it is not possible to trace this history step by step, certain general points can be made. Organs were known in cathedrals less as an exception and more as a norm, and there was usually a clear distinction between the large positive organ—with front pipes arranged from left to right—and the fixed church organ—with front pipes set in mitre form, requiring a rollerboard for the larger pipes set on each side. It is safe to assume that mechanisms were gradually achieving their forms shown on pp. 91–2. As to pipework, all the evidence suggests that only open metal flue pipes were known, although some historians have seen such phrases as *plom . . . per las horguenas* ('lead for the organs', Eglise des Cordeliers, Avignon, 1372) as evidence that lead pipes were made for distinctive tone-colours, even perhaps for stopped pipes. But this is unlikely, for either 'lead' refers to pipe-metal alloy in a general sense or it can be taken as confirming what is today assumed more and more to have been the case, i.e. that in the history of the organ as a whole tin was used predominantly only at certain periods in certain areas. In Normandy and later the central Netherlands, large organs from the end of the fourteenth century onwards often had *Trompes* or a set of ten or so large open metal Bourdon pipes placed to one side, or both sides, of the main organ-case and perhaps played by their own keyboard, manual or pedal as the case may be. Presumably the larger organs also had a *Blockwerk* or undivided chorus, although not much is known about these choruses before 1450 other than that some documents mention the approximate number of pipes they contained (e.g. 2,000 at Amiens in 1429). Presumably, too, the compass of the organs was roughly equivalent to those of men's voices, though the exact octave pitch—i.e. whether at 8′, 16′, 4′ etc.—depended on the size of organ concerned, as was still the case with the Italian organ of the sixteenth century. The arrangement of the keys themselves, so made that the chromatic or *ficta* semitones were raised in groups of two and three above the C-diatonic scale, existed from at least the beginning of the fifteenth century. Before then, plainsong could be accommodated on two octaves only, with one semitone (B♭); only during the fourteenth century do such theorists as Johannes de Muris and Jacob de Liège mention others. By the beginning of the fifteenth century, keyboards often began at what appear to be the notes B or F, but the absolute pitch of these two notes may have been similar, thus showing a tradition for two pitch-standards in keyboard instruments still evident in the Italian harpsichord of the sixteenth century and the Flemish of the seventeenth.

Corroborating evidence for such historical outlines can be found in extant fragments of old organs or in good written sources. The second is usually more trustworthy. Thus the organ at Sion, Switzerland (see Plate 1), often called 'the oldest extant playing organ' and variously dated *c*. 1380 or *c*. 1435 (Brossard 1978) is so unreliable as to its original sound, specification, compass, pitch, pressure, bellows, position, purpose and origin as to make it impossible to draw from it conclusions about how medieval organs sounded. This is true even though much of the pipework is undoubtedly old and the tone produced by the higher ranks breathy and ringing like no other organ. The casework at Sion, however, shows important details: the central mitre-shape is typical for such organs and could have been found from fifteenth-century Burgundy to sixteenth-century London or Copenhagen, though probably not in Spain or Italy; the castellated towers to left and right overhang the sides, and the doors or wings, painted and perhaps therefore made in about 1434–7, close the pipes in completely. In the National Historical Museum in Stockholm is preserved the now pipeless organ of Norrlanda, usually dated *c*. 1390 and one of a group of old Scandinavian organ-remains. It appears to be a large positive and to have had a *Blockwerk* of 3–6 ranks, with a set of twelve rollers conveying not only both pedal and manual keys to two small side-towers for the larger pipes but also the key-action from four pairs of keys to a single pipe in each instance (C♯/c♯, D♯/d♯, F♯/f♯, G♯/g♯). This last device is so advanced an idea, leading as it does to a complete c–a¹ compass, that the date *c*. 1390 must be doubted. As with the famous organ of Old Radnor, Wales, still often claimed to be 'an organ of *c*. 1500', the Norrlanda positive may be an organ built up of much older furniture-timber, however typical of early fifteenth-century positives its keyboard may be shown to be (see pp. 57–8). At Bartenstein in East Prussia, parts of an organ dated *c*. 1395 existed before World War II. It had a large chest of 27 keys (FGA–a¹?), with three chest-divisions giving the organist three possibilities: **1** a large chorus of 9 to 21 ranks, **2** the 16′ case-pipes alone, and **3** the Principals 8′ + 4′. An ingenious reconstruction of the chest was drawn by Karl Bormann in 1966, but neither date nor construction of the original organ is certain. If such mechanism blocking off the divisions did belong to 1390, Bartenstein would have had the oldest known stop-mechanism and one presumably not unlike those blocking off parts of the chests in later Dutch organs.

Written sources begin to give clearer detail from about the middle of the fifteenth century, which itself may well reflect the fact that the organ was becoming more varied and developed. Henri Arnaut de Zwolle, writing in the 1440s, deserves a separate account, for his treatise though incomplete offers the best source between Theophilus and Schlick, giving as it does important details of several actual organs, including one of *c.* 1350 (see p. 60). Church records usually establish merely the presence of an organ, and about large tracts of Europe curiously little is still known. In such countries as the Netherlandish provinces it was only during the fifteenth century that the great gothic churches were built, but this at least means that many such churches were provided with an organ as a part of the church furniture right from their original completion. The first real details in church documents occur in builders' contracts from the end of the fourteenth century, when to be unambiguous a scribe would occasionally distinguish between the *opus maius* and the *parvum opus organum* ('large work', 'small organ-work' at Utrecht Cathedral); or he might distinguish between the *principaulx* pipes and the *bourdons* ('Blockwerk' and 'Trompes' at Rouen Cathedral); or he might even refer to the art of *tastando cum pedibus* ('playing with the feet' at S. Annunziata, Florence, 1379). By *c.* 1425 some reference to stops might be made, such as the *cinch tirants* ('five draw-levers'?) in a large positive for the Court Chapel of Aragon. More often, however, the contract or chapter minute merely recorded that an organ had been commissioned and that the builder was to see that it was 'decent, good and to the honour' of the church concerned (S. Giovanni Evangelista, Venice, 1430). Moreover, terminology is very uncertain. The contract of 1345 for an organ in Barcelona Cathedral speaks of a *part* of the organ; there were three such *parts*. Does this imply sections of a *Blockwerk*? When the scribe recording alterations to the organ of Trier Cathedral in 1387 mentioned the *registers* for which iron had to be bought, is it really plausible that he was referring to stop-handles?

From written sources of any kind, the best-known fourteenth-century organ is undoubtedly that of Halberstadt Cathedral, built in *c.* 1361, rebuilt in 1495 and described by Praetorius in his *Syntagma musicum* of 1619. Praetorius by no means understood the nature of such old organs, nor does he make it clear what dated from 1361 and what from 1495; but his account is still considerably detailed. He describes four keyboards as follows: **1**, called by him the *Diskant* and playing the full chorus of case-principals and *Blockwerk* or Hintersatz mixture, with the compass B–c¹ (14 keys); **2**, also called *Diskant*, playing the case-principals only, with the same compass; **3**, called by him the *Bassklavier*, playing the 12 large bass pipes with the compass B–a¹b¹ and consisting of 12 protruding levers perhaps worked by the knee; and **4**, the pedal keyboard, having the same compass as **3** and used with—even perhaps pulling down the keys of—the top manual. The largest rank of pipes was at the sub-sub-octave level (32′), and the total number of pipes was about 1,192, from 16 ranks

D

at pedal B to 56 at top manual a^1. Although according to Praetorius's illustrations the three upper keyboards were labelled with the pitch-names given here, the pitch-standard is uncertain; it may have been a^1 = c. 505Hz. The manual chorus ranks seem to have been distributed as follows (Bormann 1966, p. 45):

B–f   16.16.8.8.8.$5\frac{1}{3}$.$5\frac{1}{3}$.$5\frac{1}{3}$.$5\frac{1}{3}$.4.4.4.4.4.$2\frac{2}{3}$.$2\frac{2}{3}$.$2\frac{2}{3}$.$2\frac{2}{3}$.$2\frac{2}{3}$.$2\frac{2}{3}$.2.2.2.2.2.2.
         1.1.1.1.1.1.

f♯–c♯^{1} 16.16.8.8.8.8.$5\frac{1}{3}$.$5\frac{1}{3}$.$5\frac{1}{3}$.$5\frac{1}{3}$.$5\frac{1}{3}$.4.4.4.4.4.$2\frac{2}{3}$.$2\frac{2}{3}$.$2\frac{2}{3}$.$2\frac{2}{3}$.$2\frac{2}{3}$.$2\frac{2}{3}$.$2\frac{2}{3}$.
         2.2.2.2.2.2.2.2.1.1.1.1.1.1.1.1.1.1.

d^1–a^1 16.16.8.8.8.8.8.$5\frac{1}{3}$.$5\frac{1}{3}$.$5\frac{1}{3}$.$5\frac{1}{3}$.$5\frac{1}{3}$.$5\frac{1}{3}$.4.4.4.4.4.4.$2\frac{2}{3}$.$2\frac{2}{3}$.$2\frac{2}{3}$.$2\frac{2}{3}$.$2\frac{2}{3}$.
         $2\frac{2}{3}$.$2\frac{2}{3}$.$2\frac{2}{3}$.$2\frac{2}{3}$.$2\frac{2}{3}$.2.2.2.2.2.2.2.2.2.2.2.1.1.1.1.1.1.1.1.1.
         1.1.1.1.

Although twenty bellows supplied the wind, Praetorius's drawing shows only two men operating them; perhaps more were needed only when the *plenum* was sounded, or perhaps Praetorius did not feel compelled to show them all. He did describe the sound of the *Blockwerk*, however, in a passage of unique interest (Praetorius 1619, pp. 99–100):

> *wegen der grösse der praestanten, und weil sich ihre Manual Clavir, der wenigen Clavium halben, nicht in die höhe zur lieblichkeit begeben können, ein solch tieffes grobes brausen und grewliches grümmeln; auch wegen vielheit der MixturPfeiffen, ein uberaus starcken schall und laut, und gewaltiges geschrey (darzu denn der geweste Windt rechtschaffen nachgedruckt hat) mus von sich gegeben haben.*
> on account of the large principals, and because the keyboard, which has [?] few notes cannot rise high enough for pleasantness, such a deep coarse rumbling and dreadful thunder must result, as too a powerful shrillness, throughout strong and loud (when the required wind has been thoroughly raised) must result from the multiplicity of mixture-pipes.

Whether the *Blockwerk* as it was in 1361 would have been described exactly in these terms by Praetorius will never be known, but the general picture is very convincing.

    According to Praetorius, builders of the period from the thirteenth to fifteenth centuries knew how to fashion pipes of various sizes and scales, which certainly suggests that distinctive tone-colours were beginning to be known. Without Praetorius we would not have known that some keys were as broad as about 8 cm or that some old keyboards had a compass of B–f^1 or c–a^1, though one could guess that these were diatonic compasses only. He made interesting conjectures about important details, such as that accidental semitones appeared from about 1200, pedals from about 1220, stopped and other pipes of the non-principal kind only after c. 1450, separate stops by about 1250 and springchests (see p. 67) before 1400. Each of these needs qualification: the first accidental semitone appeared at least two centuries earlier than Praetorius claimed (though no doubt B♭ did not have its key raised above the naturals), but all five accidental semitones appeared only a century or more later than 1200, and then probably only here and there. Evidence that stopped pipes and others of special colour appeared only in the middle or later fifteenth century is strong, and Praetorius could well be right. But for the introduction of spring chests, his date sounds a little early, as does that for separate stops—unless he was referring to small positives and portatives or meant merely that on some organs two or more distinct sounds (*Blockwerk* and principals) could be produced. For example, a document at Perpignan in 1421 speaks of four effects obtainable from the organ: *grosses y plenes* ('large and full'), *ben proporcionados* ('well proportioned'), *ben clares et ben distinctas* ('very bright and clear') and *ben afinats* ('very refined'; Dufourcq 1934/5, pp. 81–2). By dividing the chest and giving it a mechanism to allow different parts to sound at will, the builder could give his organ different sound-effects or registrations; 'full' presumably refers to a combination of principals and *Blockwerk*, 'well proportioned' to the principals alone, and 'bright and clear' to the high mixture or Zimbel; or 'very refined' refers to the principals alone and 'well proportioned' to the principals with large mixture but without Zimbel, etc.

As to pedals, the picture is confusing not because they cannot be accredited to one particular builder or one particular area but because the nature of early pedals is still understood only imperfectly. It is not only a question of whether Praetorius is referring here to true pedals or merely pulldowns but of whether any pedal keys at all before a certain period (1450? 1500? 1550?) were playing the bass pipes. At one point Praetorius remarks that some early pedals played only the bass notes, which might suggest that the large Bourdons, *Trompes* or *teneurs* (so-called at Rouen in 1382) were not necessarily operated by the feet but by a keyboard played by hands or even knees. The term *teneur* is certainly evocative, but what exactly it evokes is uncertain. Perhaps *teneur* keys played the long notes in the inner voice of a work for voices; or perhaps *teneurs* meant merely the large pipes as distinct from the small, called *menus* in the same Rouen document and *Diskant* in Praetorius's description of the Halberstadt organ. 'Bass' is a word late to evolve in musical terminology, and it is unlikely that the Rouen organist played tenor solos as such merely because he directed the Chapter scribe to refer to his larger pipes as *teneurs*. Nor can we assume that the distinction was always clear between a keyboard played by the hands ('manual') and one played by the feet ('pedal'), at least from the point of view of what part of the total sound they each produced. It could be that the French texts of the sixteenth century that refer to pedals in connection with Trompes (Angers, Fougères, Chartres, Rheims, Dijon) were reflecting a gradual but not original association between the two.

In the period around 1400, then, a large church organ in the vast area Rouen–Utrecht–Magdeburg–Orvieto–Barcelona–Rouen might have contained a *Blockwerk* of unison, 5th and 8ve ranks (perhaps with as many as 80 ranks at the top of the narrow compass), or the *Blockwerk* may have been already divided into principals and mixtures; probably all pipes were open, cylindrical and made of metal; the manual had broad keys and could have had a compass of anything between 16 and 40 or even more notes; perhaps another keyboard or other keyboards were present, in order for each to play a distinctive sound (including Trompes); perhaps here and there a second manual might have been connected to a second smaller organ placed below the first. The low pipes of the largest cathedral organs were the lowest sounds then ever heard; deep sounds were not characteristic of medieval music or instrumentation in general, and it would not be unreasonable to claim that the evolution towards the bass-dominated diatonicism of all western music from the sixteenth century onwards sprang from the large organ-pipes of the fourteenth- and fifteenth-century cathedrals.

Bibliography

BORMANN, K., *Die gotische Orgel von Halberstadt* (Berlin, 1966)

BROSSARD, P., 'Note à propos de l'Orgue XIVe (sic) de Sion-Valère', *Connoissance de l'orgue*, 27 (1978), 28–30

CALDWELL, J. A., 'The Organ in the Medieval Latin Liturgy, 800–1500', *Proceedings of the Royal Musical Association*, 93 (1966–7), 11–24

DUFOURCQ, N., *Documents inédits relatifs à l'orgue français* (Paris, 1934–5)

HARDOUIN, P., 'Les Trompes', *Connoissance de l'orgue*, 19/20 (1976), 3–12

KLOTZ, H., *Über die Orgelkunst der Gotik, der Renaissance und des Barock* (Kassel, 1975)

MEEÙS, N., 'La Naissance de l'octave courte et ses différentes formes au 16e siècle' (unpublished diss., Louvain, 1971)

PERROT, J., *L'Orgue de ses origines hellénistiques à la fin du XIIIe siècle* (Paris, 1965; Eng. trans., adapted, London, 1971)

PRAETORIUS, M., *Syntagma musicum, II. De Organographia* (Wolfenbüttel, 1619)

WILLIAMS, P., *The European Organ 1450–1850* (London, 1966)

6   The Late Medieval Positive and Portative

'Portative' is the name now given to a small portable organ held by a strap over the organist's shoulder, blown by a pair of bellows operated by the left hand, and played by the right. The compass was two octaves or less, the pipes open metal, the number of ranks one, two or rarely three. Some portatives had one or two larger bass pipes, presumably open Bourdons, and the keys were often T-shaped, like those of the hurdy-gurdy, though some look more like round buttons of the typewriter kind. Sources for such information about the stylized fifteenth-century portative are entirely iconographical: some composers like Landini and Dufay are represented in portraits playing small organs, and the instrument can be seen in many a fifteenth-century painting (particularly Venetian) of angel choirs at the Virgin's Coronation, or some similar genre-piece. Such too are the ornate and finely wrought portatives shown by named painters of the period, such as Memling—little organs that presumably sounded like a set of strong flutes played by a keyboard. But the term 'portative' is less conventionalized. French documents rarely use the word, and the so-called *petites orgues* hired and carried at Rouen Saint-Maclou in 1519 were more typical. In Germany, *portiff* might mean a portative (Frankfurt 1434), as might *organetto* or *organino* in Italy during the fifteenth and sixteenth centuries; later terms such as *organi portatili* are less ambiguous whether coined by Italian writers (Barcotto MS *c.* 1650) or English (Roger North *c.* 1715). In England, however, the distinguishing term 'positive' was rarely if ever used, so that early appearances of the words *portatives* (poem of Gavin Douglas), a *payre of portatives* (a will of 1522) or *portatyffes* (St. Andrew, Canterbury *c.* 1520) are likely to denote small, movable organs in general rather than the portative proper.

'Positive' is a somewhat better authenticated term given to organs larger than the portative, placed on the nave, quire or gallery floor but not permanently fixed to it. The fixture itself is less important than what it implies: that the bellows are part of (though often placed behind) the structure and not conducted off into their own chamber. The bellows were operated by a second person and the keys were played by both of the organist's hands. The more or less chromatic keyboards had usually more than two octaves (often, even usually, beginning at B) and the keys were short, protruding simply from the case-front. Two apparent rows of pipes would form one complete rank of open metal pipes, clearly shown in the better paintings as diminishing in diameter; cut-ups often look low and the scaling narrow; and there were sometimes a pair or more of open Bourdon pipes evidently an octave lower than the bass pipes of the main row—a kind of miniature version of the Trompes of large organs, even perhaps the original inspiration for them. It can only be conjectured what these Bourdon pipes were for or how full the chords were that the organist played, for most of the sources are iconographical and therefore unclear on crucial details. Written sources used 'positive' not to describe any particular function or playing-technique but merely to distinguish that kind of organ from those either smaller or bigger. Virdung (1511) uses both *positive* and *portative*, Arnaut de Zwolle (*c.* 1450) *portivus*, *positivo* and *organum*, while church or legal scribes soon began to use 'positive' specifically for the Chair Organ (*posityff* at Zwolle 1447, *le positif* at Saint-Laurent, Rouen in 1524)—though this last significance of the word is more ambiguous than modern historians assume.

That paintings are less helpful than is often supposed can be shown by either of the two most famous depictions of a positive organ, that of Van der Goes in the National Gallery, Edinburgh (dated 1476) and that of Van Eyck in the altarpiece at St. Bavo, Ghent (1432 or earlier). To take the latter: its beauty seems to add to its unreality, for Van Eyck 'was perfectly capable of depicting an instrument with photographic verisimilitude had he wished to do so' (Ripin 1974, p. 195), which seems not to have been the case. The front pipes, though painted with attention to detail, are not placed naturally: the tips of the feet rest right at the front of the topboard of the chest, while each pipe whatever its diameter is held up against the supporting braces, which have a constant thickness —the vertical plane is therefore unrealistic at this point. Clearly the perspective is less correct than it first seems, for the feet of the inner row of pipes are placed almost without 'depth' but each is exactly between the feet of the front row—which are, however, ranged in perspective. Particularly problematic is the compass. There must be 32 to 35 keys in the keyboard (depending on the number of bass accidentals), unless it were placed asymmetrically, running no higher than the highest note not blocked by the organist's arm; but there are only 21 pipes in the front row, which means therefore that the back row cannot have formed a second, independent rank. If both rows had 21 pipes, there would be too many for one rank, at least if each key were to have had only one pipe. Moreover, the line made by the pipe-tops corresponds neither to a completely diatonic tuning nor to a chromatic, in addition to which the scaling of the larger pipes seems unnaturally narrow. As to the latchkey hanging on the frontboard to the lower left, various suggestions have been made: that it shut off wind from one of the rows of pipes, that it brought on one or more bass pipes sounding a drone, that it was a Tremulant device, and that it operated a valve or pallet emptying the chest of wind in case of cipher or when the organist had finished playing. The last seems the most likely, for the Norrlanda organ (see p. 50) once had a similar 'key' with a pivoted hold-down apparently for this purpose, as far as can now be seen.

On the two particular questions of the keyboard/pipe-rank compass and of the latchkey, various answers can be plausibly conjectured and equally plausibly countered. For example, some of the pipes could have been dummies—but in that case the problem of tuning (diatonic? chromatic?) remains. Or perhaps some of the treble pipes were duplicated as they were in later and larger Dutch organs, one note playing two unison pipes—but in that case, either the top line of the pipes would not descend regularly (which it does) or the pipe length was only apparent and the pipes were cut away behind the front segment (which is probably a later practice). Similarly, if the latchkey operated a Tremulant, one would expect other evidence from the period to support it; if it operated drone-pipes, one would expect them to be at least obscurely visible; if it operated a complete rank of pipes to the rear, one would not expect there to be doubts about the total number of keys and pipes. A similar, if different, series of points could be made about the Van der Goes painting, and in both cases a further complication arises in that the painter seems (or painters seem) to have worked twice on the painting, probably altering

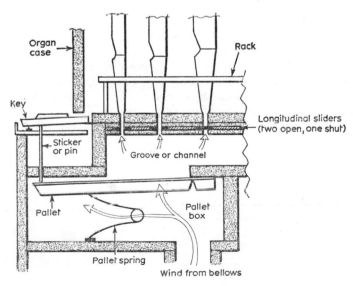

Figure 5

both the compass of the keyboard and the position of the hands, as can be shown by X-ray photography. Thus these paintings show the technical unreliability of even the most polished iconographical evidence, just as a realistic appraisal of the medieval theorists referred to in Chapter 4 shows their limitations for us today. Both reappraisals result in greater doubt rather than greater certainty.

While the little protruding keys of the Norrlanda, Van Eyck and Van der Goes organs presumably had little trackers or stickers pulling down the pallets (see p. 91), portative organs and many, perhaps most, positive or chamber organs from the sixteenth century—whatever shape, name or function—seem to have favoured the so-called pin action. In this system (see Fig. 5) the key presses down the pallet by means of a little rod or sticker. The diagram here shows an organ with three separate ranks of pipes, each of which can be made to sound separately by means of the perforated strip (the 'slider') running longitudinally between groove and pipe foot; but pin action itself does not presuppose several or separate ranks. Obviously, the grooved or 'barred' chest allowed immense development as it itself no doubt manifested builders' concern to make versatile chests and to give the organist variety of tone; but at what point between the ninth and sixteenth centuries such chests, with their pallet, groove and slider, developed into this perfected structure is only conjectural.

Bibliography

BOWLES, E. A., 'On the Origin of the Keyboard Mechanism in the Late Middle Ages', *Technology and Culture*, 7 (1966), 152–62

HARDOUIN, P., 'Twelve Well-known Positive Organs: Useful Evidence or Difficult Problems?', *The Organ Yearbook*, 5 (1974), 20–9

RIPIN, E. M., 'The Norrlanda Organ and the Ghent Altarpiece', *Festschrift to Ernst Emsheimer* (Stockholm, 1974), 193–6, 286–8

VIRDUNG, S., *Musica getutscht und ausgezogen* (Basel, 1511)

7   The Treatise of
Henri Arnaut de Zwolle

Arnaut's treatise is known from one source only (Paris, Bib. Nat. lat. 7295) and provides not a compendium of knowledge copied or culled from previous treatises but a new approach to the art of writing a technical account of organs, never completed or polished beyond draft stage, alas. It was written in Dijon between 1436 and 1454, partly by Arnaut, who is thought to have been a Dutch polymath at the Burgundian court of Philip the Good, and partly by two other authors or scribes—it is not clear which. A recent hypothesis has connected 'Zwolle' not with the city of that name in The Netherlands but with Zwollen (Stvolny) in Czechoslovakia which, if it were ever proved, would point to an interesting coincidence with Arnold Schlick, who may also have had Bohemian origins. The treatise deals with several kinds of keyboard instrument including small organs, but it also throws light on wider organ techniques of the period, perhaps as a sign of the lively cultural ties between Burgundy and the Low Countries. In general, the treatise is more practical than any known since the eleventh century, describing as it does certain *Blockwerk* or principal choruses which, after all, constitute the most characteristic of all organ sounds. For at least a century afterwards, no source was to show in such detail what a builder should do when he plans his Diapason chorus, for documents of all kinds preferred to lyricize over the new colour stops, secondary manuals and other relatively minor effects.

Arnaut's description of an organ pipe is not theoretical or Pythagorean but empirical and systematic. The scale seems to be highly tapered, i.e. bass pipes are relatively narrow (some 10 semitones narrower than the so-called *Normalmensur* at bass B), trebles relatively wide (some 7 semitones wider than *Normalmensur* at a hypothetical b''). Mouth width is about a quarter of the circumference but wider (about two-sevenths) for pipes producing a bigger tone; cut-up is a quarter of the mouth width; the diameter of the footholes a quarter of the pipe width (i.e. large). It is not clear whether Arnaut was working with two pitches ($a^1 = c.415$ Hz and $a^1 = c.435$ Hz) or with a mean pitch (*tonus cori*) of $a^1 = 415$ Hz. But he is the first writer known to describe keyboard compass in terms of specific, not merely notional, note names, referring as he does to both F and B keyboards.

Arnaut describes two chests of the positive or portative types (*ciste portivorum*). In the one, a single rank of pipes with the compass b–g'''a''' (without g♯''') is placed 'in the form of a bishop's mitre' (*ad modum mitre episcopalis*), with the tallest pipes in the middle; in the other, a single rank with the compass b–f''' is placed in straight chromatic progression, tallest to the left, shortest to the right. It is the second that is the 'usual chest' (*ciste communis*). There is also a sketch of what seems to be a standard design for a larger organ, very like that still extant at Sion and probably to be identified as the organ at Salins whose *Blockwerk* Arnaut described as a chorus rising from 6 ranks at the bottom B to 21 at the top f'', with a longest pipe of 4' (i.e. 8' sounding pitch at B).

On a further page of Arnaut's treatise appears what seems to be the first reference in known written sources to reed pipes. The page is incomplete and contains scarcely twenty words and ten figures apropos the *diapason . . . calamorum dei custodientium* ('scaling . . . of the pipes in the organ of the Dei Custodientes church'); on it occurs the phrase *l'anche de F* (or *l'anche de G[amut]*), apparently in reference to the reed and block of a reed pipe. Arnaut seems to be saying that a rank of such pipes from B to b' needs eight different sizes of block (Bormann 1966, p. 161); why he gives no other details is not known, but room was left on the page for expansion, and the handwriting seems to conform to that of the rest of the treatise.

Arnaut describes briefly several actual organs, including that in Notre-Dame, Dijon. Its compass was B–a'' and its lead pipes already old and corroded (*plumbei, antiqui et pulverosi*), hence a putative date of *c.* 1350; the pipe mouths were generally about half an octave too narrow, i.e. pipes had a mouth only as wide as one a 4th or so higher in new instruments. Since Arnaut mentions the Fourniture mixture stop, it seems that the chorus was at least partly separable, rather than a true *Blockwerk*. There were altogether 768 pipes of which 330 seem to have been those that could be separated off. The leather bellows had three folds and measured *c.* 160 cm by *c.* 70 cm, though Arnaut does not make it clear whether they belonged to the original organ.

The treatise is particularly valuable in its analyses of *Blockwerke*. Arnaut or the anon scribes express in table form four different *Blockwerk* structures:

1   compass F–e''', 8 ranks in bass, 21 in treble
2   compass BB–f'', 6 ranks in bass, 21 in treble
3   compass BB–f'', 6 ranks in bass, 15 in treble
4   compass BB–a'b', 10 ranks in bass, 26 in treble

The first of these, thought by some modern commentators to be the organ in Notre-Dame, Dijon (1447), had three parts unnamed but corresponding to Principal, Cymbale, Fourniture: this variety was produced probably by divisions within the chest rather than by separate manuals or 'stops' in any modern sense. At the top of the compass were four ranks of Principal 8', fourteen of the Fourniture, and a three-rank Cymbale including the Tierce—the first known documented proof of the 3rd-sounding rank. The Cymbale repeated, beginning at 29.31.33 and ending at 8.10.15. The whole chorus then ends with 7 unison ranks, 10 octave ranks, two 5ths, one 12th and one 10th, which hardly suggests a shrill squealing sound. Vital for the future development of the organ was the fact that the two mixtures repeated or broke back and produced the following scheme:

F–B♭	1.8	26	15.19.22.22
B–c	1.8	29.31.33	8.15.19.22.22.26
c♯–b♭	1.8	29.31.33	8.15.19.22.26 (*sic*)
b–e¹	1.1	22.24.26	8.8.15.15.19.22
f¹–b♭¹	1.1	22.24.26	8.8.8.15.15.15.15.19.22
b¹–e¹¹	1.1.1	15.17.19	1.1.8.8.8.8.15.15.15.19
f¹¹–b♭¹¹	1.1.1	12.15.17	1.1.8.8.8.8.8.8.12.12.15.15
b¹¹	1.1.1.1	10.12.15	1.1.1.8.8.8.8.8.12.12.15
c¹¹¹–c♯¹¹¹	1.1.1.1	8.10.12	1.1.1.8.8.8.8.8.8.12.12.15
d¹¹¹–d♯¹¹¹	1.1.1.1	8.10.12	1.1.1.1.1.1.8.8.8.8.12.12
e¹¹¹–f¹¹¹	1.1.1.1	8.10.12	1.1.1.5.5.8.8.8.8.8.8.8.8

One of the three other organs was that at Salins (Salin, formerly in Burgundy), which had an 8' *Blockwerk* with the compass B–f¹¹¹ or a 4' *Blockwerk* of BB–f¹¹. This was a plain, cumulative *Blockwerk* with ranks duplicating but not breaking back:

BB–E	8.8.15.15.19.22
F–B♭	8.8.15.15.19.19.22.22
B–e	8.8.12.12.15.15.19.19.22.22
f–b♭	8.8.12.12.15.15.19.19.19.22.22.22
b–e¹	8.8.8.12.12.15.15.15.19.19.19.22.22.22
f¹–f¹¹	8.8.8.12.12.15.15.15.19.19.19.22.22.22.22

The 43 notes may well have been distributed on pedal (BB–B♭) and manual (B–f¹¹), as has been recently suggested (Klotz 1975, p. 31), but there is no evidence for this.

While the old-fashioned nature of the *Blockwerk* is clear from Arnaut's table, it is the apparently arbitrary arrangement of the three-division scheme above that better repays study. Presumably the middle division—often called *Terzzimbel* today—lay between the other two on the chest itself, hence the order in Arnaut's table. It appears to have been carefully designed as an addition to the chorus produced by the sum of the other two divisions, topping or usefully duplicating that chorus as well as adding the all-important Tierce rank. Whether it was used alone with the principals of course will never be known, but some pale ghost of its effect can be conjured up by reading off the ranks.

At Saint-Cyr—probably Nevers Cathedral—Arnaut says that there were 12 *fistulas tenoris*, 'tenor pipes', almost half as long again as the longest pipes of the chorus. These Trompes had no mixture ranks (*nullas fornituras*) of their own, which presumably means that they sounded alone, perhaps from their own keyboard, but in any case confirming the tradition for calling bass pipes 'tenors'. At the Church of the Cordeliers (probably in Dijon), the ten *subdupla tenoris* pipes did have a separate keyboard, or at least ten keys placed apart from the others (*claves istas 10 eminentes ab extra*) which could be coupled to and played by the other keyboard. Arnaut refers to these Trompes being played 'by the left hand' (*manu sinistra*). The organ could then play three different sounds: the usual chorus (*modo simplicia organa*), the chorus plus *subdupla* pipes (*modo duplicia*) and two-manual play in which the right hand plays the chorus in the treble and the left plays the bass part (*simplicia organa pro discantu . . . tenorem in 10 clavibus bassioribus*). Describing the chorus in more detail, Arnaut uses the phrase 'double Principal' (*duplicia principalia*) for the basic rank, but it is uncertain whether this means two open pipes or one open and one stopped. In fact, this phrase occurs frequently in one or other form over the next hundred years, usually more ambiguous than some modern writers assume. Arnaut writes that in the case of the Dijon Court Chapel the *simplicia principalia* was 'divided into two' (*in duo divisa*), which must mean either that the usual double principals (8.8? 8.4?) could be separated from each other, which is likely, or that the single rank was halved to enable bass and treble to be played separately, though for what reason in 1450 can only be guessed. Two quints and an octave stop gave, presumably with the two principal stops, *quinque registra* or five registers— an early reference both to the idea of five stops (cf. the *cinque tirants* in a contemporary court chapel—see p. 51) and to the term *registrum*.

Arnaut also refers to Chair organs or *tergali positivo* ('back positive'), describing one (said to be that of Notre-Dame, Dijon, 1447) with 195 pipes, a compass of FG–f'' at 4' pitch, and a *Blockwerk* of octave ranks only, four in the bass and seven at the top. The front pipes were of tin, the others—the 'helpers and co-principal pipes standing behind' (*auxiliantes et posteriores coprincipales*)—of lead, very thick and nearly three times as heavy as the front pipes. The measurements of neither mouths nor footholes followed any true scaling (*nulla est . . . dyapason*), and yet everyone who heard the organ praised it. 'What would people say if the organ had been made according to the rules of the art?' asked Arnaut.

Bibliography

BORMANN, K., *Die gotische Orgel von Halberstadt* (Berlin, 1966), 147–72

HARDOUIN, P., 'Pour une histoire du plein-jeu', *Renaissance de l'orgue*, 1 (1968), 21–3; 2 (1969), 6–11; *Connoissance de l'orgue*, 10 (1974), 5–9

KLOTZ, H., *Über die Orgelkunst der Gotik, der Renaissance und des Barock* (Kassel, 1975), 31–48

G. LE CERF and E.-R. LABANDE, eds., *Les Traités d'Henri Arnaut de Zwolle et de divers anonymes* (*MS Bib. Nat. latin 7295*) (Paris, 1932; reprint with postword by F. Lesure, Kassel, 1972)

8 Developments in the Later Fifteenth Century

The division of the *Blockwerk* into different 'sounds', called *gheluut*, *registra* or *jeu* in different sources, is established by other documents from the mid-fifteenth century, in particular the contracts and agreements which begin to specify number of 'sounds', compass, keyboards and other details. Thus at Zwolle in 1447, the contract specifies a Great Organ beginning at F and a Positive 'with double Principal and three sounds' (*van dubbel principalen van dreen gelueden*; Vente 1942, p. 179). From other Dutch sources it is clear that these three sounds were 1 principals, 2 mixture and 3 the two together. Moreover, at Delft Oude Kerk in 1458 the contract specifies that the Chair Organ (Vente 1942, p. 114):

> *sal hebben een regüster daer ment mede of sluten sal die posysy als men wil ende dan salt hebben een doef gheluut als floeyten*
> shall have a register so that one may shut off the mixture at will and then have a quiet sound like flutes

The two keyboards allowed one to play the Chair Organ alone or 'with the Great Organ' at will, a remark that may—but does not certainly—suggest a manual coupler. In the important southern parts of Germany, the 'three sounds' were increased: St. Sebald, Nuremberg (1439–41) had Principal, Fourniture and Cymbale, the last perhaps of the kind described by Arnaut. This particular division of the *Blockwerk* became something of a norm in the area, with examples in Koblenz (St. Florian, 1467), Hagenau (St. George, 1491), Weimar (1492), Basel (St. Peter, 1496) and elsewhere farther west (Louvain, 1522). Yet it is exactly at this period that organs in Italy and probably parts of southern France had already become much more versatile, built with one long manual instead of two short (the Delft Great was FGA–g"a", the Chair f–g"a" only) and furnished with several separate ranks of pipes. By 1474–83, S. Petronio, Bologna, already had a full-scale, 50-note organ of nine single-rank stops (smaller than the extant organ), and the organist there can be assumed to have combined those stops in many various ways, though perhaps to a lower level of volume than his northern colleague.

Two questions sum up the major issues at this key period: Why did builders of some areas give an organ several manuals while those in others developed the single manual? And, how were stops separated from each other to produce the different colours or effects characteristic of all later organs? As to the first question, it is possible that southern builders learnt earlier than northern—perhaps because of their materials and climactic conditions—how variety can be given to one long keyboard when the chest is so made as to enable some kind of mechanism to block the wind from certain ranks at will; and perhaps northern builders found that two or even three shorter, perhaps unequal keyboards, with one or two registrations each, were more useful and reliable, even more powerful. The length of the keyboards is instructive: thus, already by 1473 S. Martino, Lucca, had a compass of 53 or 54 notes while the Hagenau organ listed above still had only 36 and 25 notes respectively. It could well be too that the required volume of sound was important, for dividing the organ into several chests is very practical from the point of view of wind supply, and the large chests of Italy must have been unsuitable for constant playing of a big *plenum*, however many the number of contrapuntal parts in the music. On the question of how stops were divided, the situation is clearer. Several documents from the middle of the fifteenth century onwards refer to the varieties of sound produced by the organ concerned and use such terms as *registra* (Henri Arnaut), *registros* (Treviso, 1436), *tirans* (Aragon Court Chapel, 1420 and Barcelona Minorite Church, 1480), *division de veus* ('division of voices' at Perpignan, 1516), *dreen gelueden* (the 'three sounds' of Dutch organs), and even *a la moderna cum registri sei* ('with six stops in the modern manner', Catarro, 1488). The terms themselves sometimes suggest the mechanism. Thus *registres* and *tirants* certainly suggest the sliderchest, as do the *registres sive tirans* ('registers or draw-stops') at Avignon in 1539; on the other hand, *division* seems to suggest that the *Blockwerk* chest was divided into two or three parts to which wind could be admitted separately.

Fig. 6 is a diagram of an ideal *Blockwerk* chest from which builders gradually departed. In this construction, the opened pallet admits wind to all the pipes belonging to one key, i.e. those placed above one groove in the chest, and amongst which pipes the player cannot choose. To obtain variety, some organs had their grooves divided laterally into two or more parts, each with its own pallet; each partial chest could have its wind cut off with a valve somewhere between bellows and pallet-box, though it is probable that most often the front half-chest sounded all the time, for its pipes were those of the case-front or Open Diapason, perhaps paired with a Stopped Diapason in some organs. In effect, the principals and the mixture of such double chests had their own wind box, the back one of which was provided with a shut-off valve for taking off the mixture. Each key in an organ whose principals did not always sound operated two pallets and two pallet-springs, and though apparently cumbersome, once made such chests were probably as reliable as they were unwasteful of wind, and it is not surprising that fifteenth-century

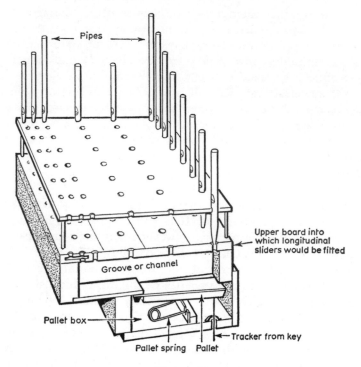

Figure 6

builders in the triangle Normandy–Rhineland–Netherlands valued them.

The Roman organ of Aquincum had sliders in so far as the player admitted wind to the pipes by means of a perforated strip (see also Fig. 3); longitudinal sliders running the length of the chest beneath one rank of pipes were different only in application. But when and where such true stop-sliders were first made will probably never be known, though it could be assumed that they first appeared on small organs. In any case, the sliderchest was the most crucial factor in the development of the organ and requires some examination.

In this construction, the opened pallet admits wind to each stop, whether single or multi-rank, by means of a perforated slip of wood sliding longitudinally in the boards between the pipe feet and the groove of the chest (see Fig. 6). The slider is pushed and pulled a sufficient distance either to allow wind to pass through ('stop drawn') or to prevent it from passing through ('stop pushed in'), and the slider end itself can be operated from a knob or lever near the player by means of a mechanism made up of rods, trundles and levers.

A third system for separating sounds was the springchest. Such chests were known probably in Italy during the fifteenth century, and Orvieto

Cathedral is said to have had an organ in 1480 with two spring stops and two slider stops (*duo ad ventum et duo ad tira*; Lunelli 1956, p. 103). The springchest was much admired in the Netherlands about 1520 when builders seem to have found it more reliable than the sliderchest for the biggest department of an organ.

In this construction (see Fig. 7), the opened pallet admits wind to each single or multi-rank stop by means of a secondary pallet or 'groove-valve' operated by the stop-lever bar, which like the slider could be connected or relayed to a position convenient to the player. The spring acting on the

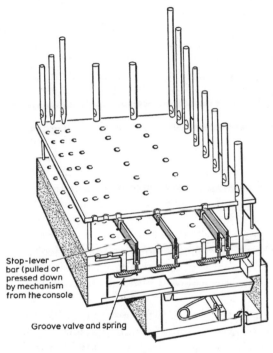

Stop-lever bar (pulled or pressed down by mechanism from the console

Groove valve and spring

Figure 7

secondary pallet causes the bar to spring back to the off-position unless prevented from doing so, e.g. by the player notching the stop-lever at the keyboard into an on-position. There were other kinds of springchest: many Italian builders from the late fifteenth century onwards placed their secondary pallets vertically rather than horizontally, with the convenience that the bar then moved horizontally. Others in sixteenth-century Italy and seventeenth-century Germany went some way to avoiding the trouble necessary for dismantling a chest, when one of the brass springs broke or lost its flexibility, by designing the chest so that all the secondary pallets belonging to a single groove could be pulled out in a strip when required.

E

Whatever the refinements, however, the springchest is troublesome to make, as later theorists such as Mersenne and Werckmeister noted, and it takes up more room than a comparable sliderchest. But it has also been said that springchests last longer, being less subject to minor change caused by warping, and that their spaciousness is itself an advantage for the acoustic development of pipe tone throughout an organ.

While the nature and purpose of the block, slider- and springchests are well enough understood today, at least in principle, there is far less certainty about other details. Thus although it is common to suppose that the 'double Principal' of the late fifteenth century denoted a rank of stopped pipes sounding with the open pipes of the case-front, the evidence is slender. In fact, the origin and development of stopped pipes are very unclear. The Quintadena is a stopped rank mentioned and often called *Schallpfeifen* early in the sixteenth century; but when exactly it appeared is not known, although no doubt the emphasis on new organ colours at this period was responsible for the development of stopped pipes in general. 'Coppel' was the name given to some stopped pipes in organs of central Europe from early in the sixteenth century onwards (Bienne, Switzerland, 1517); but it seems first to have been used for the open case-pipes themselves (Limburg, 1471), in which case the term is no doubt related to the 'double Principal' of the contracts: something 'coupled to' the case-pipes. The stopped Holpyp seems to be authenticated from Rhineland or Netherlandish sources from *c.* 1500 onwards, but probably not before. Schlick is still ambiguous about stopped pipes in 1511, which would hardly have been the case had they become accepted as a norm by then. Even flute stops at that period were open (e.g. at Bordeaux in 1510), as was indeed the case in most kinds of Italian organ for the next two and even three hundred years.

In the period around 1500, then, the average or large organ in northern Italy or southern France would probably have had a chorus of some ten separate stops, mostly or all single-rank, probably provided by a springchest if the organ were on the large side and by a sliderchest if small; upper ranks may have been duplicated in some organs. In the parts of Spain influenced by Flemish or 'German' builders the organ was accordingly more northern in style. The larger instruments of the Rhineland and Netherlands (see Plate 7) had two and even three manual departments (*Blockwerk*, Chair organ and a further small chest at Zwolle Onze Lieve Vrouw, 1454), in most instances with their own keyboard. In England, the organ seems to have been of the smaller Dutch kind (All Hallows, London, 1519), though it is possible that in secular or aristocratic circles Italian organs were known. Three characteristic dispositions are the following:

NETHERLANDS (DELFT, Oude Kerk; source, Vente 1942, pp. 113 f)
A. Pieterszoon, rebuild of 1458

Grote Werk
A *Blockwerk* of 38 keys (FGA–g''a'') based on 16', with about 6 ranks in bass to 32 in treble (total, *c.* 750 pipes)

Rugpositief
A double chest of 28 keys (f–g''a''), with two 'sounds': the *doef* (2-rank Principal 4' or 8') and the *positie* (Mixture)

RHINELAND (HAGENAU, St. George; source, Vogeleis 1900)
F. Krebs, 1491

Manual
A divided chest FG–f'' with three sounds: *driifach fleiten* (the principals 8.8.4?), *das werk* (Mixture) and *ein zymmet* (Zimbell)

Positif
A double chest of 25 keys (f–f''), with two sounds? Described in contract merely as *positif zwifach*

Tenor
Pedal or bass manual of 17 keys (FG–b), based on 16', its sounds described as *fleiten* (principals), *klein tenor* (octave principal?) and *zymmet* (Zimbel)

ITALY (PADUA, S. Giustina; source, Lunelli 1937)
Leonard of Salzburg, 1493

Manual
One manual of 38 notes (FGA–g''a'')

Tenori	8
Ottava	4
Decimaquinta	2
Decimanona	$1\frac{1}{3}$
Vigesimaseconda	1
Flauto	8

Such schemes were regional, and it may well be that when the German Bernhard Dilmano made a large 1000-pipe organ at Milan in 1464–6, it was of the larger northern type with which he was familiar, based on a divided chest giving at least the 'three sounds'; the instrument was modernized twenty or so years later, but by 1508 it still had only eight separate stop-levers. However, it is still not certain how many ranks of a local Italian organ of 1475 would have been separate; as so often, it is easy to allow knowledge of later organs to influence the interpretation of the sources.

Even when much of the original material still exists, as it does at S. Petronio, Bologna (see Plate 4), there is at present little more than conjecture that can be made about the sound of such early organs. Wind pressures and voicing techniques of this period are still uncertain, and the fact that such-and-such a pipe or stop is 'old' tells us nothing. Little therefore should be read into the present-day singing, breathy quality of the Bologna principals or the 'limpid' choruses. But it does seem that some degree of extremes was aimed at by the early builders. The sources often speak of *süss* or *lieblich* principals ('sweet, lovely' at the Kloster Maria zu den Steinen, Basel, in 1518) and of *scharf* mixtures and cymbales (*ibid.*); only with the increase of colour stops on the subsidiary manuals are other tonal qualities invoked or claimed. One major factor must have been the rivalry between one church and another, or at least the desire to be equal: a whole chapter in the history of the organ can be read into a phrase in the contract at Zwolle in 1447 when the builder was required to make the organ 'as big and good' as that in Deventer.

Bibliography

KLOTZ, H., *Über die Orgelkunst der Gotik, der Renaissance und des Barock* (Kassel, 1975), 34–60

LUNELLI, R., *Der Orgelbau in Italien in seinen Meisterwerken* (Mainz, 1956)

LUNELLI, R., 'Organari stranieri in Italia', *Note d'Archivio* (Rome, 1937), nos. 4–6

VENTE, M. A., *Bouwstoffen tot de Geschiedenis van het Nederlandse Orgel in de 16de Eeuw* (Amsterdam, 1942)

VOGELEIS, M., 'Ein Orgelvertrag aus dem Jahre 1491', *Monatshefte für Musikgeschichte*, 32 (1900), 155–61

WILLIAMS, P., *The European Organ 1450–1850* (London, 1966)

9 Arnolt Schlick and his 'Spiegel der Orgelmacher'

By 1500, organists, organ-builders and their clients were demanding special effects from their instruments. New organs in Flanders or southern France, Baltic Germany or northern Italy, were expected to provide new sounds, and builders promised them to their clients. Thus, at Antwerp Cathedral in 1509, Hans Suys promised individual stops to provide, alone or in combination—it is not clear which—the sounds of the Schwiegel flute, the Waldhorn, the Quintadena (*Scheelpijpen*), trumpets, shawms, the Zink (cornett), Rauschpfeife, drums and *noch meer andere seltseme stemmen* ('several other unusual stops more'), according to his agreement (Stellfeld 1942, p. 45). Probably most major builders reckoned to have 'other unusual stops' in their repertory, unknown to their competitors and thus superior to them. It was against this background of inventive competition that in 1511 Arnolt Schlick produced and published a splendid, forthright little book on organs—the first published book on the subject, the fellow of contemporary books on instruments by Virdung and others, but much their superior in practical and permanent usefulness. *Spiegel der Orgelmacher* ('The Mirror of Organ-makers')* was published under imperial auspices and seems to have been intended as a kind of standard code of practice for organ-builders in Maximilian I's German Empire: an organ-maker's equivalent to the books the Emperor wished to have available on various other subjects such as hunting, falconry, fishing and gardening (Biba 1969, p. 1315). Schlick himself lived in the central Palatinate court-town of Heidelberg, writing in something of a Heidelberg dialect. He may have come from Bohemia and evidently travelled quite widely in the area contained by Prague, Basel and Utrecht; he served as organ adviser, and both as composer and author exercised a major influence on Rhineland organ-art of the period. Since that area was amongst the most modern in its approach to organs, it becomes particularly important to understand what Schlick was saying and what lies behind his pithily expressed opinions.

The two ideal organs described in the *Spiegel* contained about 15 stops

---

* 'Mirror' was a common title for *incunabula* and other early printed books conveying information on practical or on technical matters.

each and were governed by his ideas that 'it is not commendable to build many registers' and that there should not be 'too many of the same type'. The chief difference between the two organs is that of the octave pitch, rather than the number of stops; the larger was the equivalent of a 16′ organ, with a bigger case-size than the 8′ organ.

Hauptwerk (F–a″, 41 notes)

die Principaln (Principal of two or more ranks, one 'long', one 'short' scale)

ein Oktaff einer langen mess (Octave of 'long measurement', i.e. open? Double length if the organ were large, i.e. of 16′)

Gemsserhörner . . . kurtz weit mess ('wide Gemshorn', an octave above the Principals)

ein Zymmel (Zimbel)

Hindersatz (large chorus Mixture, 16–18 ranks at the top)

die rauss Pfeifen (Rauschpfeife imitating the shawm; perhaps a reed stop?)

hültze Glechter (an unusual stop, a 'wooden clapper', 'whose sound resembles that of small boys hitting a pot with a spoon'; perhaps a Quintadena, i.e. with narrow stopped pipes)

der Zinck (Zink or cornett, either a reed or a mixture containing Tierce rank)

Schwiegeln (Flageolet or small flute, probably of 2′)

Register . . . gleich eim Positiff ein Regall oder ein Superregal ('stop like the regal or octave-regal of a positive organ; perhaps in the *Brust* or breastwork of the organ)

Rückpositiv (F–a″, 41 notes?)

die Principaln (Principal, 'either of wood or of tin voiced like wood')

Gemsslein (small Gemshorn, also perhaps tapered)

Hindersetzlein (small Mixture)

guts rheins Zymmelein ('good clean Zimbel', i.e. Zimbel without Tierce rank?)

Pedal (F–c′, 20 notes)

Principaln ym Pedal (Principal, perhaps transmitted from *Hw*)

Octaff (Octave, perhaps transmitted from *Hw*)

Hindersats (Mixture, perhaps transmitted from *Hw*)

Trommeten oder Busaun (Trumpet or Posaune)

In addition, Schlick said, the *Hauptwerk* might contain a Krummhorn (*Kromphörner*) and the pedal a 'Klein octaff' and 'Zymmel', but the last two are not really pedal stops. This last is an interesting detail since it shows Schlick to be post-medieval in his approach to the bass line or pedal part: organ-building and music in general were moving towards the assumption that a bass line is not merely the lowest part but one with its own deep tone and acoustic weight. However, all stops should be on separate sliders, according to Schlick, so that the pedal if required could take the *cantus firmus* or melody which, as two centuries of organists were to appreciate, suited it very well. The double Principals of 'long' and 'short' scale may well suggest open and stopped pipes; or the terminology may suggest two Principal ranks of narrow and wide scales respectively, as is said to have been the case with the 1491 Haguenau organ (see p. 69; Schlick reported on this organ in 1510) and elsewhere at the turn of the century. The Hintersatz should not contain the very low ranks of the 'large mixture' (by which perhaps he meant the old *Blockwerk*) nor the 'low pitched 3rds and 5ths' sometimes met with in organs—another interesting detail and one perhaps referring to the new *Hörnli* mixtures of central Europe, i.e. Tierce compound-stops of the Sesquialtera and Cornet family. The Hintersatz could be made of 'lead pipes', while the Zimbel was to be clear, pure and high pitched. Schlick saw little point in making $5\frac{1}{3}'$ stops or Sesquialteras, and the adding of various little chests of the *Brustwerk* kind merely increased cost and resulted in 'much sauce for little fish'.

Reeds he thought not unreliable if properly made, and it was a characteristic of the Schlick organ that it had a judicious and carefully thought-out proportion of reed stops to flutes and flue choruses. Whether his phrase *Rauschpfeife, Krummhorn oder Schalmei* meant three quite different stops or is merely a list of synonyms for one stop is not clear. It seems that reeds had a bad reputation for stability—whether of tone or pitch is also unclear—but Schlick thought a competent organist could soon learn how to make the necessary minor adjustments to them. Thus he knew an organ of principals, mixtures, flutes and reeds; two manuals and pedal; probably a manual coupler; conveniently situated stop-levers (preferably not push–pull, he thought—sliding iron levers in a major organ can still be seen in the Innsbruck Hofkirche), not too long or too heavy to work easily from the keyboards; a range of different scalings for the open metal pipes, varying in circumference to length from 1:5 through 1:6 to 1:7; and conical metal pipes. What he seems not to have specifically required—though he surely knew them by 1511—were stopped pipes and wooden pipes. The pipe metal (at least of the case-front principals) was to be mostly pure tin, and the Principal was doubled. For the smaller (and probably larger) organ that he described, he recommended a compass of F–a" in order to give a *gut frey bass contra* ('a good independent bass line')—a phrase implying much about the evolution of harmony and bass lines. He also recommended a pitch about a tone lower than that of today, with $a^1 = 374$–392 Hz, depending on the diameter of the pipe. The *Spiegel* is also of major importance to the history of temperament. While recommending an irregular tuning with an a♭ that could serve (if played embellished) as g♯ in a cadence on A, Schlick recognized that some people preferred a meantone temperament in which major 3rds were slightly larger than pure. Various interpretations of his temperament have been published (most recently in Barber 1975, Lange 1978 and the 6th edn. of Grove's *Dictionary*); he seems to have heard intervals, particularly 3rds very precisely, perhaps as a result of his blindness, and in his treatment of 5ths (all but a♭–e♭ one fifth of a syntonic comma flat) created an unequal temperament easier to tune without artificial aids than today's equal temperament. As to playing methods, it is clear that Schlick's design of the keyboards and organist's stool were such that an organist sat rather higher than today, therefore finding toe-pedalling and thumbless manual-playing comfortable.

Thus Schlick provides a complete picture of an organ or at least of the outlines of one towards which a skilled builder applies his own methods or manner of construction. His general attitudes are equally informative and have the ring of an opinion meant to be influential on organists in general. He felt that eight or nine stops in the Great Organ were all that were needed; they should be clearly different in tone; and the second manual was to be regarded as a kind of small positive, in no sense a match for the Great. He noted that the organ was used in connection with the liturgy: the priest at the altar—whether in chapel or quire—was given the note for most Mass movements from the Gloria onwards, and the organist also accompanied Masses, Magnificats and other pieces, in addition to his solo music. And since the organ had a particular part to play in music such as the sung sequences, it was placed near the choir. Moreover, its design ought to have some regard for the architecture of the church. Whether the pedal were transmitted from the Great or not, it should have stops of the same pitch as the main manual for which—though Schlick does not say so in as many words—it acts as a kind of extension. The pedal should not be composed only of low sub-octave stops, because it would then, Schlick says, invert the harmony.* Reed stops can be well made and still sound as new nine or so years later. No mixtures, whether made up of 5ths and 8ves or 5ths and 3rds should contain ranks too low; it should be possible to play full chords with the *organo pleno*; and

---

* This must refer to the facts firstly that in playing a *cantus firmus* the pedal is a tenor line and should not cross the bass; secondly that by 1511 the bass part or *contratenor bassus* was being freed from its medieval subservience or equality; and thirdly that some organs had large pipes always and only played by the pedal keyboard.

the number of mixture ranks should depend on the size of the church. Manual keys should not be too long or short, nor too wide or narrow, spaced not too far apart or too close; the pedal keys should be short and the bench position such as to enable the organist's feet to 'hang or hover over the pedals' for the toe-pedalling. The manual should be centred over the pedalboard. Schlick's measurements, like those in some earlier manuscripts dealing with technical subjects, are related to a line printed in the text (i.e. they do not depend on movable concepts like 'feet' and 'inches') and suggest that he wanted the manual keys rather stubby by today's standards (naturals $c.\ 4\frac{5}{16}''$, sharps $c.\ 2\frac{5}{8}''$), with an octave span about the same as on a modern organ ($c.\ 8''$).

Some of Schlick's own music in *Tablatur etlicher Lobgesang* (1512) is contrapuntal in a way that closely anticipates later organ chorales which use the theme imitatively in three or four parts; the frequent *cantus firmus* phrases may or may not require solo stops. In such pieces the pedal took the melody when it appeared in the bass. He also knew pedal playing in two, three and even four parts, as well as pedal runs; in the *Tablatur*, no less than four out of thirteen pieces require double pedalling. For none of these functions would the old Trompes have been useful, and it is clear that at least in the Rhineland the art of pedal playing had entered a new era. However typical or atypical further research will ever show Schlick's three- or four-part pedal playing to have been, his treatise certainly signals a sophisticated stage in the development of organ playing as a whole. The inner-voice *cantus firmus* technique, however, should not necessarily be taken at face value, any more than it should be in the Buxheim Organ Book of the previous century. Such musical notation as is found in the *Tablatur* of 1512 essentially represents an organ score; and such scores must often have been open to various interpretations or playing methods. Indeed, they must often have been intended or designed as such. As late as *c.* 1750 it is not wholly certain what J. S. Bach intended the pedal to play in some of his *Schübler* chorales, and it cannot be more certain in Schlick.

The largest chapters of the *Spiegel* are concerned with tuning, the making of chests (with sliders at the top of the chest, not running between the two top boards, according to Klotz 1975, p. 90), and the bellows. Schlick's advice is always practical: for example, the wind must be generous (for homophonic textures on full organ?), the organ should be constantly played (even during Advent and Lent though presumably not in the liturgy itself?), and only the best and most experienced organ-builders should be entrusted with a commission. Thus the book surveys the whole field of organ activity—building, playing, composing—and even the long chapters on chests and tuning are full of good, direct advice beyond that of most craftsmen-builders on one hand and most scholars-theorists on the other. Later organs such as Weingarten 1554–8 seem to follow, or at least owe a lot to, the scheme propounded by Schlick; and although the book was unknown a century later, was not mentioned by contemporary authors or by Praetorius, and survives today in only two copies, it would nevertheless be reasonable to claim that Schlick's *Spiegel*, for its size and purpose, has never been bettered.

Bibliography

BARBER, E. B., 'Arnolt Schlick, Organ Consultant and his "Spiegel der Orgelmacher und Organisten" ', *The Organ Yearbook*, 6 (1975), 33–41

BIBA, O., 'Zum 450 Todestag von Kaiser Maximilian I', *Ars organi*, 35 (1969), 1314–20

KLOTZ, H., *Über die Orgelkunst der Gotik, der Renaissance und des Barock* (Kassel, 1975), 89–93

LANGE, H. H. K., 'Das Clavecin Brisé von Jean Marius in der Berliner Sammlung und die Schlick-Stimmung', *Musikforschung*, 31 (1978), 57–79

SCHLICK, A., *Spiegel der Orgelmacher und Organisten* (Speyer, 1511; facs. with modern German translation [P. Smets], Mainz, 1959; facs. with English translation [E. B. Barber], Amsterdam, 1979?)

STELLFELD, J. A., 'Bronnen tot de Geschiedenis der Antwerpse Clavecymbel- en Orgelbouwers in de XVIe en XVIIe Eeuwen', *Vlaams Jaarboek voor Muziekgeschiedenis*, 4 (1942), 1–110

Although its type differed from country to country, soon after 1500 the organ was capable of producing more colours and effects than it had ever produced before. It did this by means of separable stops or several keyboards or both, and it is still not at all clear why a region favoured one system more than another. A great deal of any organ type is characteristic of only a restricted geographical area, and it would still be premature to assume that the northern organist required more volume of sound than his Italian contemporary, or that a Mediterranean builder's materials— particularly the kinds of wood—made a single large springchest more desirable than a pair of divided or sliderchests. Throughout organ history after the fourteenth century, the characteristics belonging to regional organ types were often strangely independent of those elsewhere, even of those in neighbouring regions. Were there to be a tradition for cultural exchange between regions—such as that between the northern Hanseatic towns or between Flanders and Catalonia—cross-currents would be clearer, and it would be easier to find connections between Amsterdam and Danzig than between cities far nearer Amsterdam such as Paris or Prague. On the whole the later the organ the more local it is likely to be, and the period from the early Benedictine abbeys to those years in which Napoleon's armies were tying the ends of Europe can be seen not as a gradual approach towards unity but, in terms of organ design, a gradual move away from it.

At the beginning of the sixteenth century there were still points in common between the regional organ types. Many new stops, in particular the flutes and reeds, were invented, and extant documents show how they were used. Such registrations or, as the document of *c.* 1510 in Saint-Michel, Bordeaux puts it, *instructions pour le jeu de l'orgue*, already use such terms as *tot lo orgue*, *orgue plè*, *grand jeu*, *Principaal* (Netherlands) and *ripieno* (Brescia) to refer to the full organ, while to distinguish the case-pipes from the full organ a more anonymous term such as *fleutes* could be found in a contract placed with any church in the stretch from Amsterdam to Barcelona. If the organ contained a set of single-rank stops, it became even more necessary not only to label each of them but to work out ways of combining them. This was the case at Bordeaux, and it would be reasonable to suppose that many an Italian and Spanish organist had similar ideas. The Bordeaux specification is not clear, but a plausible interpretation is as follows (Douglass 1969, p. 34):

BORDEAUX, St-Michel
L. Gaudet, 1510

1	Prestant	16 (F-compass)
2	Octave	8
3	Fifteenth	4
4	Nineteenth	$2\frac{2}{3}$
5	Twenty-second	2
6	Twenty-sixth	$1\frac{1}{3}$
7	Twenty-ninth	1
8	Flute	8
9	Flute	4

grand jeu: all stops except the first
jeu de papegay: 1, 2
les cornès: 1, 5, 6
jeu de grans cornaiez: 1, 5, 6, 9
la fleuste: 1
les cimbales: 1, 2, 6, 9
les chantres: 1, 8 (or 1, 2, 8)
les fleutes d'Alement: 3, 8
la petite cimbale: 1, 6
les gros cornetz: 1, 2, 5, 6
le grand jeu doulx: 1, 2, 3, 8 9

Three points stand out from this registration list: firstly, that there were subtle gradations between full organ and single stops; secondly, that builders and players were already finding fanciful names for the combinations; thirdly, that mutations were already taking their place in imaginative colour-building. Schlick too wanted stops drawn in different combination and those combinations frequently changed. The Bordeaux list also shows an important detail: only for one registration are more than four stops drawn. For at least the next two centuries—up to and beyond the registrations of Gottfried Silbermann—all known directives for organ stops centre on imaginatively combining only a handful of stops. Old organs 'restored' during this century and given modern wind-raising apparatus trap most organists—particularly those working for the record companies—into habits of gross over-registration.

Quite as important as the fanciful Bordeaux registrations were the more general references found in other documents, such as Daniel van der Distelen's agreement with Antwerp Cathedral in 1505, where the 'sounds' are put in distinct groups: principals, flutes, reeds, mixtures. Mutations, whether scaled as principals or flutes, were more familiar in the southern organ at this period, but at Antwerp there were at least four reed stops, all designed (at least in name) to imitate particular instruments: cornett, bagpipe-regal, trumpet and crumhorn/dulcian. Such imitations became so important during the sixteenth century that both reeds and compound flue stops were employed to produce the desired imitation. Often it is unclear from the sources whether a particular Zink, Cornet, Nachthorn or Rauschpipe were flue or reed, although in the case of trumpets and crumhorns it seems always to have been a question of reeds. Also unclear is whether the various kinds of flute were open or stopped. In most cases they were probably open, presumably wide in scale, while stopped pipes were reserved for even more special colour stops like the Quintadena or for the Bourdons that automatically sounded when the open principals of the case-front were drawn. The remarks made by the builder at St. Mary Magdalen, Basel in 1518 may hint at a common fault with early stopped ranks: he promised to make his stopped pipes 'bold and sweet' (*tapferer und liblich*), 'not too puerile' (*nit zu kindlich*) but audible throughout the church (Flade 1963).

The early sixteenth-century organ was full of colour: manual reeds, regals in little chests (*Brustwerk, Rückpositiv*), pedal reeds; stopped pipes of various kinds (Quintadena, Rohrflöte and plain Gedackt at Alkmaar in 1511); flutes of distinct colour (Gemshorn, Hohlflöte, Sifflöte), not least at mutation pitches (Schwiegel $1\frac{1}{3}'$). Both construction and octave-pitch of these various stops are often unclear, as too is the origin of those stop names that must always have indicated mutations ('Nasard', 'Larigot'). Tremulants, bird-stops and moving statuary were all known by the end of the fifteenth century, particularly in those areas with the most advanced organ-designs, for example the Upper Rhineland. As is often the case, there is very little reliable connection between the types of organ known by *c.* 1525 and the extant music of that period supposedly written for them, and it is even difficult to see the exact relationship between Arnolt Schlick's own music and the instrument he described in the *Spiegel*. Connections seen today between a south German organ of 1525 and the group of south German organ-tabulatures written in the same period are far more speculative and tentative than they often appear. But there can be no doubt that organs were registered imaginatively. Directions at Trier in 1537 show some basic ideas governing the music played on such instruments, with such registrations as the following (Klotz 1975, pp. 120–3):

TRIER, Cathedral
P. Breisiger, 1537

Two manuals and pedal (compass FFGGAA–g''a'' 50 notes, FGA–g''a''
38 notes and FGA–b 16 notes respectively)

Principael: Prinzipal, Quintaden, Mixtur, Zimbel
Hohlpfeife und Zimbel: Quintaden, Hohlpfeife 4', Zimbel, with pedal
   Quintaden, Prinzipal and Hohlpfeife
Quintaden, Zimbel und Flötenbass: Quintaden, Zimbel, with pedal
   Flöte 2'
two manuals and pedal:
1. Quintaden, Prinzipal, Hohlpfeife, Zimbel, with *Positiv ripieno* and
   pedal Prinzipal and Hohlpfeife; or
2. Quintaden, Nachthorn [flue Cornet], with *Positiv* Quintaden,
   Rauschwerk [reed] and pedal Quintaden, Prinzipal, Trompete

---

The two dozen or so registrations at Trier are all witness—despite the
inevitable ambiguities—to an imaginative use of two manuals, pedal solos
and manual colours. Single-manual organs, like that in the Dresden
Court Chapel (made in 1563 by H. R. Rodensteen), allowed a wide range
of combinations from one to four stops, as the original registrations
show here too; indeed, theoretical calculation of how many combinations
or permutations could be computed from a given number of ranks
became rather a pastime with some seventeenth-century theorists. At
Dresden, some typical registrations were as follows (Flade 1932/3,
pp. 7 ff):

any of the 16', 8', 4' and 2' ranks alone
flutes: 16.8, 16.4, 16.2, 16.8 reed, 16.Zimbel, 8.8.4, 8.4.Zimbel
full organ: 8.8.4.Mixtur.Zimbel

The last was the only registration of more than four stops. At Bayreuth in
1597, T. Cumpenius's registrations were also careful to add the pedal
(Hofner 1972 p. 8), for example:

full organ: manual 8.8.4.2⅔.Mixtur.Zimbel, with pedal Subbass, Principal and Posaune
pedal solo: pedal Subbass, Cornett, with manual Gedackt
flutes: manual Gedackt, Sifflöte, Tremulant, with pedal Subbass
single 8': manual Principal with pedal Principal

Specifications of some characteristic organs follow, organs to which the previous developments were leading. All these were sophisticated schemes, traditional in some details, innovatory or formative in others. The first is from the Netherlands (Vente 1958, pp. 67–75; see also Edskes 1969):

AMSTERDAM, Oude Kerk
Hendrik & Hermann Niehoff, with Hans Suys, 1539–42

Das Prinzipal		*Oberwerk*	
Probably FGA–g^{ll}a^{ll}		F–a^{ll} (with g$\sharp^{ll}$?), two chests	
Prinzipal	16	Prinzipal	8
Oktave	8 ∣ 4	Holpijp	8
Mixtur		Offenflöte	4
Scharf		Quintadena	8 or 4
		Gemshorn	2
		Sifflöte	1 or 1$\frac{1}{3}$
Rückpositiv		Zimbel (?)	III (?)
F–a^{ll} (with g$\sharp^{ll}$?), two chests		Trompete	8
Prinzipal	8	Zinck (treble)	8 (?)
Oktave	4		
Mixtur		*Pedal*	
Scharf		FGA–c^l	
Quintadena	8	Coupler to *Prinzipal* manual, F–d^l	
Holpijp	4	Nachthorn	2
Krummhorn (?)	8	Trompete	8
Regal	8	Pedal stops on *Prinzipal*	
Baarpijp (regal)	8	chest?	
Schalmei	4		

Six bellows (probably single-fold)
Wind-pressure *c.* 90 mm
Couplers uncertain, perhaps *Ow/Rp* only
Tremulant, probably in the main trunk
All chests probably springchests (*Rp* sliderchest?)
Keyboards: *Ow* aligned above *Rp* but *Hw* probably a 4th to the left or 5th to the right
First four *Rückpositiv* stops 'make the Prinzipal'
Holpijp ranks, probably chimney-flutes; Nasard and Gemshorn conical?

This instrument, modified in 1544, was that known to Sweelinck and shows the 'Brabant organ' at its most typical: a big Principal chorus ('strengthened' in 1544), large flute ranks on the upper chest (Nasard replacing the Quintadena in 1544), smaller stops producing great variety in the Chair organ (Sifflöte 1⅓' replacing the Krummhorn in 1544), and a pedal department with two clear functions (coupled *plenum* and strong solo stops for melodies). The manuals encouraged variety for which the partitas on psalm tunes, popular over the next two or more centuries in reformed churches, were very suitable, as too the size and splendour of such organs encouraged the new taste for weekday organ-recitals in such buildings. From surviving examples of Niehoff's pipework, it seems that the inner ranks were of thick, hammered lead of good quality, the principals narrow in the bass and round-toned in the treble, the whole with a mild-voiced, singing quality quite different from the baroque organ of the next century. Flutes were wide, sometimes very wide; reeds were penetrating and powerful, particularly in the bass. Whether it can be argued that the 'very difficult runs in 3rds and 6ths' in Sweelinck's music proves Niehoff to have made light actions and shallow key-falls (Vente 1958, p. 138) is doubtful, since there are too many questions begged when instrument and music are so directly related. Similarly, the wide stretches written in Sweelinck's Fantasias, chiefly in their first sections only, are poor evidence that he required the pedal (Klotz 1975, p. 200), since other explanations could be conjectured. But certainly the Amsterdam springchests were considered superior to the sliderchests so often made for the small organs of large churches (e.g. Alkmaar small organ, sliderchest of 1511) or for the Chair organs of the larger instruments. Some of the 'Brabant organs' also had large pedal departments, at least in the instruments of the kind Niehoff fathered in Cologne, Würzburg, Lüneburg and elsewhere; and the music for which they were made gained some circulation amongst the many widely scattered composers directly or indirectly under Sweelinck's influence.

Two largely extant organs representative of sixteenth-century central Europe and northern Italy respectively are those of Innsbruck and Brescia (Eberstaller 1955, p. 9; Antegnati 1958 edn., preface, p. 11):

INNSBRUCK, Hofkirche
G. Ebert, 1555–61 (restored J. Ahrend, 1970)

Hauptwerk CDEFGA–g''a''		*Rückpositiv* FGA–g''a''	
Prinzipal	8	Prinzipal	4
Gedackt	8	Gedackt	4
Oktave	4	Mixtur	III–V
Quinte	2⅔	Hörnlein	II (new)
Superoktave	2	Zimbel	II (new)

Hauptwerk		Pedal	
Hörnlein	II	CDEFGA–b♭	
Hintersatz	V–X	operating own row of pallets in	
Zimbel	II	*Hw* chest (? 16th century)	
Trompete	8 (new)		
Regal	8 (new)		

Seven or eight bellows
Pitch, $a^1 = 445$ Hz
Wind-pressure, 90 mm
Meantone tuning, with pure thirds and e♭/d♯ mean
Rp pallets in lower part of main organ (conduits below organ stool)
Regal placed in the front of the organ on a *Brustwerk* chest (with its own
 pallets) below *Hw* chest
Suspended action (i.e. keys hanging from trackers)
Tremulant in main trunk (the fewer the undulations the larger the pipes being
 played)
Case-pipes 76·7% tin, inner pipes 57·8% tin

BRESCIA, S. Giuseppe
G. Antegnati, 1581

CCDDEEFFGGAA–g"a"	(53 notes)
Principale	*8 (halves)
Ottava	4
Quintadecima	2
Decimanona	$1\frac{1}{3}$
Vigesimaseconda	1
Vigesimasesta	$\frac{2}{3}$
Vigesimanona	$\frac{1}{2}$
Trigesimaterza	$\frac{1}{3}$
Trigesimasesta	$\frac{1}{4}$
Flauto in ottava	4
Flauto in duodecima	$2\frac{2}{3}$
Flauto in quintadecima	2
Fiffaro	8 (treble only)

* Pitch-names from C (i.e. 16′ Principale from CC, etc.)

Pedal pulldowns (original compass uncertain)
Originally a springchest
Pitch, about one semitone above $a^1 = 440$ Hz
Wind pressure, *c.* 42 mm

At *Brescia*, the low pressure and the average-to-narrow scalings (said to be untransposed and therefore original) give a soft, round, mild tone very cantabile in character. Low pressures may explain the absence of reeds in such organs, though the argument could be reversed. The downward compass of such Italian organs ideally varied with the size of the church: the larger the church, the longer the bass compass. The top note was almost always a'', the bottom (depending on size) c, G, F, C, GG, FF or CC. The fifteenth-century organ at S. Petronio, Bologna, went to AA or perhaps GG at 16' pitch, i.e. into the 32' octave. When pedalboards were added later to such organs, they were thought of as mechanical conveniences for pulling down the bass keys and were usually made of simple strips of wood sloping upwards into the organ. The classical Italian organ had only open metal pipes; the ranks of the separate high stops break back an octave at or no higher than the pipe sounding c♯'''''', thus producing in the treble an accumulation of ranks usually no higher than the Principale 2'. In fact, the top of the Brescian treble cannot have been so different from a *Blockwerk* a century or more earlier. The lower ranks of such organs were often divided at b/c', requiring separate stop-levers for treble and bass and encouraging solo effects on a single manual. Costanzo Antegnati's rules for registration (1608) show the particular tone produced by a stop, the style of music it was made for, and the moment at which it played in the liturgy to be intimately connected. Thus the *ripieno* or *tutti* was drawn for sustained music of the so-called *durezze e ligature* style ('with suspensions and discords'), which in turn was employed for such moments as the toccata at the end of the *Deo gratias*. Flute stops of all pitches were played 'in solo music' (*da concerto*), not for accompanying motets or for filling out the *ripieno*. The undulating Fiffaro was drawn with the Principale alone and was heard in slow music played 'as smoothly and legato as possible', often with melodic phrases in the right hand such as one sees in the later toccatas of Frescobaldi. Pedal pipes were good for the long notes in toccatas, half-stops 'for playing in dialogue' (*per far dialoghi*), and the 2⅔' or 2' flutes for adding to the Principale in 'quick passages' and canzonas, i.e. lively fugues. Moreover, as Diruta showed, some keys or church modes were associated with particular moods and hence required particular registration. Although Diruta could be said to typify the Monteverdian age in his belief 'that certain registrations enhance the ethos of *affect* peculiar to each of the modes' (Soehnlein 1979), his registrations and remarks sprang from experience with organs of the previous century. Thus he thought that the mournfulness of E minor (Phrygian) needs the 16' with the Flauto 8', while D minor (Dorian) was full and grave, requiring either 16.16 or 16.8 combinations; F major (Lydian) was moderately gay and could have the Flauto 4' added to the 8.4 principals, while G major (Mixolydian) was lively and mild, requiring 8.4.2. Once again, both theorists work on the understanding that three or four stops are adequate and that the big *ripieni* ($16.8.4.2\frac{2}{3}.2.1\frac{1}{3}.1.\frac{2}{3}$ in Antegnati) are heard only once or twice in the service. While it is probable that the organs of Rome, Naples and many other cities were more modest than those of Brescia or Bologna, there is a striking uniformity about the Italian organ of the period (see Plate 11). Its greatest development since the fifteenth century lay rather in the design of the cases themselves, from gothic to renaissance and so to a wonderfully poised organ-shape worthy of that particular country in that particular century.

The cases of the organ at *Innsbruck* are very shallow, that of the Chair organ less than 50 cm, the Great about double. The chests are spacious, however, and both parts of the organ are contained in resonant closed wooden boxes, unlike so many Italian and Iberian organs partly open to the back and held by walls at the sides. The tone is very strong, unsuitable for accompanying a choir from either manual. Since all the Chair stops have equivalents in the Great yet at an octave above—a common idea in the late fifteenth and sixteenth centuries—the two manuals can be regarded at least in part as extensions of each other, as if one long compass had been broken into two and partly duplicated. Similar points could be made about even later Chair organs, e.g. H. Compenius's *Rückpositiv* at Fritzlar in 1590, where the stoplist is almost a literal repeat of the *Hauptwerk* only an octave higher (T. Schneider 1976, p. 995): Hw $8.4.2\frac{2}{3}.2.IV.II.16.8.4.8/Rp$ $4.2.1\frac{1}{3}.1.II.I.8.4.2.8$. But such similarities are more apparent than real, for at least four of the Rp ranks were flutes not principals. At Innsbruck and other organs of its area and period, the similarity between the two manuals was more real: for example, the Hw Gedackt 8' and Rp Gedackt 4' have scalings virtually identical. In any case, even the stopped pipes at Innsbruck are very strong in tone, with a big mouth (high cut-up characterizes all pipes of the organ) and a tone colour ranging from vague flute sound in the wide bass to a strong, breathy, colourful treble. All the pipes of the Hw Mixtur and Zimbel and the Rp Mixtur and Zimbel had (and now have) the same scale as the Hw Oktave 2', which is itself much the same as the Oktave 4', i.e. somewhat narrower then the Prinzipal 8'. The two Hörnli stops, restored by Ahrend and very characteristic of the period and area, are very keen, repeating Terzzimbeln, perhaps direct descendants of the little mixtures Henri Arnaut described. Throughout the organ there is a marked change of tone from bass to treble, showing that for the builder uniformity was not of paramount importance for any given rank of pipes, and enabling the treble keys to produce a solo-like quality when playing a line above accompanying chords. In the historical *aperçus* it offers the thinking player, the Innsbruck organ is unique and without doubt one of the most important organs in the world (see Salmen 1978).

For the French organ, Gisors has been taken for some decades now as the most instructive example from the late sixteenth century (Dufourcq 1971, pp. 122 ff):

GISORS, St-Gervais and St-Protais
N. Barbier, 1580

Grand orgue		*Positif*	
CD–c'''		CD–c'''	
Montre (tin)	16*	Bourdon (lowest 8ve wood)	8
Montre (lead)	8*	? Prestant (lead)	4
Bourdon (lead)	8*	? Doublette (lead)	2
Prestant (tin)	4*	Petite Quinte (tin)	1⅓
Flûte (lead)	4	Cymbale (tin)	II
Nasard (lead)	(II)2⅔	Cromorne	8
Doublette (tin)	2*		
Sifflet (lead)	1		
Fourniture (tin)	IV*	*Pédale*	
Cymbale (tin)	III*	Jeu de pédale (wood)	8
Quinte-flûte (lead)	1⅓ (?)	(from C?)	
Cornet (from c¹)	V	Sacquebouttes (tin)	8†
Trompette	8	(from FF)	
Clairon	4		
Voix humaine	8		

* *serviront pour le Plain Jeu* ('will serve for the full organ')
† perhaps 16′

Positif built within the main case (4′ rank perhaps stopped)
Tremulant, perhaps in main trunk
Coupler: *Pos/GO*
Pedal reeds on two chests either side of the *GO*
Four bellows (5′ × 2½′, Flemish foot measurement)
GO 1⅓′ and possibly *Pos* 1⅓′ rank, *à biberon* (chimney flute)
Principals and reeds had tin bodies with lead feet
In 1618, C. Carlier added a Chair organ

What music was written for the Gisors organ is uncertain, as it is indeed for all French types of organ before the Parisian standardization at the end of the seventeenth century. French organs of 1520 to 1575 often had a full palette of colours, whether they belonged to the Bordeaux–Italian traditions of the south or to those of the north, more Flemish-inspired in their variety of reeds and choruses. Reeds of 16′, 8′ and 4′ were frequently found on larger organs of about 1575 and as usual had instrumental names (sackbut, clarion); quint mutations were common; most organs had 8' and 4' stopped ranks (some had 16'), either of wood or metal; a few obsolescent ranks such as 1' Prinzipals could still be found; and so could a much more important stop, the mounted Cornet, often called 'Flemish horn' and conducted off to its own little half-chest above the inner front ranks of the *Grand Orgue* pipework. In some respects, the Gisors scheme was Flemish: the *Positif* location (for reasons not at all clear, the Chair Organ had become temporarily rare in France), the springchest, the CD–c''' compass, the quint flutes of 1⅓', the 8' pedal stops, and the *grand ravalement* or long compass for the pedal reed. No doubt the sound of the Gisors organ was closer to the Netherlandish conception than it was to the late classical French organ of F.-H. Clicquot.

In the Iberian peninsula, organs were often built either by Italians (Évora Cathedral, 1562) or Netherlanders (El Escorial, *c.* 1580). Although there were hardly yet distinct Spanish characteristics, Évora certainly had more Mixtures than an Italian organ, while El Escorial had its secondary manual in the form of a typically southern internal positive, rather than a Dutch–German Chair organ. The Lérida organ was typical of one kind of Spanish instrument (Anglès 1948):

LÉRIDA, Cathedral
M. Tellez, agreements of 1543 and 1544

Orgue major		*Cadireta*	
CDE–a''?		CDE–a''?	
Flautat	8	Flautat	4
Octava	4	Plè	
Plè [pleno]		Címales	
Címales [Zimbel]		Flautes tapades	8
Flautat	8	Flautes octaves	4
Flautat	4	Flautes quincenas	2
Trompetas	8?	Clarins de mar	8
Xaramellat	4?		
Clarins de galera	8?		

Six nightingales, seven tremulants, drums, a large Zimbelstern

As other interpretations of these contracts, which were written in medieval Catalan, show (Klotz 1975, p. 144; Williams 1966, pp. 238–9), there is much doubt about Tellez's terminology, so much so that it is not even clear whether one phrase refers to an eight-note pedal or merely to the twenty ranks of the main chorus. Certainly, however, some elements are clear: the ingenuity of the various toy-stops, the signalling function of the wheel-bells and the 'gallery trumpets', the balance of two choruses, two sets of flutes and two sets of colourful reeds ('trumpets of the sea', *xaramellat* or shawm). It is tempting to see the reeds as hinting at what was to come in Iberian organs and to dismiss the ambiguity over the pedals as characteristic of so many organs south of a line Bordeaux–Venice.

Bibliography

ANGLÈS, H., 'El Órgano de la Catedral de Lérida en 1543–56', *Anuario Musical*, 3 (1948), 205–7

ANTEGNATI, C., *L'Arte Organica* (Brescia, 1608; Ger. trans. [P. Smets], Mainz, 1958)

DIRUTA, G., *Il Transilvano* (Venice, 1593)

DOUGLASS, F., *The Language of the Classical French Organ* (New Haven, 1969)

DUFOURCQ, N., *Le Livre d'orgue français*, I 'Les Sources' (Paris, 1971)

EBERSTALLER, O., *Orgeln und Orgelbau in Oesterreich* (Graz/Köln, 1955)

EDSKES, C. H., 'The Organs of the Oude Kerk in Amsterdam at the Time of Sweelinck', appendix 1 in A. Curtis, *Sweelinck's Keyboard Music* (Leiden & London, 1969), 163–200

FLADE, E., 'Hermann Raphael Rottenstein-Pock', *Zeitschrift für Musikwissenschaft*, 15 (1932–3), 1 ff

FLADE, E., 'Literarische Zeugnisse zur Empfindung der Farbe und Farbigkeit bei der Orgel und beim Orgelspiel in Deutschland *c.* 1500–1620', *Acta musiocologica*, 28 (1963), 176–206

FOCK, G., 'Hamburgs Anteil am Orgelbau im niederdeutschen Kulturgebiet', *Zeitschrift des Vereins für Hamburgische Geschichte*, 38 (1939), 289–373

HOFNER, H., 'Der ostfränkische Orgelbau', *Archiv für Geschichte von Oberfranken*, 52 (1972)

KLOTZ, H., *Über die Orgelkunst der Gotik, der Renaissance und des Barock* (Kassel, 1975)

SALMEN, W., ed., *Orgel und Orgelspiel im 16. Jahrhundert* (Innsbruck, 1978). Symposium of essays including J. Ahrend and E. Krauss, 'Die Restaurierung der Ebertorgel', 184–207

SCHNEIDER, T., 'The Compenius Family: Organ Builders', *ISO Information*, 14 (1976), 979–98

SOEHNLEIN, E. J., 'Diruta and his Contemporaries: Tradition and Innovation in the Art of Registration', *The Organ Yearbook*, 10 (1979)

VENTE, M. A., *Die Brabanter Orgel* (Amsterdam, 1958)

WILLIAMS, P., *The European Organ 1450–1850* (London, 1966)

11 Some Structures and Mechanisms Before 1600

While it is true that a fully detailed history of the way organ-mechanism developed has still to be written, certain lines of development are clear enough. By the early seventeenth century, when Michael Praetorius was compiling his treatise, all essential attributes or properties of the organ already existed. Only in tone and purpose did the organ change during the next two hundred and more years, and only with the new key actions and bellows structures of the middle of the nineteenth century was anything developed that was basically new to the organ.

Wedge bellows seem to have become fairly standardized. Whether single-fold (*Faltenbalg*) or multi-fold (called *Spanbalg* by Praetorius), they were made of hinged wooden boards (*Span*) with ribs attached to strips of leather (see Fig. 8). Although larger versions with levers are illustrated here, bellows types can be made small and simple, worked either by hand or by the body weight of the bellows-blower. They are said to produce steadier wind than the ribless cuneiform 'forge bellows' of earlier period. The drawing shows other important details of construction: the alternation between two bellows; the position of the weight (stone or lead) to increase the heaviness of the upper board which, when

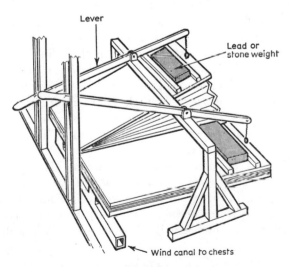

Lever

Lead or stone weight

Wind canal to chests

Figure 8

cocked, falls to expel air under pressure; and the wind trunk going from bellows to chest, without collecting in a reservoir and without being given any stabilization other than that which might result from the cushioning of air within the wind trunk. Such *Spanbälge* as these were made to supply wind at an average pressure at the pipe foot of 75–100 mm.*
During the later eighteenth century, several builders in England, Germany and elsewhere gradually worked more with reservoirs, adding such 'collectors' between bellows ('feeder bellows') and chests. Two other types of feeder bellows were also found, though neither necessarily had a reservoir. These were the square, lantern-shaped bellows (*soufflets à lanterne*, illustrated by Mersenne) and the box bellows (*Kastenbalg*) known during the seventeenth century but perfected only by about 1825. Both had a topboard raised by pulley: in the first, the board fell and made the square multi-fold bellows collapse, expelling wind; in the second, the board was the top of a wooden box falling slowly within a second larger but tight-fitting, open-topped box, from which wind was thereby expelled. The advantage of the first was economy of space, the advantage of the second that it involved no perishable leather hinges. All types of bellows and hydraulis-cisterns suck in air through an aperture opened by an intake valve but closed as soon as the full bellows begin to expel wind; all had a further valve in the trunk which allowed wind to pass from the bellows but stopped it from being sucked back as soon as the feeders were inflated again.

Key mechanism had achieved full maturity by the early sixteenth century. The general principles behind the construction shown in a drawing (see Fig. 9) of the Oosthuizen organ of *c*. 1530 were known to many a builder from at least 1400 onwards (Peeters and Vente 1971, pp. 24, 29). This design can be assumed to be that behind most fixed church organs (e.g. Plates 2, 3, 5, 6, 8, 9). If the organ were larger, other chests could be added: a *Brustwerk* or little chest 'in the breast' of the organ above the music desk (*positive forn an die brust*, Schlick 1511; *voer yn dye borst*, Amsterdam Oude Kerk 1539); a Chair organ behind the player's back (*positiff en rück*, Schlick 1511; *Positieff*, Delft 1461; *la cheyere*, Valenciennes 1515; *in den stoel*, Amsterdam 1539); a pedal section behind the main chest, or to the sides of it. The case itself soon began to lose its simple, shallow altar-like shape, although some of the better case-designs of later centuries—Province Holland in the late seventeenth century, Pugin's 'gothick' cases of the nineteenth, certain enlightened revivals in the twentieth—have been made with reference to this classic shape. The key action of such organs often varied in detail, having splayed trackers or backfalls instead of a rollerboard, etc.

* That is, the pressure of air is sufficient to cause the level of water in one side of an open-ended U-tube to rise until it is 75–100 mm higher than the other.

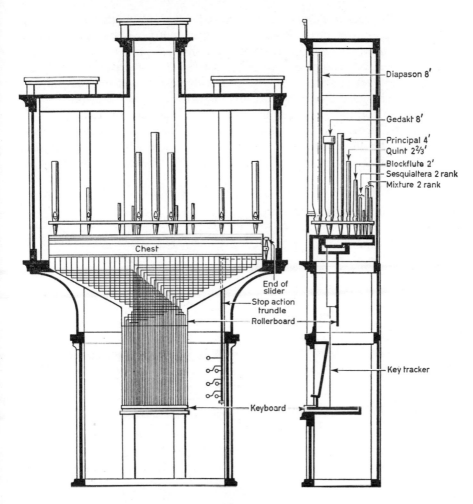

Figure 9

Tracker, backfall and rollerboard are illustrated in Fig. 10. The first drawing shows the layout and names for a simple mechanical action. Some builders, particularly in France, gradually perfected the *mécanique suspendue* in which the sticker pulled down the pallet directly without backfall; such a system can be seen in Fig. 9. This required even finer engineering than the action illustrated in Fig. 10, but the resulting lightness and immediacy of touch are incomparable and persuaded the best eighteenth-century (and twentieth-century) builders to apply it not only to the main manual but to the little treble chests (French classical builders) and even to the complete upper manuals (e.g. J. Wagner). The second drawing here shows manual and pedal actions enabling the pipes to be placed some way from the keys that play them, both laterally and vertically distant: leverage is conveyed by means of the roller and could be more direct than that shown—see Oosthuizen (Fig. 9) above—or even less direct, allowing the builder to scatter chests over a wide aural field and making the touch more difficult for the player. This second figure shows all the mechanical elements belonging to a theoretically complete 'tracker action', as it has become called.

From the many enormous and apparently shapeless organ-specifications cited by Praetorius in the early seventeenth century, it may be thought that the German builders of the late sixteenth century had

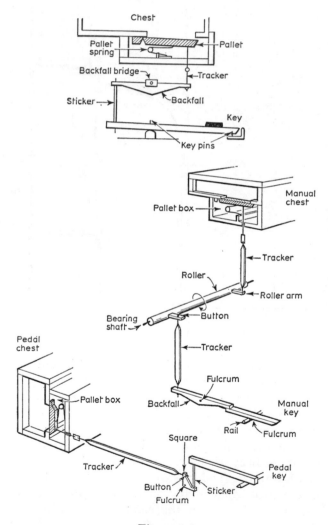

Figure 10

advanced their technology beyond what was required or even suitable for the music itself. The aristocratic court chapels in particular seem to have encouraged builders to try their hand at welding an instrument together from many chests, manuals and families of stops. Praetorius's description of stops, in particular the flutes (metal, wood, wide, narrow, open, stopped, cylindrical, tapering, outward-tapering, narrow-stopped, narrow-conical, over-blowing, etc.) and the reeds and regals (metal, wood, narrow, wide, long, short, cylindrical, conical, plain, fanciful, etc.) is itself an attempt to give order to an embarrassing luxury of choice and should not be seen for more than what it is. Any modern stop-glossary that concentrates on Praetorius or uses him for more than a passing reference to ephemeral, provincial ideas of seventeenth-century Germany is based on a misunderstanding of his historical position. No other organ type of Europe had such variety; German ingenuity was exercised to the full, and it is doubtful if the organist of Gröningen Court Chapel— to take an example of an organ still extant in part—knew what to do with the myriad colour-stops provided by his builder, other than ringing the changes for sets of Protestant chorale-partitas (Praetorius 1619, pp. 188–9):

GRÖNINGEN, Court Chapel
D. Beck, 1592–6
Casework since 1770 in the Martinskirche, Halberstadt

Im Oberwerk Manual (manual stops on main chest)		Quintadeen Bass	16
		Klein Octaven Bass	4
Principal	8	Klein Quintadeen Bass	4
Zimbeldoppelt	(II)	Rauschquinten Bass	
Gross Querflöit	8	Holflöiten Bass	2
Mixtur		Holquinten Bass	($5\frac{1}{3}$)
Nachthorn	4	Nachthorn Bass	4
Holflöiten	8	Mixtur	
Klein Querflöite	4		
Quinta	$5\frac{1}{3}$	*Fornen in der Brust zum Manual* (manual stops in the *Brustwerk*)	
Octava	4		
Grobgedact	8		
Gemsshorn	8	Klein Gedact	2
Gross Quintadehna	16	Klein Octava	1
		Klein Mixtur	2
Im Pedal auff der Oberlade (pedal stops on upper chest)		Zimbeldoppelt	(II)
		Rancket	8
Untersatz	16	Regal	8
Octaven Bass	8	Zimbel Regal	2 (*sic*)

Im Rückpositiff		Gross Principal Bass	16
(Chair organ)		Gross Gemsshorn Bass	16
Principal	4	Gross Querflöiten Bass	8
Gemsshorn	4	Gemsshorn Bass	8
Quintadehn	8	Kleingedact Bass	4
Spitzflöite	2	Quintflöiten Bass	$5\frac{1}{3}$
Gedact	4	Sordunen Bass	16
Octava	2	Posaunen Bass	16
Quinta	$1\frac{1}{3}$	Trommeten Bass	8
Subflöite	1	Schallmeyen Bass	4
Mixtur			
Zimbel	$2\frac{2}{3}$	*In der Brust auff beyden Seiten*	
Sordunen	16	*zum Pedal*	
Trommet	8		
Krumbhorn	8	(pedal stops on *Brustwerk*	
Klein Regal	4	side-chests)	
		Quintflöiten Bass	$10\frac{2}{3}$ (*sic*)
		Bawrflöiten Bass	4
In den beyden Seit Thörmen zum		Zimbel Bass	$2\frac{2}{3}$
Pedal		Rancket Bass	8
(pedal stops in the two side-		Krumbhorn Bass	8
towers)		Klein Regal Bass	4

Colourful combinations were certainly what was intended; a century or more later, Werckmeister noted that the organ had such narrow pallets and channels that not many stops could be drawn at once (Werckmeister 1704). But in any case, some of the organs listed by Praetorius are scarcely credible. Prague Týn Church is said to have had a large 70-stop, four-manual organ built between 1556 and 1588; but perhaps different departments were built at different points over those years, resulting in a conglomerate instrument that was never playable or ready all at once. At Gröningen, hundreds, even thousands, of possible stop-combinations could be computed from the stoplist, particularly those all-important combinations of two or three stops. The registrations at the Court Chapel of Dresden in 1563 (see p. 80) were all for three stops or less, apart from the three principal choruses of four or five stops. Quite apart from what this might imply about the wind-raising techniques of the later sixteenth century, it suggests that many organs of the period were geared towards subtle colour. The many chests must have been operated by a complex action, with double pallets (enabling a rank to be played by more than one set of keys, manual or pedal), extensions (enabling a pipe to be played by keys at different octave-pitches) and other transmission systems still not always clear despite attempts to categorize them (Bunjes 1966).

The most useful of the complex layouts was also the oldest and longest lived, namely the double or multiple pedal division in which the biggest bass-pipes were placed on their own chests and the higher solo stops placed on another. A *Sperrventil* or blocking valve would prevent wind from entering any chest not immediately needed, so that stops could be 'prepared' by being drawn but not sounding until required. This had obvious advantages for the player, in that he could register in advance, while for the builder the advantages of separate chests were that they could save wind and that low pressure could be better sustained if no chest were above a certain size.

The first such 'multiple actions' may have been built early in the century in the Netherlands (Diest, 1523), although the evidence is less conclusive than has been claimed. At Antwerp in 1505, Daniel van der Distelen seems to have planned but did not make—because the authorities 'were too little versed in the innovations of the day' (Klotz 1975, p. 85)?—a pedal keyboard couplable to the Great and playing ranks both in the Chair organ and in the *Brustwerk*. But the terminology is vague and depends on our assuming that e.g. '12 large Bourdons' in the Chair organ really were pedal pipes (Vente 1958, p. 33). It was some years before the wealthy court chapels of central Germany had what were indeed some of the richest mechanical layouts ever known before pneumatic action suddenly made the distancing of keys from pipes so much more feasible. Praetorius's descriptions centre on three main kinds of complex layout: **1** the double action, allowing one keyboard to play on two or more chests, **2** the transmission chest with more than one pallet, allowing certain ranks to be played by more than one keyboard, and **3** octave and quint extension, i.e. a chest so constructed as to allow a rank of pipes to be played at unison, octave or quint pitches. The third was very rare but important in view of later developments; presumably the pipes were placed on a solid panel in which were bored three channels to each pipe—channels to each of which the wind was admitted by a pallet controlled by the key. Couplers and blocking valves were also important to organs with complex actions, both of them increasing the registration possibilities. But all such mechanical aids have the effect of giving too much importance to the Great Organ, reducing the status and power of the secondary manuals, lessening the independence of the pedal, and inviting builders to cultivate fanciful workmanship as an end in itself. In the major church organs, however, the Chair organ kept its usefulness and helped to produce the right conditions for the most idiomatic organ music of the seventeenth century, in Germany, France, the Netherlands, Scandinavia and even England.

Bibliography

BUNJES, P., *The Praetorius Organ* (St. Louis, 1966)

KLOTZ, H., *Über die Orgelkunst der Gotik, der Renaissance und des Barock* (Kassel, 1975)

MERSENNE, M., *Harmonie universelle* (Paris, 1636; partial Eng. trans. [R. E. Chapman], The Hague, 1957)

PEETERS, F. and VENTE, M. A., *De Orgelkonst in de Nederlanden van de 16de tot de 18e Eeuw* (Antwerp, 1971; Eng. trans. [P. Williams], Antwerp, 1971)

PRAETORIUS, M., *Syntagma musicum, II. De Organographia* (Wolfenbüttel, 1619)

PRAETORIUS, M., *Theatrum instrumentorum* (Wolfenbüttel, 1620)

VENTE, M. A., *Die Brabanter Orgel* (Amsterdam, 1958)

WERCKMEISTER, A., *Organum Gruningense redivivum* (Quedlingburg, 1704)

12 Organs Built According to the 'Werkprinzip'

The visual characteristics of an organ built on the *Werkprinzip* ('principle of independent chests') were all known by the end of the fourteenth century, and indeed it would not have occurred to a builder to follow any other plan: it is the natural form for an organ. To a single main case could be added the Chair organ in front (see Plates, 12, 13, 14); to these, one or two separate pedal-towers could be added. Although these elements were known by the fifteenth century, the *Werkprinzip* conception reached full maturity in the more northerly parts of Europe only over the period 1550–1750 and deserves separate consideration, not least since it is the most important principle behind the best organs of today.

In Fig. 11 (Zwolle Grote Kerk, drawn in Peeters and Vente 1971, p. 16), the pedal chests could be understood as being placed to the front of the gallery on the left and right side of the main case, of which Fig. 11 is a cross-section. In most organs of the seventeenth and eighteenth centuries, the pedal chests would have been placed behind the main case or incorporated deep within it, thus losing the acoustic immediacy and resonant balance of the true *Werkprinzip*. In Roman Catholic countries (Austria, Bohemia, Silesia) the space between the organist and the Chair organ was often large enough to accommodate a full choir and orchestra, particularly by the later seventeenth century. Further small chests could be conducted off the main chest shown in Figure 11: in France during the seventeenth century the 'mounted' Cornet, in southern Germany somewhat later various kinds of echo chests, in Spain and Portugal during the eighteenth century whole manuals and subsidiary chests (see Plate 33), in most countries one or more kinds of toy stop (cuckoos, nightingales, star-bells, etc.). In addition, one or more departments could be enclosed in a Swellbox, particularly in those countries (Spain, England) or periods (from the later eighteenth century) in which the *Werkprinzip* was rarely applied in its purest form. A more traditional device applied to one or other chest, or to each main wind trunk as the case may be, was the Tremulant, a sprung flap either allowing the wind to escape in short puffs from the trunk (*à vent perdu*) or beating within the trunk to give the wind an uneven impulse (*tremulant doux*).

Essentially the manual supplying the true balanced chorus pitted

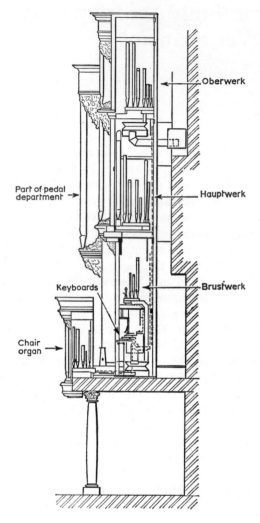

Figure 11

against the Great is the Chair organ, but in order to lower expense or to avoid potentially heavy action or to reduce the clear-ringing contrast between rich Great and penetrating Chair, builders of many countries and periods have preferred other secondary manuals: for example, interior positives in sixteenth-century France, seventeenth-century Iberia, eighteenth-century England and Saxony, nineteenth-century Germany. But the Chair organ has had a varied character: the strong Principal choruses in the sixteenth century must have been very different from the colourful palettes found in a seventeenth-century *Rückpositiv* of northern Europe, which in turn was far more versatile than the pretty echo effects and little flutey sounds produced by the Chair organ of e.g. an eighteenth-century Bohemian Jesuit church. Even pedal towers differed, and it is a mistake to relate either Chair organ or pedal towers as found in a mature organ of *c.* 1675 to those briefly described by Henri Arnaut. It is not even certain whether in 1450 a given Chair organ had the same pitch as the Great, whether its keyboard were aligned with it or even whether it was playable in the same sitting position as that needed to play the Great.

Although the side towers of the old French and Dutch Trompes held large bass pipes, they were not necessarily played by the pedal, nor can they be seen as the direct inspiration for *Werkprinzip* pedal towers. After all, a crucial factor in the construction and function of the *Werkprinzip* towers was that they also held solo melodic stops suitable for pedal *cantus firmus* lines, and indeed held them in the front of the gallery only a few feet away from the congregation sitting in or below the organ gallery. Presumably the larger organs of *c.* 1550 had pedal towers which collected both solo stops and equivalents to the old Trompes (i.e. both high and low stops), but the true *Werkprinzip* organ reached its highest form hundreds of miles to the north and east of the cathedrals with medieval Trompes.

One of the attributes and advantages of the *Werkprinzip* was that an organ could be added to at any point in its history. Thanks to skill in building chests extra to the main department, many of the organs of northern Germany reached states they did not originally have—chests and manuals were added, and the end result was an agglomeration of parts built at different times. One example by no means exceptional was the Jakobikirche, Hamburg (Fock 1974, pp. 54–5):

HAMBURG, Jakobikirche
a stops of 1512–16 (Iversand, Stüven), *b* 1576 (Hoyer), *c* 1588 (Scherer), *d* 1590–92 (Scherer, Bockelmann), *e* 1605 (Scherer)

Oberwerk (*Hauptwerk*)		Scharp *a*?	
FGA–g''a'', chest *a*		Mixtur *a*?	
Principal *a*	16		
Octava *a*	8		
Quintadeen *b* 1569	16	*Brustwerk* (lower)	
Holpipe *a*	8	FGA–g''a''	
Holflöit *d*	4	Krumborn *b*	8
Querpipe *d*	8	Quintflöit	$2\frac{2}{3}$
(16', overblowing)		Waltflöit *c*	2
Russpipe *a*?		Spitzflöite (treble)	4

G

Pedal			Kleinflöite	2
CDEFGA–c¹d¹			Klingende Zimbel	III
Principal from F a	32		Trompette	8
Mixtur a (based on 16')			Regal	8
In Hoyer's side-towers:			Zincke (f–a'')	8
Principal b	16			
Grossbass (1598)	16		*Rückpositiv*	
Octava b	4		CDEFGA–c''', chest b	
Gemsshorn Bass			Principal b	8
Spitzquinte b?			Octava b	4
Zimbel b			Scharp e	
Mixtur b			Mixtur e	
Spillpipe d	4		Gedact d	8
(8', overblowing)			Quintadeen b	8
Krumbhorn	16		Holflöit c	4
Bassaune c	16		Blockflöit e	4
Trommete c	8		Gemsshorn c	2
Cornett c	2		Ziflöit c	(1⅓)
			Klingende Zimbel b	
Brustwerk (upper)			Schalmeyen	4
entirely of 1590–2, a kind of			Baarpfeiffe	8
Oberwerk				
Principal	8		Tremulants (*b*)	
Holpipe	8		18 little bellows	
Flöite	4		3 manuals	
Offen Querflöite	4		Pedal F♯, G♯ and c♯¹ added in	
(overblowing, of 1605)			1622	
Nasatt	2⅔		Bellows replaced and compass	
Gemsshorn	2		completed in 1635–6	

In particular it is possible that the reed choruses for which such organs were famous—15 reeds out of a total of 54 stops in the Marienkirche, Lübeck, by the time that Buxtehude was organist—were frequently revoiced, rescaled, renewed and even remade. The famous Totentanz organ of Lübeck, destroyed in 1942, had four departments which clearly reflected their respective periods: Great Organ of the fifteenth century, Chair organ of the mid-sixteenth, *Brustwerk* of the seventeenth, and an enlarged pedal of the mid-eighteenth. Other famous instruments of the area, such as the Johanniskirche, Lüneburg, are composite instruments accumulating different *Werke* which were constantly altered in their contents, compass, tuning and no doubt voicing by builder after builder. The big organs of the great builder-families—the Niehoffs, the Scherers, Compenius, Fritzsche—were like living organisms, changing their shape and style from generation to generation. It is this very mutability that makes what few organs of this type still exist so unreliable as historic witnesses. Except for the large chamber organ in the chapel of Frederiksborg Castle, Denmark, none remains in anything like its original state—despite claims made on record sleeves and in other ephemera—and it will be some years yet before any can be justly claimed to sound as the builder, perhaps himself only one of a series of builders, left it. A significant recent success in the art of restoration is the Hoyer–Schnitger organ of Stade (see p. 210 and Plates 20, 21, 22).

The chief characteristics of the *Werkprinzip* emerging in the northern Europe of the seventeenth century were: contrast between a full, round *Hauptwerk* (sometimes called *Oberwerk*) and a thin, versatile and penetrating *Rückpositiv*; a pedal department with well-developed solo and chorus potential; and an overall clarity and directness of sound evidently desirable in average-sized parish churches of little reverberation. In most cases it was the Chair organ that was understood to be the solo manual, not the Great. The characteristics of the music played on such instruments seem to have been sufficiently well defined for the organist to have needed little in the way of advice on how to register, for balanced contrast could be easily achieved between any two departments if the same number of stops were drawn on each. Which builder is responsible for which particular detail is not possible to say, but attempts have been made to credit Gottfried Fritzsche with the introduction of certain features (Williams 1966, p. 105), many of which would be found on his rebuilt organ for the Hamburg Jakobikirche in 1635–6: the fourth manual (a high chest); more regular use of 32' and 16' reeds, also of C-compass; inventing or introducing rare stops, both flue (Viol, Schwiegel, imitative flutes) and reed (Sordun, Rancket); clear contrast between narrow 'male' and wide 'female' stops (e.g. Quinte 2⅔' and Nasard 2⅔' on the same manual); thinning of the old Scharf mixture to a high repeating two-rank Zimbel; greater use of tin in the pipe metal, and also of wooden pipes for flues, reeds, open and stopped pipes. Probably not a single one of these belongs to Fritzsche—for example, little repeating two-rank Zimbeln must have been common on sixteenth-century positives, even in England—but they do suggest an organ becoming refined in detail.

The Hamburg *Werkprinzip* organ reached maturity and even a *ne plus ultra* in the work of Arp Schnitger, celebrated in his day across Germany, holder of many official privileges and, with Gottfried Silbermann, the inspiration for the German Organ Reform of the 1920s. Despite recent researches (e.g. Edskes 1969), and despite many claims to the contrary, curiously little is known about Schnitger—in what way or to what extent he was responsible for his instruments (his workshop employed a series of strikingly good and individual builders), how he conceived his scalings (which vary widely, depending on the church, the pitch, the amount of old pipework he incorporated in a so-called new organ, etc.), what his pitch and tuning were, why when he rebuilt an old organ he usually replaced multifold bellows by large single-fold bellows, why he dropped the Chair organ in his late work in the area around Berlin, who designed his organ-cases (see Plate 19), and so on. Work in progress by such practical scholars as George Taylor, Cor Edskes (see Winter–Edskes 1977), Harald Vogel and Jürgen Ahrend should gradually yield better details on the work of Schnitger. His wind pressure seems to have varied between *c*. 94 mm or higher (large organs in Hamburg) and *c*. 67 mm, an average being *c*. 85 mm (Nikolaikirche, Flensburg). The following scheme is that of his first four-manual organ, built for the Nikolaikirche, HAMBURG, in 1682–7 and destroyed in 1842 (Fock 1974, p. 48):

Hauptwerk			
Principal (case)	16	Sub Bass	16
Quintadena	16	Octav	8
Rohrflöte	16	Saltzianell	8
Oktav	8	Rauschpfeife	III
Spitzflöte	8	Octav	4
Saltzianell	8	Nachthorn	2
Quintpfeife	5⅓	Mixtur	VI–X
Octav	4	Posaunen	32
Flachfloet	2	Posaunen	16
Rauschpfeife	III	Dulcian	16
Superoctav	2	Tromett	8
Mixtur	VI–X	Crumphorn	8
Scharf	III	Tromett	4
Tromett	16	Cornett	2

Brustpositiv		*Oberpositiv*	
Principal	4	Holtzflöte	8
Blockflöte (wood)	8	Weidte Flöte	8
Weidte Rohrflöte	4	Rohrflöte	8
Quinte	2⅔	Quintadena	8
Walflöte	2	Octav	4
Nasat	1⅓	Spielflöte	4
Tertian	II	Nassat	2⅔
Scharff	IV–VI	Gemshorn	2
Baarpfeife	8	Scharff	V–VII
Dulcian	8	Zimbel	III
		Tromett	8
Pedal		Krummhorn	8
Principal	32	Vox humana	8
Octav	16	Tromett	4

Rückpositiv		3 Tremulants
Principal	8	5 Sperrventile
Bordun	16	2 Zimbelsterne
Quintadena	8	1 Pauke (drum-stop)
Gedact	8	*Ow/Hw, Bw/Hw, (Rp/Hw?)*
Octav	4	
Blockflöte	4	Compass: manual CDEF–c^{III},
Querflöte	2	pedal CD–d^{I}
Sifflöte	$1\frac{1}{3}$	
Sesquialtera	II	
Scharff	VI–IX	16 *Spanbälge* (bellows 10′ × 5′)
Dulcian	16	WP, *c.* 71 mm
Trecht Regall	8	Pitch, about $\frac{1}{4}$ tone above
Schalmey	4	a^{I} = 440 Hz

Such large organs give an optimal survey, a highest common factor, of the instruments known to such composers as Buxtehude, Lübeck, Bruhns, Böhm and (in his early years) J. S. Bach, and on which the toccatas and organ chorales of the older composers (Scheidemann, Weckmann, Tunder) were still played. In many parts of northern Europe such organs remained the ideal until at least 1850.

Bibliography

EDSKES, B. H., 'Nieuw-Scheemda', *Arp Schnitger en zijn Werk in het Groningerland* (Groningen, 1969)

FOCK, G., *Arp Schnitger und seine Schule* (Kassel, 1974)

PEETERS, F. and VENTE, M. A., *De Orgelkonst in de Nederlanden van de 16de tot de 18e Eeuw* (Antwerp, 1971; Eng. trans., Antwerp, 1971)

WILLIAMS, P., *The European Organ 1450–1850* (London, 1966), 97–120

WINTER, II., EDSKES, C. II. and BOECK, U., 'Die Schnitger-Orgel in Cappel', *Orgel-Studien*, 2 (Hamburg, 1977)

13 The French Classical Organ

Only in the middle of the seventeenth century did the French organ achieve its classical form. Even then, one should rather say 'Parisian' than 'French', for the chief builders and the composers of the idiomatic organ music closely tied to such organs were mostly Parisian by origin or residence. Indeed, the apparent standardization that overcame both music and organ in France is the result of a Parisian monopoly not least in printing and publishing, as a result of which the Parisian musicians of that period still dominate the thoughts and approaches of contemporary musical historians. Already in the 1670s a builder would refer to Paris as his point of departure: Jean de Joyeuse promised at Béziers in 1679 to give the organ *une harmonie semblable aux orgues les plus accomplies de la ville de Paris*, at Perpignan in 1697 new bellows *montés à la mode de Paris* and at Auch in 1688 (see Plate 17) something even more specific —the composition of a Fourniture VI *comme sont les meilleurs plains jeux de la ville de Paris* (Dufourcq 1958, pp. 44, 62, 70, 57). Clearly, the metropolis was a reference point, and the very number of *livres d'orgue* published there suggests a unified organ school, as no doubt it was meant to. A characteristic of this school was that every stop in a French organ of about 1700 came to have its own function, and the *livres* from Nivers (1665) to at least Marchand (*c.* 1715) show the seventeenth-century Parisian organist to have been exceptionally independent of outside influences past and present.

But a century earlier, Flemish influence had been as strong in northern France as Italian had been and was often to remain in parts of what is now south-west France. In Rouen, Titelouze's full organ had probably produced much the same kind of sound as that of a Dutch composer, though for colours he had a non-Flemish Tierce stop. Even that most characteristic stop of the French organ, the Cornet, originated in the Netherlands and could be found from at least 1565 onwards (Antwerp). Yet although certain details in Mersenne's *Harmonie Universelle* (Paris, 1636) may have been influenced by a reading of Praetorius—just as Dutch and English musical theorists of the seventeenth century were then influenced by Mersenne—the Parisian organ of Mersenne's period was beginning to approach that written for in the *livres d'orgue* appearing in the reign of Louis XIV. Both narrow and wide-scaled Tierce ranks soon became common (narrow at Saint-Nicholas-des-Champs in 1618, wide at Saint-Jacques-de-la-Boucherie) as were the flute mutations at $1\frac{1}{3}'$ and $2\frac{2}{3}'$; the $1'$ rank disappeared, however, as did pedal $16'$ ranks on smaller organs. Tin became usual for the diapason chorus stops but not for the mutations—for which, as one builder of 1701 noted, *l'étain est trop piquant* (Hardouin 1977, p. 11). For Mersenne, the Tierce was used both in *plein jeu* and solo registrations, and it was a rank usually, perhaps always, found on the new short-compass keyboards used for solo melodies. These little manuals are characteristic of the *livre d'orgue* organ; they also became characteristic of certain Belgian and most English organs of the eighteenth century. The little 25-note Cornet manual or *récit* at Saint-Séverin, Paris in 1610 set the fashion, though it seems to have been intended at first merely to give the raised Cornet chest its own row of keys. If such a half-chest were placed in the space below the *Grand Orgue*, instead of in the space behind its upper case-pipes, it would have a more distant sound, be called the *Echo* manual, and perhaps have a longer keyboard. By 1660, a French classical organ of larger size could then be expected to have four manuals (or two and two half-manuals), giving the Great/Chair contrasts familiar in the contemporary Hamburg *Werkprinzip* organ but also an array of right-hand solo effects for the various Organ-mass movements, with melodies said to derive from the *récit dramatique* of the opera.

As an example of the accomplished French classical organ, there follows the stoplist of the instrument played by Nicholas Lebègue, one of the organists to the king (Dufourcq 1971, pp. 250–3):

PARIS, St-Louis-des-Invalides
A. Thierry, 1679–87

Grand Orgue		Cornet	V
CD–c'''		Trompette	8
Montre	16	Clairon	4
Bourdon	16	Voix humaine	8
Montre	8		
Bourdon	8	*Echo*	
Prestant	4	c–c'''	
Flûte	4	Bourdon	8
Grosse Tierce	$3\frac{1}{5}$	Flûte	4
Nasard	$2\frac{2}{3}$	Nasard	$2\frac{2}{3}$
Doublette	2	Quarte	2
Quarte de Nasard	2	Tierce	$1\frac{3}{5}$
Tierce	$1\frac{3}{5}$	Cymbale	II
Fourniture	V	Cromorne	8
Cymbale	IV		

Positif		*Récit*	
CD–c³		c¹–c³	
Montre	8	Cornet	V
Bourdon	8	Trompette	8
Prestant	4		
Flûte	4	*Pédale*	
Nasard	2⅔	AA–f¹ (30 notes;	
Doublette	2	AABBCDE–f¹?)	
Tierce	1⅗	Flûte	8
Larigot	1⅓	Trompette	8
Fourniture	III		
Cymbale	II	Tremulants	
Cromorne	8	*Rp/Hw* push-coupler (*Hw/P?*)	
Voix humaine	8	Pitch unknown (but see below)	

Standardization was one of the chief aims of this organ-type, and rarely can music and instrument be so closely related as the works of Raison, de Grigny, François Couperin and Lebègue himself can be to such an organ. Pitch, at least from *c.* 1680 onwards, was a semitone below a¹ = 440 Hz; but how exclusively such low pitch was characteristic of the Parisian organ is not yet certain. Pipe metal was as usual hammered, including the lead pipes of the Bourdons. The keyboards had a lightness of action equalled only by certain Italian and French harpsichord-makers of the next century; keys of the *Grand Orgue*, *Récit* and *Echo* were usually pivoted at the distal end and the mechanism suspended from pallet-box to keys. The *Positif* stickers connect with a lever raising the pallet, which is placed above the end of the channel near the player's seat. That the French classical organ was on one hand relatively standardized as to repertory and function in the liturgy and on the other very accomplished as to structural or engineering skill is clear from two recent studies, on the music (Higginbottom 1976) and on the key-action (Legros 1976).

Registrations were conventionalized and—as often happens in organ history when a certain kind of organ is standardized over a large area or for a long period—frequently described in the books of music. The most important were as follows:

1. *Plein jeu.* To obtain the full diapason chorus or *plein jeu* for those movements of the Mass or Office conventionally associated with it, the organist drew the Principals 16', 8', 4' and 2', added the Fourniture and finally the Cymbale. The last two had the following composition, or one very like it:

C–e	15.19.22.26.29	C–B	(26).29.33.36
		c–e	(22).26.29.33
f–e¹	8.12.15.19.22	f–b	(19).22.26.29
		c¹–e¹	(15).19.22.26
f¹–c¹¹¹	1.5.8.12.15	f¹–b¹	(12).15.19.22
		c¹¹–e¹¹	(8).12.15.19
		f¹¹–c¹¹¹	(5).8.12.15

Such mixture-composition was described by Dom Bedos de Celles at the end of the classical period but can be taken as a kind of constant norm: for example, the maximum of six ranks suggested by Mersenne for the Fourniture is not known to have been exceeded in the whole period 1630–1700 (Hardouin 1977, p. 12). It was important to the overall sound that the Cymbale broke back more often than the Fourniture, thus duplicating it in the treble—such a mixture frequently repeating was called *cymbalisée*. Fourniture/Cymbale duplication was followed by e.g. Gottfried Silbermann in Saxony. No rank is higher than 2' pitch at c¹¹¹ (i.e. no pipe is shorter than about 28 mm long), and ranks were not duplicated in either of the mixtures. The resulting *plein jeu* was rarely brilliant, never shrill, and far from the German full organ of the twentieth century, built in an imaginary neo-baroque style; rather it was another 'colour' of the organ.

2. *Grand jeu.* This was a totally different chorus for which the organist drew a varying combination of reeds, Cornet, Prestant 4' and Tierces. The reeds gave the volume and brilliance; indeed, the true *grand jeu* depends on the *élan* characteristic of the fine French reed-voicing of the classical period, removed on the one hand from the blare of Spanish horizontal reeds and on the other from the thinner, more discreet reeds that seem typical of many German organ types. In the *grand jeu* the Cornet boosted the thin trumpet trebles, the Tierce implemented the rich overtone content, and the Prestants strengthened the basic unison tone without taking too much wind from the reeds or adding any obtrusive 8' flue sound. Such registrations were often recommended by the composers for their fugues; and other fugal registrations—such as Tierce-combination with Tremulant—must also have given a *ton* to the organ fugue totally different from that of German or Italian fugues in the period 1650 to 1750. On larger organs after about 1750 a pair of Trompettes on the *Grand Orgue* gave an extra flavour to the timbre peculiar to French reeds, with their depth of tone in the bass (often sounding as if a flue stop were drawn with them) and their brilliance in the treble. Late in the classical period, a Trompette was also sometimes put into the *Positif* (which meant a roomier case) and, after Thierry's organ at Notre Dame, Paris in 1733, Bombarde manuals were also occasionally made—a

keyboard coupled to the *Grand Orgue* and playing the large-scaled Bombarde 16' on its own chest, which perhaps had one or two other large reed-stops with it. One purpose of this arrangement was to give the the special reed-ranks their own wind supply; pressure at the end of the classical period was often high (125 mm at Poitiers Cathedral). In the same way, it was the necessary boosting of the treble by the Cornet that led in the next century to higher pressure throughout and to double-length harmonic resonators for the reeds. The reed-basses, both of the Trompette and Cromorne types, remained the chief glory of the French *grand jeu*, encouraging composers from about 1650 onwards to write special *basse de trompette* music requiring the reeds *de grosse taille* ('of large scale') frequently specified in late seventeenth-century contracts.

3. Solo and other effects. Only a handful of stops were involved in most of the characteristic French registrations, and even for the *pleins jeux* the French organ was not overdrawn. Throughout the classical period, builders could afford to build narrow channels and small wind trunks. The colourful effects were not only ingenious—much of the art of stop-combination from at least 1500 onwards had been the result of ingenuity —but highly codified and conventionalized, leaving little room for any single organist's own inventiveness. He would know, for example, that a piece marked *Tierce en taille* would contain the following elements: (a) left hand on *Positif*, with Bourdon 8', Prestant 4', Doublette 2', Nasard, Tierce and perhaps Larigot, playing an expressive and spacious melody in the middle of the texture, rather like a viola da gamba obbligato; (b) right hand on *Grand Orgue*, with the *jeux doux* or soft flue stops, Bour-dons 16', 8', 4', playing an accompaniment above and around the melody; (c) pedal playing the bass line on Flûte 8', or perhaps coupled to *Grand Orgue* Bourdon 16', etc. The result is without doubt one of the most beautiful and idiomatic effects of which an organ has ever been capable.

The theorists differed from each other in some of their suggestions: Bedos, for example, did not like 16' manual stops in the accompanying *jeux doux*. But despite their gradual corroding of Lebègue's formulas, the French did not change their ideas on the suitability of Nasard and Tierces for creating good solo lines, as the Germans seem to have done during the eighteenth century. Tierce-combinations were particularly characteristic. A Cornet solo for the right hand on the *Grand Orgue*, for example, could be accompanied in dialogue by the left hand playing a *jeu de tierce* combination on the *Positif*, i.e. ranks of 1.8.12.15.17.19. This stop-combination corresponded to the treble Cornet's make-up of 1.8.12.15.17, but it was not so wide-scaled, not so uniform in overall tone (some of the ranks were not wide open flutes), and it ran the full compass instead of beginning on middle c'.

As to the pedal, its chief purposes were to play 8′ and 16′ *cantus firmus* lines derived from the plainsong in Mass movements and to 'be able to play the trios' (*pour pouvoir jouer les trios*), according to Joyeuse's contract at Auch cathedral in 1688. This latter aim agrees with such known *livres* as that of d'Anglebert (1689), in which quartets and trios were registered for three different tonal colours, including the pedal line. Using the big pedal reeds for *cantus firmus* solos had long been traditional and every builder must have planned his reeds and wind supply accordingly. But the biggest drain on wind supply was not so much the occasional *plenum* as the slower, sustained music written for the combinations called *concert de flûtes* and *fonds d'orgue*, i.e. registrations made up of all available Montres, Prestants, open Flûtes and Bourdons in various combinations of the kind much admired in the decades leading up to the Revolution.

Like the Dutch organ of 1700, the Spanish of 1800 and the English of 1860, the French organ on the eve of the Revolution of 1789 must have been vastly superior to the music written for it. Yet the very decadence of the music of that period draws out the powerful contrasts, the very loud and very soft effects, the brilliant reeds, round flutes, distant echoes and other colours available on the late instruments of Saint-Maximin-en-Var (J. E. Isnard, 1773) and Poitiers Cathedral (F.-H. Clicquot). At Poitiers, it seems likely that the basic flue ranks were all very flute-like and almost anonymous in tone, leaving all the colour to be supplied by the mutations on one hand and the big reed choruses on the other. The result is a series of very marked and distinct organ effects which builder and composer joined in expecting and to which they assumed the organist would be restricted. Quite how the French organ would have developed had it not been for the disruption of the Revolution is particularly difficult to conjecture, for with such instruments as Poitiers it reached the end of a line. It was ripe for development during the very years in which Clicquot's sons were in the army, but not until Saint-Denis in 1841 were some of the assumptions underlying Saint-Maximin and Poitiers carried to their logical end by a builder of great ability.

Bibliography

BEDOS DE CELLES, F., *L'Art du facteur d'orgues*, 4 vols. (Paris, 1766–78)
DOUGLASS, F., *The Language of the Classical French Organ* (New Haven, 1696)
DOUGLASS, F., 'Should Dom Bedos play Lebègue?', *The Organ Yearbook*, 4 (1973), 101–11
DUFOURCQ, N., *Jean de Joyeuse et la pénétration de la facteur d'orgues Parisiennes dans le Midi de la France au XVIIe siècle* (Paris, 1958)
DUFOURCQ, N., *Le Livre d'orgue français*, I 'Les Sources' (Paris, 1971)

FELLOT, J., 'L'Orgue classique français', special number of *Musique de tous les temps* (1962)

HARDOUIN, P., 'Naissance et élaboration de l'orgue français classique d'après sa composition', *L'Orgue français: Double numéro de la Revue musicale*, 295–6 (1977), 7–34

HIGGINBOTTOM, E., 'French classical organ music and the liturgy', PRMA, 103 (1976), 19–40

LEGROS, H., 'Étude sur la mécanique de l'orgue Clicquot de Souvigny', *ISO Information*, 15 (1976), 15–32

MERSENNE, M., *Harmonie universelle* (Paris, 1636; partial Eng. trans. [R. E. Chapman], The Hague, 1957)

14 The Organ of J. S. Bach

Although the fact that 'on no single organ that Bach is known ever to have played would all of his music have sounded at its best' (Williams 1972, p. 70) may well cause problems for the organist of today, the organ-historian need find it of no particular disadvantage, since the many influences on and cross-currents in the music of J. S. Bach are reflected in the various organs he is known to have played and admired. The organs of Thuringia, Weimar and Saxony show the same kind of German traditionalism or provincialism tempered by outside influence (particularly French and Italian) as J. S. Bach's organ music, and 'the Bach organ' becomes rather more difficult to understand than the organ of Frescobaldi, Buxtehude or de Grigny.

J. S. Bach is known to have been intimately acquainted with organ music of several countries and periods, not least some of that by these same three composers, Frescobaldi, Buxtehude and de Grigny. Although most of his contemporaries in central Germany had, like him, a compositional technique derived from old German *Figurenlehre*,* what is surprising is that some of them (particularly Bach and J. G. Walther) knew so much organ music of other areas. Probably no French, Italian, Spanish, English or north German organist of the early eighteenth century knew so many different kinds of organ music. Perhaps that cosmopolitanism was short lived. At least, when C. P. E. Bach noted that his father registered the organ 'in his own manner' so as to 'astound organists' when he played on their instruments (Schulze 1972, p. 284), he was almost certainly referring to frenchified registrations—a style not known to the younger organists who thought that 'the art died with him' and for whom a *grand jeu* on one of the larger Gottfried Silbermann organs (see Plate 26) must have been an unusual sound. Not that the French element in J. S. Bach should be overstated. When his pupil J. F. Agricola reported that 'real connoisseurs'—probably meaning J. S. Bach—complained that Silbermann's mixtures and Zimbel were 'over-weak', giving insufficiently 'sharp penetration . . . especially in larger churches' (Dähnert 1970, p. 23), we should read that as meaning that

* *Figurenlehre*, the doctrine or practice of composing music by inventing contrapuntal lines based on 'figures' or short groups of notes arranged in certain patterns recognized and listed as specific motifs by such theorists as J. C. Printz (*Satyrischer Componist*, 1696) and J. G. Walther (*Praecepta*, 1708). Most if not all of the *Orgelbüchlein* chorales, for example, can be shown to have been so composed.

J. S. Bach did not appreciate a basic French principle, namely: the *plein jeu* is merely one of the many colours of an organ rather than an all-embracing *tutti*.

The whole area of Germany from Hanover to Breslau had produced and was to produce great organ-builders of versatility (the families of Fritzsche, Compenius, Casparini—see Plate 23, Silbermann, Wagner, Engler, Hildebrandt, Schulze) and a group of very influential organ-theorists (Praetorius, Werckmeister, Sorge, Adlung, Agricola, Knecht, Seidel, Töpfer). Its composers and builders included many who travelled to hear organs elsewhere—J. S. Bach went to Lübeck to hear Buxtehude and in 1720 applied for the organist's post on the Schnitger of the Jakobikirche, Hamburg—or who settled in another part of Germany, forming major schools of keyboard music around them (Froberger, Pachelbel, Handel, C. P. E. Bach). According to some viewpoints, the organ of J. S. Bach's native Thuringia was rather 'impure'; the traditions were not for Chair organs and pedal towers but for interior second manuals, for a range of 8′ colour stops, for few mutations, a plain pedal and one main chorus only. Gradually during the seventeenth century the emphasis had shifted towards west-end organs, placed in a gallery near to the congregations who by 1700—earlier in some cities—expected to sing the chorales with the organ in what has become the familiar manner. The result of this process was a plain organ of which that played by J. S. Bach at Arnstadt from 1703 to 1707 is typical (David 1951, p. 83):

ARNSTADT, Neue Kirche (Bonifaciuskirche)
J. F. Wender, 1699, 1703

Hauptwerk				
CDE–d'''		Violone		16
Prinzipal (tin, case)	8	Prinzipal (tin, case)		8
Quintaden	(8?)	Hohlflöte (stopped)		8
Viola da gamba (tin)	8	Posaune (wood)		16
Gemshorn	8			
Grobgedact	8	*Brustwerk*		
Oktave	4	CDE–d'''		
Quinte		Stillgedact		8
Mixtur	IV	Prinzipal (tin, case)		4
Zimbel	III	Nachthorn		4
Trompete	8	Quinte		
		Spitzflöte		2
Pedal		Sesquialtera		II
CDE–d'		Oktave		2
Subbass (wood)	16	Mixtur		IV

Hw/P, Hw/Bw
Tremulant (*Hw*)
Two tuned Zimbelsterne
  ('Glockenaccord')
Pipes of 'metal' unless otherwise
  shown (case-pipes 87·5% tin,
  Gamba 50%)

Uncertain: Quintaden 16' or 8'?
  Hw Quinte $5\frac{1}{3}'$ or $2\frac{2}{3}'$?
  Bw Quinte $2\frac{2}{3}'$ or $1\frac{1}{3}'$?
  Hohlflöte, *Pedal* or *Bw*?
  Hw/P later addition?

This was also the kind of organ known to Pachelbel. The Sesquialtera
served for solo lines of chorales and fantasias, and there were various flue
choruses on the manuals, not least for whatever *continuo* part the occasional cantata required the organ to play. The Weimar organ for which
the *Orgelbüchlein* and so many of the preludes, fugues, fantasias and
chorales were written, seems to have had a similar character, with the
important difference that, being a court-chapel organ, it was placed very
high on the top gallery of a narrow, tall church and presumably produced
a more distant effect.

When J. S. Bach lived in Lüneburg in 1700 or visited Lübeck in 1706,
he would not have heard organists there—Georg Böhm in the first,
Dietrich Buxtehude in the second—mixing the families of organ stops,
i.e. drawing more than one rank of any given pitch at the same time. The
Werkprinzip organist did not draw two stops of the same pitch because
according to Werckmeister (1698, pp. 71–3) one can always hear them
separately (this must reflect the strong character of each stop in a
seventeenth-century organ), the wind is uneven (i.e. bellows and trunks
were not made for such combinations), and temperament problems may
then arise. But only twenty years later in Hamburg, Mattheson was
suggesting that the *plenum* of a large church organ could contain all the
manual stops but reeds—Principals, Bourdons, Salicionals, Rausch-
pfeifen, Quintatöne, Octaves, Superoctaves, Fifths, Mixtures, Scharfe,
Tertian, Nasards, Sesquialteras—a view he stated more than once,
presumably as a demand for builders to bear in mind (Mattheson 1739,
p. 467). While Mattheson was no average professional organist and often
leaves his meaning unclear, he does seem to be showing here a crucial
change taking place in the eighteenth-century organ. Somewhat later,
Adlung thought good modern bellows ought to allow an organist to draw
such choruses on manual or pedal as the following (Adlung 1768,
pp. 167 f):

manual Prinzipal 8', Gedact 8', Gemshorn 8', Rohrflöte 8'
pedal Contrabass 32', Posaune 32', Subbass 16', Violon 16', Posaune 16',
  Oktave 8', Gedact 8'

whereas formerly it seems that one did not draw together both the lowest flue and reed stops in the pedal, only one or the other (Klotz 1975, p. 335). Solo lines were also thickened over the years, and such composers as D. M. Gronau (died 1747) recommended:

Prinzipal 8′, Flöte 8′, Oktave 4′, Flöte 4′, Salicet 4′, Trompete 8′, Oboe 8′

for the solo lines of an organ chorale (Frotscher 1935, pp. 1028–32). Perhaps the big organs of the Hanseatic churches in Mattheson's Hamburg or Gronau's Danzig had always encouraged such registrations; but by 1750 they were certainly common and no doubt builders endeavoured to make bellows capable of producing enough wind. Thus it was that during J. S. Bach's lifetime, and to a large extent within his area of work, ideas about the full chorus or *plenum* changed, as they did too about the number and kind of solo stops thought desirable.

In Hamburg, Lüneburg and Lübeck, J. S. Bach knew organs with *Rückpositiven*; but in his own area, Chair organs were almost unknown in new instruments from about 1710 (see e.g. Plates 23, 25). Moreover, at Mühlhausen the *Rückpositiv* had a stoplist quite different from the brilliant array of a Dutch or French organ: 8.8.4.4.2.2.1⅓.II?.III. Where ceiling height allowed it, builders preferred to carry such secondary chests within the Great case, usually placed above the *Hauptwerk* and ideally in a vertical line with it. This kind of 'Oberwerk' was different in origin and nature from the old *Oberwerk* of the Brabant organ of the sixteenth century, which had served to take off the non-chorus ranks from the Great Organ. As Chair organs disappeared during Bach's lifetime, pedals too became increasingly less able to provide solo colour for *cantus firmus* lines; indeed, *cantus firmus* music as a whole became a dying genre, though as so often in organ music it is impossible to say which demise came first.

It is a curious fact that several less-than-ideal features are found in some of the most beautiful organs ever made, those of Gottfried Silbermann in Saxony (see Plate 25). They had *Oberwerk* instead of Chair organ, small pedal departments of limited musical use, deep cases (chamber-like and no longer planned as free-standing shallow boxes), few manual reeds, narrow manual and pedal compass, and (at least on paper) a stereotyped nature admitting little major development throughout his total work-span. In practice, however, the strength and beauty of tone, the immensely colourful palette, the strangely versatile pedal 16′, the easy key-action (as light 'as a clavichord', Silbermann claimed at Freiberg in 1710), and the carefully reasoned contrast-with-equality between the manuals produces an organ on which the spirit of much of Bach's organ music is most easily understood. Silbermann was the privileged organ-builder to the court of Saxony, a native Saxon said to have learnt the art in France and Alsace*, returning to make the friendship of such composers as Kuhnau and J. S. Bach. Here, in such organs as the standard model at Fraureuth, is not a mass of colour stops but a unique blend of Saxon and Parisian elements, full of well-thought-out balance between manuals and requiring a mode of registration needing to be learnt by the organist (Dähnert 1953, pp. 209 f, 216 f; Flade 1926, p. 96):

FRAUREUTH
G. Silbermann, 1739–42

Hauptwerk			*Oberwerk*			*Pedal*		
CD–c'''			CD–c'''			CD–c'		
1 Prinzipal	8		11 Gedact	8		19 Subbass	16	
2 Rohrflöte	8		12 Rohrflöte	4		20 Posaune	16	
3 Quintadena	8		13 Nasat	$2\frac{2}{3}$				
4 Oktave	4		14 Oktave	2				
5 Spitzflöte	4		15 Quinte	$1\frac{1}{3}$		Manual push-coupler		
6 Quinte	$2\frac{2}{3}$		16 Sifflöte	1		*Hw/P*		
7 Superoktave	2		17 Sesquialtera	$1\frac{3}{5}$		Tremulant		
8 Tierce	$1\frac{3}{5}$		(Tierce, rep.					
9 Mixtur	IV		at c')					
10 Cornet	III		18 Zimbel	II				

Combinations were noted by the priest of Fraureuth:

Pleno: 1, 2, 4, 5, 6, 7, 9, coupled to 11, 12, 14, 15, 16, 18 with 19, 20
'Sharp, clear combination': 1, 2, 4, 7 coupled to 11, 12, 14, 16 with 19, 20
Cornet: 1, 2, 4, 5, 10 accompanied by 11, 12 and 19
Stahlspiel ('steel-play', glockenspiel): 11, 13, 16, 17 accompanied by 2, 4 and 19
Nasat: 11, 12, 13 accompanied by 2, 4 and 19
Sifflöte: 11, 12, 16 accompanied by 2, 4 and 19
Tremulant: with 1 or 2 or 3 alone, accompanied by 11 and 19
Tertien-Zug zweystimmig ('Tierce registration in two parts'):
　　　　rh 　　1, 2, 4, 6, 7, 8 with or without 9
　　　　lh 　　11, 12, 13, 14, 15, 16
　　　　pedal 　19, 20

* There is, however, a distinct possibility that Gottfried Silbermann learnt not (or not only) with his brother Andreas in Alsace but with Schnitger (or in Schnitger's workshop) in Berlin, up to the years before his first big contract at Freiberg Cathedral in 1710. Work in progress today (Bernhardt Edskes, Marc Schaefer) will probably lead to a re-assessment of Silbermann's early career.

H

Silbermann's voicing is strong, particularly of the principals; his smaller village organs have power and energy, and his wind pressure may have been higher than usual in 1700: *c.* 94 mm for manuals and *c.* 104 mm for pedals. While there is little direct connection between any of Bach's organ music and such instruments,* the Fraureuth registrations do suggest the registrations that may have been drawn for whichever of the unpublished organ sonatas (the so-called 'Trio Sonatas') an organist in Saxony might have been exceptional enough to have known. Were Bach himself to have been called upon to design an ideal organ, which may have been the case for Hildebrandt's large instrument at St. Wenzel, Naumburg, 1743–6 (Dähnert 1970), he would probably have chosen to combine the features of several distinct organ-types: three manuals, including a large Chair organ; a big stoplist of 53 stops including solo pedal stops; and each manual designed as an entity, with its own semi-chorus stops such as Viola, Fugara, Unda maris, Weidpfeife and Spillflöte. As in all the organs known to have been played often by J. S. Bach, Naumburg has several string-toned stops, either narrow cylindrical or conical. Though much altered, the organ still gives some idea of the wide range of colour available. Tierce ranks, alone or as part of the Sesquialtera or Cornet, were indispensable for solo lines in a chorale, whether a congregational hymn or an organ-piece; manual reeds, however, were never numerous and even at Naumburg accounted for less than ten per cent of the total. What reeds there were had a place only in the chorus, except for the Chalumeau and Vox humana. The result is an organ as suitable for *Clavierübung III* (1739) as Arnstadt was for the earlier organ chorales, preludes and fugues. Indeed, this question of chronology is particularly relevant to our understanding of 'the Bach organ', for not only do the earlier works require an organ different in overall concept from the later works, as implied in general terms here, but also an organ different in specific details: for example, it would probably be reflecting the composer's circumstances, if not his intentions, to suppose that *Clavierübung III* requires an organ of lower pitch than the *Orgelbüchlein*.

In view of the changing habits of registration characteristic of his period, it is not surprising that J. S. Bach left only a few registrations, and those only of an unspecific nature. The published Schübler chorales (*c.* 1746?) make clear whether the pedal is at 16′ (like a *basso continuo*) or at 4′ (with a *cantus firmus* line) but do not specify colour. Giving any direction at all may be because of the 'open score' appearance of the page as engraved, i.e. the 'registrations' suggest to organists used largely to

* It is not known from the sources, but can hardly be doubted, that Bach knew the Silbermann organs in Rötha (a few miles from Leipzig) and Freiberg (whose cantorate was second only to Leipzig in the Saxon circuit). He certainly knew the Dresden Silbermanns at the Frauenkirche and Sophienkirche.

two-stave organ notation how to interpret the three staves. What is more, in one or two cases the 'registration' offers only one possible interpretation of the score (e.g. in 'Wachet auf!' BWV 645, the pedal would not be unsuitable for the tenor melody). Similarly, while for the *Orgelbüchlein* chorale BWV 600 the autograph MS registers manual Prinzipal 8′ and pedal Trompete 8′, the true point of the rubric is to show that in the cramped two-stave score the pedal and manual chorale-melody stand to each other as a canon at the 8ve: something not immediately clear. In the concertos it is rarely certain on whose authority the manual-changes have been specified in the known copies, though in the case of the Dorian Toccata BWV 538 the manual contrasts are part of the rhetorical scheme for the movement and must have been part of the composer's original conception. In the case of the chorale 'Ein' feste Burg' BWV 720, the registrations given in modern editions come from J. G. Walther's copies of the work and are more likely to be Walther's way of suggesting how such chorale-fantasias could be registered than specific directions given or even authorized by the composer himself. But while our knowing the precise colours intended or expected by J. S. Bach for any of his music may well be out of the question, certain general points are clear enough. The familiar baroque tinkles heard today for the contrapuntal lines of a trio sonata—i.e. such combinations as $8.2\frac{2}{3}.1$, with 'gaps' between ranks —belong to a different era and area. No manual-changing for the episodes of a fugue is—however subjectively plausible today—authenticated by the Bach sources. Most organists now over-register most organ chorales. And, finally, Bach-playing as a whole is still at a highly conjectural and arbitrary level, very unreliable not least in connection with 'the Bach organ' itself, its changing nature, its various ideals, its kinds of tone, manuals, registration, touch, compass, pitch and countless other details.

Bibliography

ADLUNG, J., *Musica mechanica organoedi*, 2 vols. (Berlin, 1768), with notes by
    J. F. Agricola
DÄHNERT, U., *Die Orgeln Gottfried Silbermanns in Mitteldeutschland* (Leipzig,
    1953)
DÄHNERT, U., 'Johann Sebastian Bach's ideal Organ', *The Organ Yearbook*, 1
    (1970), 20–37
DAVID, W., *Johann Sebastian Bach's Orgeln* (Berlin, 1951)
FLADE, E., *Der Orgelbauer Gottfried Silbermann* (Leipzig, 1926)
FROTSCHER, G., *Geschichte des Orgelspiels und der Orgelkomposition*, 2 vols.
    (Berlin, 1935)
KLOPPERS, J., 'A Criterion for Manual Changes in the Organ Works of Bach',
    The Organ Yearbook, 7 (1976), 59–67

KLOTZ, H., *Über die Orgelkunst der Gotik, der Renaissance und des Barock* (Kassel, 1975)

KNECHT, J. H., *Vollständige Orgelschule* (Leipzig, 1795)

MATTHESON, J., *Der vollkommene Kapellmeister* (Hamburg, 1739)

SCHULZE, H.-J., ed., *Bach-Dokumente*, III (Leipzig, 1972)

SEIDEL, J. J., *Die Orgel und ihr Bau* (Breslau, 1843)

SORGE, G. A., *Der in der Rechen- und Messkunst wohl-erfahrene Orgelbaumeister* (Lobenstein, 1773)

TÖPFER, J. G., *Lehrbuch der Orgelbaukunst*, 4 vols. (Weimar, 1855)

WERCKMEISTER, A., *Erweiterte und verbesserte Orgelprobe* (Quedlingburg, 1698; Eng. trans., Raleigh, N.C., 1976)

WILLIAMS, P., *The Organ Music of J. S. Bach* (London, 1972)

15 The Spanish Baroque Organ

Spanish and Portuguese organs of the baroque period differed widely from region to region. But all the major instruments had special qualities in common, however individual each could be shown to be, and these special qualities join to make an organ very distinct from those of the rest of Europe. Yet in 1500 Spanish organs stood at much the same point as those of northern France or the Netherlands. The influences were Dutch rather than French or Italian, at least in Catalonia where such builders as Pedro Flamench ('Peter the Fleming') worked at Barcelona in 1540. Even the terminology was influenced by the Dutch, for example *fleutes* for the principals from which the later term *flautado* was no doubt derived. Apparently Dutch builders brought new kinds of stop to add to the principals and mixtures (*Mixturas, Forniment, Simbalet*), and by the 1550s new organs of major dimensions could be expected to have chimney flutes, Quintadenas and large-scaled reed stops. Some extant positives of the later sixteenth century show an accomplished technique in making sliderchests for regals, reeds and wooden flues. The big reeds began to have colourful names: *trompetas naturals a la tudesca* ('full-scaled trumpets in the Dutch-German style'), *clarins de galera, molt sonorosos* ('gallery trumpets, very resonant') at Lérida in 1554 (see pp. 87–8),or *clarins de mar molt clas y alegres* ('trumpets of the sea, very clear and arresting') in the same church in 1543 (Anglès 1948). Sea or gallery trumpets were probably clarions used for signal purposes on the kinds of ship sent for South American gold or for the quelling of Elizabeth I. Organ stops of the name were certainly not horizontal, but the evocative names must have played some part in their remarkable evolution during the next century.

As Flemish singers and painters were called to Philip II's new court chapel in Madrid, so Flemish organ-builders (notably the Brebos family) were commissioned to make organs, particularly for the new monastery-palace of El Escorial. Their work there in the years around 1580 resulted in a large Dutch Great Organ of two chests, flue and reed choruses, and solo mutations, like an old Brabant *Hoofdwerk* and *Oberwerk* combined. The pedal was also up to date (16.16.8.4.Mixt.8.8.4) and indeed in advance of any other native Spanish pedal department for the next two centuries (Vente 1958, pp. 122–3). But there was no Chair;

the second manual was a *Brustwerk* based on 4′ Principal (4.8.8.4.2⅔.2. 1⅓.III.III.8.8.8), and though this too remained exceptional, the organ as a whole did set the scene for the single-case Spanish organ in which the second manual is almost always contained in the main case, high up or low down as the case may be. The Dutch flavour of the Catalonian organ is confirmed by the somewhat old-fashioned registrations left at S. Juan de las Abadesas in 1613, which recommend such combinations as 8.1⅓ or 8.Zimb.Trem, as well as a total *plenum* of 8.8.4.2.1⅓.II.1.III (Baldelló 1946, p. 225). It was also the Brebos organs that were particularly familiar to Cabezón (at the Escorial Palace itself) and to Vittoria (at the Descalzas Reales monastery within the Escorial). In general, 'it is not unreasonable for us to assume that the Spanish organ-aesthetic at the turn of the seventeenth century had much in common with those known to Cornet and Titelouze; even Sweelinck's would not have been totally different' (Wyly 1977, p. 42).

The origins of both the most striking of the Spanish features, horizontal reeds (see Plate 33) and swellboxes, are obscure. Perhaps the first reeds to be placed *en chamade* were regals, and possibly towards the end of the sixteenth century. The term itself is French, used in the eighteenth century and originally referring to the trumpet calls when a parley is summoned on the battlefield (Lat. *clamare*, 'to summon'). Placing reeds horizontally gave them a penetrating quality desirable in churches where the organ did not directly face any congregation; it also left them easily accessible for tuning, kept the dust out of the reed, looked splendid and enabled the cathedral to dispense with the more expensive trumpeters employed for the myriad festivals of the Spanish liturgical year. It is impossible to say which of these factors played the biggest part in their popularity. Perhaps full-length reeds *en chamade* date from *c.* 1650 and were first found in the south. At least, Joseph de Echevarría claimed to have invented the *clarines* at Eibar in 1659, a stop 'placed in the main cornice like cannons, which will beautify all the façade of the organ' (Wyly 1977, pp. 42–3):

EIBAR, S. Diego de Alcalá de Henares
J. de Echevarría, 1659

Flautado de 26	Principal 16′
Flautado de 13	Principal 8′
Flautado menor	Octave 4′
Dozena clara	Twelfth 2⅔′
Quincena	Fifteenth 2′ (II)
Diecinona	Nineteenth 1⅓
Compuestas de lleno	Mixture IV

Zimbala	Sharp IV
Sobre Zimbala	Cimbale II
Flautado suave	Open flute (8'? 4'?)
Flautado tapado	Stopped flute (4'? 8'?)
Nasarte mayor	Nasard $2\frac{2}{3}'$
Nasarte mediano	Flute 2'
Nasarte menor	Nasard $1\frac{1}{3}$
Tolosana (Chirumbela)	Tierce mixture
Claron	Tierce mixture (wide scale?)
Flautado 1°	Principal* (*lh* only? stopped?)
Flautado 2°	Principal* (*lh* only? stopped?)
Corneta real	Mounted Cornet VI
Corneta	Echo Cornet, enclosed
Clarines	Trumpet en chamade, treble
Clarines en eco	Trumpet enclosed, treble
Trompetas reales	Interior trumpet
Dulzainas	Regal 8', probably en chamade
Orlos	Crumhorn 8', probably en chamade
Trompeta mayor	Trumpet 16', treble
Bajoncillos	Trumpet 4', bass
Voz humana	Vox humana
Pedal, 8 peanas	Pulldowns (also wooden bass pipes?)

---

* accompaniment for the right-hand Cornets

But documents rarely specify whether the reeds were to be horizontal or vertical, just as documents before the end of the eighteenth century rarely say whether any *Eco* chest or any internal solo stops like Cornet or Trumpet were placed in a Swellbox, and if so of what kind. It is always possible that the reeds often extravagantly described in the documents of the seventeenth century were horizontal. In *c.* 1680, for example, Joseph de Echevarría called reeds 'warlike stops of brass', saying that there could be three kinds of Trompetas reales and Orlos (the latter of which sounded like 'the guitar or harpsichord', a comparison by no means unknown in documents of the 17th century), as well as a Trompeta mayor, a Bajoncillos, Voz humanas, Dulzainas and even angel-statues on either side of the organ, blowing trumpets operated by a footlever (Donostía 1955). Doubtless at least some of these were *en chamade*.

By 1700 or soon after, any large Iberian organ would have a big battery of reeds, both vertical and horizontal, complete with several flue choruses (with and without Tierce ranks), large Swell departments for solo stops, a pedal rank or two, and from time to time even a subsidiary chest in the gallery-front. So thorough was the rebuilding of old Spanish organs during the eighteenth century—because organists wanted the new reed stops and Swellboxes—that the oldest authentic playing organ of any major size in Spain seems to be the late seventeenth-century instrument in Salamanca Cathedral. The famous old organs of Toledo and elsewhere succumbed to fashion as completely as an organ in Hamburg or Paris. The organ type that resulted was highly idiosyncratic. A look into such an organ would discover several chests arranged at different levels, often divided into bass and treble, usually conducted off from one pallet-box and presenting a somewhat disorderly array. No large Spanish organ could be called 'typical' (see Plates 34, 35, 36), for as in Italy during the next century, the larger the organ the less it was like any other and the greater the variety of solo stops. An average-to-large organ typical of the period can still be heard in Braga Cathedral, Portugal, where a pair of identical-looking cases contains a single-manual and a double-manual organ. The big organs of Granada (1746), Toledo Cathedral (1796), Madrid Royal Palace (1778) and elsewhere merely enlarged the possibilities of such instruments and, though fine pieces of engineering, did not offer anything essentially different (Vente and Kok 1957, pp. 203 f):

BRAGA, Cathedral, larger organ on the Gospel side
Anon builder, 1737–8

Organo grande
Originally CD–c'''?

left-hand stops		right-hand stops	
Flautado	16	Flautado	16
Flautado	8	Flautado	8
Oitava	4	Oitava	4
Docena	2⅔	Quincena (15.19)	II
Quincena (15.19)	II	Corneta real	VIII
Nasardos	IV	Simbala	IV
Simbala	IV	Resimbala	IV
Resimbala	IV	Compuestas	IV
Compuestas	IV	Trompeta real	8
Trompeta real	8	*Clarim de batalha	8
*Clarim de batalha	8	*Trompeta magna	16
*Baixao de zinho	4	*Clarom	8
*Clarom	8	*Dulzaina	8
*Dulzaina	8		

Cadireta

Second manual with one chest and one set of pallets: six stops in an *Eco* within the main case, four stops conducted off to a small Chair organ

Eco

left-hand stops		right-hand stops	
Viola	8	Flauta dolce	8
Flauta	4	Flauta	8
Compuestas	(2)	Corneta real	VIII
Tenor	(8)	Clarom	8
Trompeta castarda	4	Clarim	4
Clarom	8	Cheremia	8

Chair Organ

left-hand stops		right-hand stops	
Flautado	8	Flautado	8
Oitava	4	Pífano	4
Simbala		Simbala	
Compuestas		Compuestas	

Pedal

Contras	16

* en chamade

The registration guides to the Spanish baroque organ that are known today date from the middle or later eighteenth century. Dávila's direction for the *plenum* at Granada was simply to draw the Principals 16.8(front). 8(rear).8(stopped).$5\frac{1}{3}$.4.4.$2\frac{2}{3}$.2.$1\frac{1}{3}$.IV.III.III (Wyly 1964, p. 79). The fuller directions at Segovia Cathedral in *c.* 1770, though colourful and evocative, suggest the organists of these extravagant creations to have wanted them only for certain conventionalized effects. These include registrations for frenchified *dialogues* (two-part pieces with mutation ranks or reeds in each hand), regal solo (e.g. Dulzaina in either hand), half-stops for each hand on the same manual (a technique familiar since the later sixteenth century and amply illustrated by Correa de Arauxo in his *Facultad Orgánica*, 1626), echo effects and manual contrasts or antiphony, flutes pitted against reeds (presumably in homophonic or sectional music), coupling of the reeds *en chamade* with those inside, *grand jeu* combinations of Cornets and reeds 8.4 or 8.2 (Walter 1973). Because the stops were so often halved and their pitch-levels dependent on symmetry—i.e. the right-hand trumpet played by key d' might have the same length resonator as the left-hand trumpet played by key D—the right hand could produce a melody below the accompaniment played by the left. In the Segovia registrations, pedal is ignored. More significant still is the fact that the Swell is mentioned not for crescendo or diminuendo effects but merely as a means of softening certain registrations, i.e. making the echo-box yet more distant in effect. In the documents dealing with Fernando Antonio's large organ for Jaén Cathedral in 1789, the builder describes clearly the stop changes brought about by his four footlevers of the kind 'common amongst many organs'. Working the footlevers in conjunction with the knee-levers (see Plate 36) produces quick stop changes, particularly from principals alone to the big solo effects with Trompeta de batalla or with Corneta (de Graaf 1976, pp. 81 f). Such gadgets were also known in England at that period— 'shifting movements', 'composition pedals'—but simpler and on a smaller scale.

Over the whole baroque period, most Iberian bellows were multifold (see Fig. 8) and generally operated by hand. Wind pressure was low— 55 mm for the large organ of the Royal Palace, Madrid—though some examples of 90 mm are known. The chests were always sliderchests, usually divided into bass and treble, not as elsewhere C-chest and C#-chest. The mechanism is usually *suspendu*. Neither bellows nor the wind trunks and channels are capacious enough for stops of different families to be combined. Subsidiary chests like the Echo are placed on the floor of the main case (the *cadireta interior*) and operated by a sticker action; if there is a Chair organ, the pallets are immediately below the keyboard and the channels run below the organist's seat. The main manual may also operate pallets (or conduits) of chests placed behind the rear case-front of the organ, facing a side aisle. There are no manual couplers. Pedal keys are short, sometimes cup-shaped, sometimes simple sticks of wood, usually of a few notes only. Although there may be a rank of eight or ten wooden pipes, most pedals are pulldowns, presumably used mostly for *points d'orgue* and cadences. The hinged lid of the Swellbox, probably first used for Cornet chests by *c.* 1675, was raised by a rope and pulley operated by a footlever that needed to be held down if the lid were to remain open.

The scaling of Iberian principals is generally narrow, the tone restrained, and the effect thinner and softer than a French Montre (for some scalings, see Flentrop 1975). Flutes are gentle and the Cornets reedy, but again thinner than the French in tone. The brash reeds were made to fill the spaces of a large Spanish church outside the immediate environs of the enclosed quire or *coro*. As well as bass or treble solos, reeds also played chords, not only for the celebrated *batallas* or battle-pieces that must have spurred builders on to more and more realistic heights but also for *intradas* or entrance-pieces on the many feast days. The cases themselves often give the appearance of there being more chests or chest-levels than is usually so; as in Italy, the amount of empty space within a Spanish organ must absorb many higher partials in the chorus and be one of the factors producing the mild colour of the flues

Bibliography

ANGLÈS, H., 'El organo de la catedral de Lérida en 1543–56', *Anuario musical*, 3 (1948), 205 f

BALDELLÓ, F., 'Órganos y organeros in Barcelona, siglos XII–XIX', *Anuario musical*,1 (1948), 195 f

DONOSTÍA, J. A. DE, 'El organo de Tolosa (Guipúzcoa) del año 1686', *Anuario musical*, 10 (1955), 121 f

FLENTROP, D. A., 'The Organ in Santa Engracia, Lisbon', *ISO Information*, 13 (1975), 927–36

DE GRAAF, G. A. C., 'A Spanish Registration List of 1789', *The Organ Yearbook*, 7 (1976), 76–89

VENTE, M. A., *Die Brabanter Orgel* (Amsterdam, 1958)

VENTE, M. A. and KOK, W., 'Organs in Spain and Portugal', part 4, *The Organ*, 36 (1957), 203 f

WALTER, R., 'A Spanish Registration List of c. 1770', *The Organ Yearbook*, 4 (1973), 40–51

WYLY, J., 'The Pre-romantic Spanish Organ: Its Structure, Literature, and Use in Performance' (unpublished diss., Kansas City, 1964)

WYLY, J., 'Registration of the Organ Works of Francisco Correa de Arauxo', *Art of the Organ*, I.iv (1971), 9–23

WYLY, J., 'Historical Notes on Spanish Façade Trumpets', *The Organ Yearbook*, 8 (1977), 41–55

16 The Italian Baroque Organ

By 1575 or earlier, the north Italian classical organ—the 'Brescian organ', as it has been called—had achieved its total character. It had a large, shallow case, rather like an altar in shape and enclosing a good deal of empty space behind the case-pipes; whatever the precise design, the case-front would have an upper tier of smaller pipes, always non-speaking (see Plate 11). There was one chest at or about the level of the footholes of the main case-pipes, and the chest would have been a springchest, mortised with well-spaced channels, which were themselves often of uniform size. All but the case-pipes were of highly leaded metal, thick-walled, with a principal scaling relatively narrow in the bass and the flutes wider but smaller mouthed. The compass rose to a'' or c''', and usually all the ranks were separate, those at the higher octave and fifth pitches breaking back at regular points to form a kind of composite mixture in the treble. Any second manual was exceptional and one probably made for a special church by a foreign builder; second manuals were rare enough for each known example to have had a quite individual character. Tuning was in some form of meantone temperament, as elsewhere, but the pitch itself varied from organ to organ (*come si vuole*, 'as you like', according to Antegnati p. 72). Antegnati's phrase implies that one chose a pitch convenient to the voice, and during the next century Barcotto noted that pitch still differed from city to city. Some Brescian organs had an octave or so of pedal pulldowns: short keys sloping upwards into the organ like a reading desk, hence the name *pedali a leggio*. In the seventeenth century a few organs had a set of open wooden principals for the pedals. Registration was standardized, and each combination of stops suggested a particular key or a particular moment in the Mass and Office (see pp. 84–5).

Italian builders gradually added their own ideas to such standard schemes but left the outlines clearly recognizable even in the large Serassi organs of 1850. Each city or region had its own variants of the standard scheme (see Plates 18, 19), and only further work in the parts of Italy still inadequately understood—Naples and Calabria in particular —will reveal how uniform the Italian organ* actually was. By 1600,

---

* A similar uniformity once claimed for the Italian harpsichord over the period 1500 to 1800 has been examined and dismissed in recent years (see e.g. J. Barnes, 'The Specious Uniformity of Italian Harpsichords', *Keyboard Instruments*, ed. E. M. Ripin (Edinburgh, 1971), 1–10).

the Flemish builder Fulgenzi Fiammengo (Wolfgang the Fleming) had already introduced stopped pipes at $2\frac{2}{3}'$, chimney flute at $2'$, conical flute at $1\frac{1}{3}'$, reeds $8'$ and regals $4'$ at Orvieto Cathedral (Lunelli 1956, pp. 102 f). Stopped pipes were known for the rare second manuals (S. Maria in Aracoeli, Rome, 1585) as of course they must have been for countless positive or chamber organs; their exclusion from the 'Brescian classical organ' was therefore intentional. By the later seventeenth century, the borderland in the Tyrol saw organs with mixtures and Cornet, as well as the C–c^{III} compass gradually becoming a norm in northern countries; such details probably owed their existence to other foreign builders such as Eugenio Casparini (Johann or Eugen Caspar), who naturally enough was forced into a kind of macaronic language for some of his terms, for example *flautt spizosa alla fiammenga in sesta* for the Sesquialtera or 'Flemish Spitzflöte in 6ths' at S. Giusto, Trieste in 1668 (Lunelli 1960, p. 37). Second manuals remained exceptional, and that made by the Dalmatian builder Pietro Nacchini (Peter Nakič) for S. Antonio, Padua in 1743–9 presented a stoplist still very much like that at S. Maria in Aracoeli, Rome in 1585–7 (Lunelli 1956, p. 117; Lunelli 1958, pp. 14–15):

Rome   *manual I*   6 Ripieno ranks, Flauto $2'$, Trombani $8'$, drum, bird-stop, tremulant

       manual II 5 ripieno ranks, regal $8'$

Padua *manual I*   7 Ripieno ranks, Flauto $4'$, $2\frac{2}{3}'$ and $1\frac{3}{5}'$, Voce umana, Tromboni $8'$, drum

       manual II 4 Ripieno ranks, Flauto $4'$ and $1\frac{3}{5}'$, Voce umana, Tromboni $8'$

       pedal   Contrabassi

One major difference, however, did gradually begin to make itself felt: builders began collecting the upper ranks of the Ripieno onto one slider, thus producing a mixture not so very different from the French *Fourniture cymbalisée* (see p. 107). During the eighteenth century, the taste for Tierce ranks also grew. These and the flute ranks drawn with them ($2\frac{2}{3}'$, $2'$) were usually called 'Cornetto' by the Venetian and northern Italian builders who liked them, no doubt as some reference to the Cornet stops found north of the Alps. In one instance (S. Apollinare, Rome, in 1666) a Flemish organ was built with a Tierce rank on both of its manuals, and its builder (S. Hay) registered them in several ways, most interestingly for a two-manual dialogue of Tierces (Culley 1967, p. 223). Indeed, such 'exceptional' organs are important to the history of the Italian organs since they were always conspicuous and therefore influential.

During the eighteenth century, the taste for exceptional or even experimental organs developed yet further, often resulting in fanciful instruments built on special commission and impressing with their extravagance the gullible from Bergamo to Sicily. But although rivalry with the fine organs 'at Marseilles, Trent and Hamburg' was an avowed motive behind the designing of the four-manual organ at S. Stefano dei Cavalieri, Pisa in 1733–7, as it may well have been elsewhere, the result was very unlike any of them. In its disposition of chests—Great, Chair, two Echoes, Pedal—Azzolino della Ciaia's organ of Pisa would not have been out of place in Castille; in its little fifth manual that slid out and played a spinet (*per l'uso del Saltero*, 'to use as a psaltery'), it had something in common with a few exceptional German organs of the previous century; in its stoplist, it did what all Italian organs have done for the last four hundred years—supplemented the classical chorus with stops chosen from other organ-cultures, particularly French (documents in Baggiani 1974). The yet larger 55-stop, five-manual, three-console organ at Catania, Sicily, made by Donato del Piano in 1755, was little more than a collection of several classical Italian organs gathered together and larded with a host of flutes and echo-colours of the kind much admired in that decadent period and highly influential on the large Italian organs of the next century.

Throughout the seventeenth and eighteenth centuries, however, not only did the average Italian organ follow the classical plan with or without regional variation, but many old organs remained to be constantly played, heard and copied: probably more than in any other area of Europe. An interesting exception to this general pattern is Venice, where very little from the earlier period remains and where, despite a report in 1697 that the city then had some 147 organs (dalla Libera 1973, p. 20), nobody now knows what they were like. The eighteenth century must have seen a deliberate and systematic replacing of the older instruments for a new, clearly characterized kind of organ. Indeed, the Venetian organ of the mid-eighteenth century was widely influential, being found along the Dalmatian, Istrian and Venetian coasts and some way inland beyond the border of the Veneto. Nacchini and his successor Gaetano Callido built hundreds of such single-manual organs and many with a second manual—the pipes of the second were enclosed in a Swell-box from about 1785—disregarding the more extravagant instruments of Italy and giving their organs a straight-forward tone, somewhat coarser than Antegnati's. The building of such organs was highly systematic: Nacchini's pipe-scales were the same however large the church, but he widened the spectrum with stopped flutes, Tierces, regals and small pedal department, the ripieno ranks breaking back and all so voiced as to suggest again that 'the feeling of Italian organs was turned towards the ideal of the vocal sound' (Šaban 1973, p. 98). A stoplist typical of the larger Venetian organs is the following (Giacobbi and Mischiati 1962, pp. 16–19):

CANDIDE, S. Maria Assunta
G. Callido, 1797–9 (Op. 367)

Organo grande		*Organo piccolo*	
FF–f'''		C–f'''	
Principale	8 (halved)	Principale	8 (halved)
Ottava	4	Ottava	4 (halved)
Quintadecima	2	Quintadecima	2
Decimanona	$1\frac{1}{3}$	Decimanona	$1\frac{1}{3}$
Vigesimaseconda	1	Vigesimaseconda	1
Vigesimasesta	$\frac{2}{3}$	Voce umana	8 (treble)
Vigesimanona	$\frac{1}{2}$	Flauto	4 (halved)
Trigesimaterza (to f)	$\frac{1}{3}$	Flauto	$2\frac{2}{3}$
Trigesimasesta (to f)	$\frac{1}{4}$	Cornetto	$1\frac{3}{5}$ (treble)
Voca umana	8 (treble)	Tromboncini	8 (halved)
Flauto in ottava	4 (halved)	Violoncello (regal)	8 (halved)
Flauto in duodecima	$2\frac{2}{3}$		
Cornetto	$1\frac{3}{5}$ (treble)	Pitch-levels as at C	
Violetta (fluc)	4 (halved)	Manual coupler	
Tromboncini (regal)	8 (halved)	Tamburo (drum-stop)	
		Second manual chest, on floor to	
Pedal (*coupled*)		left of keyboards, with vertical	
CDEFGA–b♭		shutters (originally horizontal)	
Contrabassi	16	Halved stops divide at a/b♭	
Ottava	8	Sliderchests	
Ottava	4	All flutes tapering	
Tromboni	16 (8?)	Higher ripieno ranks break back	
OG/P (new)		Manual lever for the *tiratutti*, i.e.	
Suboctave OG/P		to draw the ripieno	

The wide-scaled principals of such organs were responsible for the so-called *Italienisch Prinzipal* found in many German organs of the twentieth century, but more widely typical of the Italian organ are narrow principals, closer in many respects to the Spanish. A further coincidence with the Spanish organ is one detail of the short and small-scaled reeds and regals found in such Venetian organs: they stand vertically in front of the case-pipes, and do so for the convenience of tuning. It has been recently shown that Callido seasoned the metal plates from which he made his pipes by leaving them in the sun under certain conditions (dalla Libera 1973, p. 23); certainly the 'limpid purity' of his voicing testifies to a careful builder.

The registrations Callido provided for his organs show orchestral imitation to have been important to organists of the period; there is no subtle play of two manuals, the Tierce can be used in the chorus, and (as in Spain) the Swell shutters seem to have been used either open or shut but not expressively. At Candide, Callido not only suggested instrumental imitations such as the following (Giacobbi and Mischiati 1962, pp. 52–5):

> oboè e viola: Principale bassi, Viola bassi, Tromboncini soprani, with Contrabassi
> flauto traversiè: Flauto 4′, Violetta (soprani and bassi)
> arpa: Ottava, Tromboncini (soprani and bassi)

but gave several choruses or *ripieni*:

1 ripieno semplice: Principali and tiratutti, with Contrabassi
2 ripieno misto: *ditto*, adding Flauto $2\frac{2}{3}'$ and Cornetto
3 ripieno ad uso di orchestra: as 1, with Tromboncini (complete) and Tromboni
4 ripieno ad uso di Marcia: as 2, with Tromboncini (complete), Tromboni and Tamburo

Nevertheless, though these choruses obviously belong to 1800, Callido's next registration had been typical of the previous two or three hundred years, and except for the pedal, any organist of Antegnati's period would have recognized it:

for the Elevation: Principali and Voce umana, with Contrabassi.

Bibliography

ANTEGNATI, C., *L'arte organica* (Brescia, 1608; edn. referred to: Ger. trans. [P. Smets], Mainz, 1958)

BAGGIANI, F., *L'organo di Azzolino B. della Ciaia nella Chiesa Conventuale dei Cavalieri di S. Stefano in Pisa* (Pisa, 1974)

CULLEY, T., 'Documenti d'archivio—Organi fiamminghi a S. Apollinare a Roma, II', *L'organo*, 5 (1967), 213–24

GIACOBBI, V. and MISCHIATI, O., 'Gli antichi organi del Cadore', *L'organo*, 3 (1962), 3–58

LIBERA, S. DALLA, 'Organs in Venice', *The Organ Yearbook*, 4 (1973), 18–30

LUNELLI, R., 'Un Trattatello di Antonio Barcotto colma le lacune dell'*Arte Organica*', *Collectanea Historiae Musicae*, i (Firenze, 1953), 135ff

LUNELLI, R., *L'arte organaria del Rinascimento in Roma* (Florence, 1958)

LUNELLI, R., *Der Orgelbau in Italien* (Mainz, 1956)

LUNELLI, R., 'Eugenio Casparini, un organaro italiano per i tedeschi e tedesco per gli Italiani', *L'organo*, 1 (1960), 16–48

ŠABAN, L. and FAULEND-HEFERER, I., 'Umjetnost i Djela Graditelja Orgulja Petra Nakiča u Dalmacij i Istri', *Arti Musices*, 4 (1973)

17 The English Organ Before 1800

Full attention though this subject has received in English books on organs over the last century and a half, it is one of comparatively minor interest from an international point of view since few if any of its builders have ever had much influence outside Britain and its Empire, despite some outstanding successes at home. Moreover, because so few technical details of the English organ have ever been published and so few documents ever properly assembled, particularly as they deal with the two critical periods of 1660–90 and 1820–50, it could even be thought that no history of the English organ can yet be written, despite the attempts that have been made. At this stage, therefore, it is possible only to hint at the influences to which the English organ has been subject and at the topics which further research ought to develop.

Over a century ago, E. F. Rimbault claimed that the John Roose, Brother of the Order of Preaching Friars, who 'repaired and restored the organ at the altar of the B.V.M. in the Cathedral Church of the City of York' in 1457, was 'the first English organ builder of whom we have any authentic account' (Rimbault 1864, p. 25). But Roose was almost certainly not English, for a builder of that family name lived in Utrecht in the sixteenth century, built the organ in the Wasserkirche, Münster in 1572 and even left registrations for it (Klotz 1975, p. 194). John Roose may have been an earlier member of that family; he was probably a Dutch Dominican, placing the York organ near the B.V.M. altar in the Dutch manner; and he certainly personifies the Dutch or Flemish influence on the English organ during the late medieval period. At Louth in about 1500, there was reference to a pair of Flemish organs being set up on the rood-screen (Hopkins & Rimbault 1877, p. 53); it was unusual for documents to specify an instrument's origins in this way, but the organ may well have been typical. The unique document concerning Antony Duddyngton's organ at All Hallows, Barking in 1519—quoted by Rimbault in 1864 and copied unverified ever since— also seems to imply a Flemish or Dutch organ (Rimbault 1864, pp. 75–7):

> . . . of dowble Ce–fa–ut that ys to say, xxvij playne keyes, and the pryncipale to conteyn the length of v foote, so folowing wt Bassys called Diapason to the same, conteyning length of x foot or more:

I

And to be dowble pryncipalls thoroweout the seid instrument, so that the pyppes wt inforth shall be as fyne metall and stuff as the utter parts, that is to say of pure Tyn, wt as fewe stoppes as may be convenient.

There have been as many interpretations of this passage as there have been historians of the English organ; and until it can be verified that the contract does say e.g. *wt* ('with') and not *wc* ('which'), certain details will remain entirely conjectural. Nevertheless, the passage can be understood as a reference either to a Dutch *Principael* (*Blockwerk*) or to an Italian *Ripieno* (Diapason chorus of separate stops) with certain features that are clear enough: **1** the compass was of 27 natural keys from C (probably CDEFGA–g''a''), as were those of so many organs throughout Europe in *c*. 1520, **2** the *pryncipale* was not a single stop but the whole chorus, the case-pipes of which perhaps could be played singly, **3** the largest pipe in that chorus was of 5', below which there was some kind of suboctave rank, **4** the case-pipes were of tin, those inside tin-and-lead ('stuff' corresponds to the northern French builder's term *étoffe*, already in use). Quite unclear, however, are the following: **5** the foot-standard employed by builder and/or scribe (how long was 5'?), **6** the meaning of the phrase 'wt Bassys' (with a separate rank of suboctave pipes? a few Trompes-like bass-pipes? or implying only that the biggest pipes, i.e. those in the case-front, could be played separately?), **7** whether 'dowble pryncipalls' denotes less or more than a *Blockwerk*, **8** whether 'with as few stops as may be convenient' can be taken at its face value and if so, what exactly 'as may be convenient' means. Only speculation can answer these puzzles, but it should be noted that Henri Arnaut also used the phrase 'double principals' and that already in 1519 the specifically English terms 'diapason' (for a rank of large pipes, literally 'running through all' the gamut or compass) and 'stops' (for hand-operated register-mechanism?) do seem to have their familiar meaning.

No known English documents give any definite detail of the contents of a single major organ before 1606 (King's College, Cambridge), which certainly suggests that they were small standardized instruments, with one chest containing a chorus in Dutch or Italian manner. It is not known whether any English organ before 1600 had separate quint ranks, but the inventories of Henry VIII's instruments—small and chamber-like though they doubtless were—mention more than one 'Cimball' stop of two ranks (another French term?), one rank of which was presumably at least sometimes a quint (see Russell 1973). But in any case, it is not known whether these organs of Henry VIII were English-built. By 1550, churches were already resisting the spending of adequate sums on organs, and this miserliness—fortunately for the clergy, coinciding with reformist attitudes to music as a whole—remained a most important factor in English organ-building for the next three centuries. If a church had an organ at all by 1600, it would certainly have been no more than a single-manual, large-scaled positive of half a dozen stops, probably with sliderchest, perhaps with long compass. If those ranks were all separate and single, as was the case in organs of the earlier seventeenth century, the influences during Elizabeth's reign must have been Italian rather than Flemish, as would not be unlikely in that cultural climate. But that some organ colour was known is suggested by occasional references to Tremulants (Elizabeth's organ for the Sultan in 1599, King's College in 1605–6) and regals (St. Martin-in-the-Field 1561, Henry VIII's inventory of 1547), for they must all have been rather striking. As far as looks are concerned, Italian influences are not paramount: architectural analysts could find various French and Flemish elements in the extant late sixteenth-century organ cases at Tewkesbury, Gloucester (early seventeenth century?) and Framlingham.

The standard English 'Double Organ' of the seventeenth century was an instrument of some musical potential, stunted by political and puritan developments, but promising as far as it went. An early example was the Worcester Cathedral organ of 1613 (Thomas Dallam); that at York Minster in 1632 was a little fuller (Sayer 1977):

YORK, Minster
R. Dallam, contract of 1632

Great Organ

Open Diapason (case-front)	8	Two and Twentieth	1
Open Diapason (case-front*)	8		
Stopped Diapason (wood)	8	*Chair Organ*	
Principal (case-front*?)	4	Diapason (wood; stopped?)	8
Principal (case-front?)	4	Principal (case-front, tin)	4
Twelfth	$2\frac{2}{3}$	Flute (wood)	4
Small Principal	2	Small Principal (tin)	2
Recorder	2	Recorder (tin)†	

Both Diapasons 'to stand in sight, many of them to be chased'

* in the rear case-front?

† 'unison to the voice', thus 8', beginning at c'?; or perhaps a misreading for 'unison to the same', i.e. Principal 2'

Compass of 51 notes—CD–d''e''? GGAABB♭BBCDE–c'''?
Both manuals with a 'rowler board' (i.e. pipes arranged in mitre forms)
Three bellows

The 'drawing stoppes' listed amongst the mechanism for the Chair organ is a term analogous to the French *tirants* of an earlier period. The 51-note compass could also suggest one or other European tradition, in particular the long compass of the Italian organ. Also Italianate may have been the voicing, like the nomenclature itself ('Two and Twentieth', etc.), for these were accompanying-organs vital to the choir below and near the north side of the choir stalls over which the Chair organ at York presumably hung. In other cathedrals, it was the screen position—possibly a Flemish element, known already at Louth and no doubt elsewhere by 1500—that led to a tone for the organ perhaps not so far removed from that of the *organi da legno* or wooden organs used in Italy for continuo purposes at that later period. Even the relationship of the manuals at York resembles that of the occasional two-manual Italian organ to be found then (see p. 127).

The internal positive or second manual, as distinct from the Chair organ, was also known in seventeenth-century England, firstly in the large secular organs such as Chirk Castle (1631) and Adlington Hall (*c.* 1650), which were very likely made by Dutch or Dutch-trained builders. Adlington even has double pallets to enable the Stopped Diapason to be played by either manual. Mutation ranks had also gradually begun to appear, and it is possible that some 1' stops broke back to be $2\frac{2}{3}$' or $1\frac{1}{3}$' for the upper part of the compass (Clutton and Niland 1963, pp. 58–9). The Adlington Great has what appears to be an original specification of $8.8.4.2\frac{2}{3}.2.2.1\frac{3}{5}.1\frac{1}{3}.1.8.8.$, though it is possible that some of these may date from a later seventeenth-century rebuild. Either way, Adlington was still some way from the stoplist projected by Robert Dallam in 1654 for the Great Organ of Lesneven Priory: $8.8.4.4.2\frac{2}{3}.2.2.1\frac{3}{5}.1\frac{1}{3}.1.III.II.V.8.8.8.4.$ Although this scheme is obviously French, even to the Cornet V, a reed battery and several mutations, it could not be called a classical Parisian *Grand Orgue*, for it had high stops, a regal, but no 16' Bourdon. By 1654, Dallam was at work in northwest France, while in England the Civil War of 1642–9, the Puritan interlude and the eventual Restoration in 1660 changed the direction of the English organ; but in general the French influences should always be seen in terms of Brittany and perhaps Normandy, rather than the Île-de-France or elsewhere in that country.

Though probably exaggerated by historians, the French influences on the English organ after the Restoration, chiefly through the work of the Harris family, were certainly important. Grandson of Thomas Dallam and son of another builder (Thomas Harris or Harrison), Renatus Harris sometimes had occasion to rebuild organs made by his ancestors. At Magdalen College, Oxford in 1686, he replanned his father's organ of 1638, taking out the duplicated ranks of the kind found in the York stoplist above (they were difficult to keep in tune, he said, and gave little return in increased volume) and turning the 1638 Great of 8.8.4.4.2.2.1.1. (all open) into a new 8.8.4.2⅔.2.1⅗.II–III, in which the two 8′ stops were open and stopped respectively. Already in 1661, Robert Dallam had suggested for New College, Oxford, a complete French organ of two manuals and 24 stops, with French mixtures, i.e. the Fourniture breaking back once every octave, the Simbale twice.

While the Harris family gave impetus in the French direction, Bernard Smith gave it in a Dutch-German. He must have had experience in the Netherlands and may have been born there (Boeringer 1976); his Chapel Royal organ is a typical compromise scheme, suggesting that any north European influences in his work were dominated by Harris's French conceptions of the manuals, with all their Breton limitations (Pearce 1911, p. 84):

LONDON, Chapel Royal, Whitehall (Banqueting Hall)
B. Smith, 1699

Great Organ		*Choir Organ*	
GGAA–c'''		GGAA–c'''	
Open Diapason	8	Stopped Diapason	8
Stopped Diapason	8	Principal	4
Principal	4	Flute (wood, c♯')	2?
Flute (wood)	4?	Vox humana	8
Block Flute (metal, c♯')	2?	Cremona	8
Twelfth	2⅔	*Echo*	
Fifteenth	2	ga–c'''	
Sesquialtera	III	Open Diapason	8
Cornet (c♯')	III	Principal	4
Trumpet	8	Cornet (12.17)	II
		Trumpet	8

Source: Leffler's MS of *c*.1810 (now in private possession), where the Echo is said to be 'placed immediately over the Keys—behind the Music Desk—and not as usual enclosed in a box', i.e. it was a conventional *Brustwerk*. Smith may have called the cornet a 'Sesquialtera', and the Great Sesquialtera 'Mixture'; a *Brustwerk* Stopped Diapason would be more usual than open.

Smith won the two best-known contracts, those for the Temple Church in 1683–7 and for St. Paul's Cathedral in 1694–9, introducing to the Temple such Germanic names as Prestand, Holflute, Sesquialtera, Gedakt, Mixture, Spitts Flute, Violl and Super Octavo. But terminology is a poor guide; judging by the double voluntaries of such composers as John Blow, for example, 'Sesquialtera' was a common name for a kind of Bass Cornet, and no builder or composer in London at that period seems to have used it in any sense that would have been immediately clear to a visiting Dutchman or Thuringian. Even in terminology, the classical English organ was a strange compôte, though the prime influences may well have been French, whatever Burney and Hawkins liked to think a century later; even the first English treatise on organs (James Talbot *c*. 1687) was much indebted to a French theorist (Marin Mersenne) and to a frenchified builder (René Harris).

Much is still uncertain about the Harris–Smith organ. Were the internal Choir chests placed in the upper or lower part of the organ? Was the Whitehall *Brustwerk* unusual? Were the reeds French? Did the earliest Sesquialtera chorus-mixtures have a Tierce rank, or were they not meant for the chorus? Were the Diapason-scalings, voicing, key action, chest construction, bellows types and trunking French? What were the pitches and temperaments in use? Although such questions are only now being answered (*BIOS* 1978), some general points have long been clear. Both Harris and Smith had foreign experience; by the 1680s Smith was making frenchified schemes; traditional English influences—i.e. old Dutch and old Italian—were still strong enough for builders to dispense with pedals, though not necessarily pedal pulldowns which, like Tremulants and Couplers, were merely mechanical appurtenances and may not always have been specified in contracts; builders preferred longer compass than in France, the Netherlands or Germany (from GG in most organs, FF at the Temple, CC planned for St. Paul's); and no organ was larger than 30 stops, though two-and-a-half manuals were common. Musical potential was more limited than it need have been. For example, although Harris enlarged the organ of Salisbury Cathedral by adding French mixtures and mutations, noting that the Tierce was 'a Stop of much variety' for the organist (Williams 1970, p. 18), the instrument was still not able to produce the full effect of a *Tierce en taille*. But nor were comparable instruments on the fringe of the Île-de-France classical organ, such as those in Brittany or southern Flanders; in all three countries (England, Brittany, Flanders), at least Tierce dialogues, Cornet *récits* and various *basse de trompette* or *basse de cromorne* registrations were possible. It must have been this array of frenchified colours that encouraged solo-stop registration in the English organ-fantasias of the later seventeenth century and hence directly— though how has not yet been fully discovered—to the voluntaries of John Stanley and others. Here is a large organ of the Harris kind on which all eighteenth-century English organ music could have been played (Sumner 1973, pp. 186–7):

BRISTOL, St. Mary Redcliffe
Harris & Byfield, 1726

Great Organ		*Chair Organ*	
CC–d$^{'''}$ (63 notes)		GG–d$^{'''}$ (56 notes)	
Open Diapason	8	Stopped Diapason	8
Open Diapason	8	Principal	4
Stopped Diapason	8	Flute almain	4?
Principal	4	Flute	2?
Twelfth (from GG)	2$\frac{2}{3}$	Sesquialtera	III
Fifteenth (from GG)	2	Bassoon	8
Tierce (from G)	1$\frac{3}{5}$		
Sesquialtera	V	*Swell*	
Cornet (from c$^{'}$)	V	G–d$^{'''}$ (44 notes)	
Trumpet	8	Open Diapason	8
Clarion	4	Stopped Diapason	8
		Principal	4
Pedal		Flute	4
1 octave pulldowns		Cornet (complete)	III
		Trumpet	8
Four bellows		Hautboy	8
CO/GO?		Cremona	8
Tremulant?		French Horn	8

'Consort pitch' (i.e. *ton de chambre* a^{1} = 415 Hz?)
The Echo was 'made to swell or express Passion' (i.e. a Swellbox?)
Chair Organ Flute almain, perhaps 8', treble only
'An Invention, which by drawing only a Stop, makes it almost as loud again
　as it was before . . . tho' there are no new Pipes added to the Organ, or any
　keys put down by it' (i.e. an internal octave coupler on the long-compass
　Great Organ?)

Extant examples, as well as written documents, show that the reeds that
could be expected in an average English organ from about 1700 onwards
were French in character, though the earlier French of Robert Clicquot
rather than the rich *fin-de-siècle* French of François-Henri Clicquot.
Amongst musicians of the period there was a common opinion that both
reeds and mixtures were unnecessary. In about 1720 Roger North wrote
about reeds that they have three disadvantages: they soon lose their
tuning, they speak slowly, and 'the bases will always snore, and that
defect cannot be conquered, so that in Organs they are rather an in-

cumbrance than useful' (Wilson 1959, p. 232). Some 70 years later, Jonas Blewitt still thought that mixtures and mutations 'were put in by Organ Builders, merely to make a show of Stops to draw, at a small expense . . . they only encumber an organ'. Between those two opinions, neither of which flatters the British builder, can be read a great deal about the English organ before the mid-nineteenth century. As for the unwanted pedals, Harris himself recommended them in his 1712 scheme for St. Paul's on the grounds that the organist would then 'be able to do as much as if he had four hands' and that 'Pedals are used in all the great Organs beyond the seas' (Sumner 1973, p. 152). But no pedal pipes are known to have been made in England before the 'six large Trumpet Pipes down to 16 foot tone to be used with a pedal or without' at St. Paul's in 1720–21 (*ibid.* p. 183), and then it is clear that they could be played from the Great Organ keyboard; not until 1778, at St. Catherine-by-the-Tower, are true pedal-pipes known to have been made. Of much more interest to the English builders was the device first shown at St. Magnus, London Bridge, in 1712: a Swellbox. Abraham Jordan, the builder, claimed his Swell to be an original device, and certainly giving the traditional echo-box expressive powers by fastening its raisable flap-lid (or its sliding front-panel) to ropes and levers fixed near the player was a device of beguiling potential. But similar devices had been tried for the solo stop or two of many a Spanish organ over the previous half century, and Harris himself claimed to have tried out some swelling mechanism at Salisbury (Sumner 1973, p. 152). Either way, by 1730 every average new organ in England had a Swellbox; a century later it was ousting the Choir organ as the chief second manual; and only in the last decade or two have a few voices been raised against the Swellbox as an irrelevance. But on the technical side generally, the Harris school was obviously very competent, with their double pallets (a device probably learnt in France—see Hardouin 1976, p. 28), four manuals (Salisbury Cathedral, one of them 'communicated'), Swells, improved wind supply (regulation of the bellows by means of springs at St. Dionis Backchurch) and long compass.

That the insular British traditions were strong is also clear from the work of John Snetzler, a German Swiss who had learnt with the Passau firm of Egedacher and, like many other central European makers of organs, harpsichords and pianos, went to work and live in London, in his case early in the 1740s. Certain of Snetzler's techniques, in particular the voicing, may have resembled the Egedachers' and certainly seem to reflect the taste for fine, even over-refined tone then common in Hapsburg Europe. But his specifications are totally English, as were those of his contemporaries and compatriots then working in the English colonies (e.g. J. Klemm in New York, *c.* 1740). Only Snetzler's first organs show obvious foreign elements, such as the 16' Bourdon at King's Lynn in

1754; however, he does seem to have tried introducing other central European colours, such as Viola da Gamba, Salicional, overblowing German Flute and overblowing Dulciana. Of these, only the easiest to be made—the narrow-scaled open cylindrical Dulciana—proved popular, soon becoming *de rigueur* on all new organs larger than about four stops and betraying the English organist's limited ideas of organ tone quite as much as do Swellboxes and pedal-less *plena*. Builders such as Samuel Green seem to have let the Dulciana and the Swell govern their total designs, even to enclosing whole organs behind Venetian Swells of the kind used by some English harpsichord-makers in the 1770s (see Plate 31).

Snetzler's organ of 1757 in the Savoy Chapel had such foreign features as manual coupler, Tremulant and pedal pulldowns, none of which had immediate progeny or cast wide influences. However, this organ is important in one respect. The Savoy Chapel was a German church and points to an interesting factor in all English music-making, including organ-building in particular, over the period 1750–1875: any advanced ideas were tried out not on Anglican church organs but on those in non-establishment circles—the embassy chapels, the Methodist meeting-houses and those of other evangelical groups, the many new concert halls. At the same time, travellers like Burney were reporting on organs they heard abroad—and reporting on them usually to their detriment—and visiting virtuosi like Abt Vogler brought in ideas on pedal-playing during a period when in any case the solo-stop voluntaries of John Stanley and the others were going out of fashion. In these various ways, both instrument and its music were ripe by 1790 for the German influences burgeoning early in the next century.

Bibliography

BLEWITT, J., *A Complete Treatise on the Organ* (London, *c.* 1790)

BOERINGER, J., 'Bernard Smith (*c.* 1630–1708): A Tentative new Chronology for the Early Years', *The Organ Yearbook*, 6 (1975), 4–16

CLUTTON, C. and NILAND, A., *The British Organ* (London, 1963)

FREEMAN, A., *Father Smith, Otherwise Bernard Schmidt* (London, 1926; edited and enlarged by J. Rowntree, Oxford, 1977)

HARDOUIN, P., 'Pierre Thierry', *Connoissance de l'orgue*, 18 (1976), 27–31

HOPKINS, E. J. and RIMBAULT, E. F., *The Organ, its History and Construction* (London, 1855, 3rd edn., 1877)

KLOTZ, H., *Über die Orgelkunst der Gotik, der Renaissance und des Barock* (Kassel, 1975)

PEARCE, C. W., *Notes on English Organs ... Taken Chiefly From the MS of Henry Leffler* (London, 1911)

RIMBAULT, E. F., *The Early English Organ Builders and their Work* (London, 1864)

RUSSELL, R., *The Harpsichord and Clavichord* (London, 1959, 2/1973), 155–160

SAYER, M., 'Robert Dallam's Organ in York Minster, 1634', *British Institute of Organ Studies Journal*, 1 (1977), 60–68

SUMNER, W. L., *The Organ, its Evolution, Principles of Construction and Use* (London, 1952, 4th edn., 1973)

THISTLETHWAITE, N., 'Smith Pipework. A Study of Scaling, Voicing, Pitch and Layout', *British Institute of Organ Studies Journal*, 2 (1978)

WILLIAMS, P., 'The First English Organ Treatise', *The Organ*, 44 (1964), 17 f

WILLIAMS, P., 'Pour une histoire du plein jeu, X', *Renaissance de l'orgue*, 4 (1970), 17–20

WILSON, J., *Roger North on Music* (London, 1959)

18 Some Masterpieces of the Northern European Organ, 1640–1800

Two distinct histories of the organ after 1500 could be written: the one concerned with the average organ and its potential in the music of the period, the other concerned with the really large organs, all of which were by nature exceptional and, however obviously summing up their period or area, were removed to a greater or lesser extent from most of the organ music contemporary with them. A problem with the more extravagant organs of 1650 to 1750 is that it is rarely clear what they were meant to play and how they were meant to sound, while a problem with organs of 1750 to 1850 is that the music for which they were known to be built, often with great technological skill, is difficult to admire. The relationship between organs and organ music is more complex and tangled than summary histories make it seem. Builders must often have been inspired by other organs, irrespective of the needs or expectations of the composers. Moreover, certain periods produced batches of organs which have features in common whatever their country of origin. Thus between 1725 and 1750 a number of large and particularly important organs were built: the great organs of Haarlem (see Plate 24), Gouda, Weingarten (see Plate 27), Herzogenburg, Naumburg, Dresden (see Plate 26), Breslau, Potsdam, Uppsala, Catania, Pisa, Tours, Paris, Granada, Braga and so on. Whatever the builder of any of these organs knew about the others—and there were some obvious rivalries—they were all designed to do a different job from the great organs of 1650: they were all made to fill their churches with big, even total sound, and they were made to bewitch the ear with delicate, colourful effects. The new west-end organ was usually the only instrument in the building if the church itself were new; this itself was a departure from tradition. Extremes of sound were even more the ideal of the next generation of builders: the creators of Saint-Maximin, Toledo (see Plates 34, 35, 36), Madrid, Poitiers, Hamburg Michaeliskirche, Rostock Marienkirche (see Plate 32), Arnhem, Nijmegen, Ottobeuren, Amorbach, St. Florian, Oliwa, Milan. The theorists who planned yet bigger organs—Dom Bedos de Celles, P. Mauritius Vogt—had the same crude extremes in mind.

Two different organs of about 1650, described below, sum up the kinds of instrument from which the eighteenth-century giants developed. Others could be taken, in particular the Dutch organs of Alkmaar (see

Frontispiece) or Amsterdam Westerkerk (see Plate 15), from which a line of increasing crudity led to the German-built organs of Haarlem, Amsterdam Oude Kerk, Kampen, Nijmegen and elsewhere. But more typical of the two extremes of central European organ-art—i.e. organ-building, organ playing and organ-composing—are Klosterneuburg (see Plate 16) and Stralsund Marienkirche, each exceptional but each demonstrating important features of the organ-landscape around them, and each built for a noble, well-developed musical style. Both have been somewhat rebuilt, but from both can still be learnt much about seventeenth-century tone (Hradetzky 1973, p. 74; Prost 1975, p. 138):

KLOSTERNEUBURG, Augustinerchorherrenstift
J. Scherer, *c.* 1550; J. G. Freundt, 1636–42

Hauptwerk
CDEFGA–c'''

Prinzipal	8
*Prinzipalflöte (wide)	8
Coppel (wide)	8
Quintadena	8
Oktave	4
Offenflöte (wide)	4
Dulcian (Tolkaan)	4
Oktavcoppel (wide)	4
Quinte	2⅔
Superoktave	2
*Mixtur (4')	XII–XIV
Zimbel (½')	II
*Posaune (1950)	16
*Posaune (1950)	8

Rückpositiv
CDEFGA–c'''

Nachthorngedackt (wide)	8
Prinzipal	4
Spitzflöte	4
Kleincoppel	4
Oktave	2
Superoktave	I
Zimbel	II
Krummhorn	8

Brustwerk
CDEFGA–c'''

Coppel	4
Prinzipal	2
Spitzflöte	2
Regal	8

Pedal
CDEFGA–b♭

Portunprinzipal	16 (casc-front)
*Subbass	16
Oktave	8
Choralflöte (open)	8 (wide)
Superoktave	4
Mixtur (4')	VI–VIII
Rauschwerk (2')	III
*Posaune	16
*Posaune	8

Rp/Hw
Pitch, about 1 semitone above
  a¹ = 440 Hz
WP, 55–65 mm
All pipes made of metal; certain
  stop-names of uncertain origin
Hw and pedal ranks on chests
  together (those marked * on a
  separate chest at the back)

STRALSUND, Marienkirche
F. Stellwagen, completed 1659

Hauptwerk			*Oberpositiv*	
CD–c'''			CD–c'''	
Prinzipal	16		Prinzipal	8
Bordun	16		Hohlflöte	8
Oktave	8		Oktave	4
Spitzflöte	8		Blockflöte	4
Hohlquinte	5⅓		Quintadena	4
Oktave	4		Nasard	2⅔
Hohlflöte	4		Gemshorn	2
Flachflöte	2		Scharf	IV–VII
Rauschpfeife	II–IV		Trompete	8
Mixtur	VI–X		Krummhorn	8
Scharf	IV–VI		Schalmei	4
Trompete	16			

Rückpositiv			*Pedal*	
CD–c'''			CF–f'	
Prinzipal	8		Gross Prinzipal	32
Quintadena	16		Prinzipal	16
Gedackt	8		Untersatz	16
Quintadena	8		Oktavbass	8
Oktave	4		Spitzflöte	8
Dulzflöte	4		Oktave	4
Feldpfeife	2		Nachthorn	4
Sifflöte	1⅓		*Feldpfeife	2
Sesquialtera	II		Mixtur	IV
Scharf	VI–VIII		Posaune	16
Zimbel	III		Trompete	8
Dulzian	16		Dulzian	8
Trichterregal	8		Schalmei	4
Regal	4		Cornett (reed)	2

Zimbelstern
Trommel (drum-stop)
Vogelgeschrei (bird-stop)
Tremulant (originally for whole
  organ)

* Overblowing, double length
Unsteady wind
WP, 85 mm (*Ped*), 65 mm (*Hw, Rp*), 55 mm (*Ow*)
Ow Blockflöte 4', the only wooden stop in the organ
Rp/Hw, Ow/Hw shove-couplers (now replaced)

Although Klosterneuburg and Stralsund are amongst the most important organs of the world, such crucial details as their original pitch, their tuning, and the historic reliability of their mechanical parts (key action, wind raising and conveyancing) are still uncertain, and it will be some years yet before the true character of such instruments can be fully drawn. Some of the uncertainties are themselves suggestive of their musical nature: for example, did the original Klosterneuburg organ have manual reeds other than the Regal? Were the 16′ case-front pipes originally meant for the *Hauptwerk* rather than pedal? Is it completely certain that the *Hw* Mixtur did indeed originally have the following, *Blockwerk*-like, composition?

C	8.15.15.19.22.22.26.26.29.29.33.33
c	8.12.15.15.19.19.22.22.26.26.29.29
c^1	8.8.12.15.15.15.19.19.22.22.26.26
c^{11}	8.8.8.12.12.15.15.15.15.19.19.19.22.22
c^{111}	8.8.8.12.12.12.15.15.15.15.19.19.19.19

Depending on the answer to such questions is the kind of music they were meant to play. For example, the south German toccata would require a large manual chorus, majestic, rather static, without any particularly well-developed pedal department, even without independent pedals at all. Klosterneuburg is typical of a tradition for organs in which neither the *Brustwerk* nor even the *Rückpositiv* is a match for the Great, either in sound or in visual impact. It could even be claimed that such organs are not so much three-manual instruments as a collection of three separate organs: *Hauptwerk* for the big postludes, *Rückpositiv* for interludes in the service, *Brustwerk* for *basso continuo* work, etc. While reeds and mutations were few, colour was given by a striking array of 8′ and 4′ ranks, and throughout the whole area Vienna–Ulm–Prague–Vienna various 8′ ranks were becoming popular as extra stops. Stoplists of such organs make them look bigger than they were, practically speaking; half of the stops in the pretty organ of Prague Týn Church are played by the main manual, but no less than four of the 8′ ranks were for colour variety, not for increasing the *organo pleno* (Němec 1944, pp. 85–6):

PRAGUE, Týn Church
J. H. Mundt, 1671–3

Hauptwerk		Flöte (open wood)	8
CDEFGA–c^{111}		Salizional	8
Bourdon	16	Coppel (wood)	8
Prinzipal	8	Quintadena	8

Oktave	4	*Rückpositiv*	
Coppel	4	CDEFGA–c^{III}	
Quinte	2⅔	Coppel (wood)	8
Superoktave	2	Prinzipal	4
Quinte	1⅓	Coppel	4
Sedecima	1	Oktave	2
Mixtur (2')	VI	Quinte	1⅓
Zimbel (1')	IV	Superoktave	1
		Rauschquint (1⅓')	II
Pedal		Mixtur (1')	III
CDEFGAB♭Bcc♯dd♯efF♯			
gG♯a (*sic*)		*Hw/Rp* shove-coupler (no original	
Subbass (open wood)	16	*Hw/P?*)	
Subbass (stopped)	16	Two Zimbelsterne	
Oktave (wood)	8	* Originally 2⅔', changed in 1673	
Quinte (wood)	*(5⅓?) 2⅔		
Superoktave	4		
Mixtur	IV		

Such stops as Salicional 8' and Viola 8' were characteristic of this part of Europe during the late seventeenth century; Salicet 4', Fugara 4' and Dulciana 4' (a stop brought to England by the *émigré* builder Snetzler) were common by the early eighteenth century. All reeds, except for an occasional pedal 16' or 8', gradually disappeared. 8' colour stops were another feature brought to the fore by P. Mauritius Vogt, a Cistercian writer of 1719 whose enthusiasm typified the decadence of an Order once highly critical of the Benedictine organs and other toys. Similarly, for such registration rules as those given by J. B. Samber, a Salzburg organist, in 1704, the conical colour-stop Viola 8' was very useful in many kinds of combinations:

for *continuo*: Viola 8'
for fantasias (i.e. improvisations?): Viola 8', Flöte 4'
for fugues: Viola 8', Mixtur III
for versets: Viola 8', Zimbel II
for choral accompaniment: Prinzipal 8', Coppel 8'; Prinzipal 8', Viola 8'

Soon after Klosterneuburg, organ cases of the Hapsburg lands were more and more often divided into separate units in the west-end gallery, with one case for the *Hauptwerk*, one for the pedals and one for the second manual (Waldhausen, 1677). These divided cases are superficially comparable to the northern *Werkprinzip* organ, but quite apart from the sound they produced, they belong to quite different traditions, they were usually scattered around spacious galleries (not vertically aligned, like the

Werkprinzip organ), and they remained standardized. Most new Austrian organs of the mid-eighteenth century were divided in this way (see Plate 30): pedal in one case, *Hauptwerk* in the other, *Rückpositiv* standing in the gallery front between the other two (as seen from the altar). By 1740 the keyboards would be usually placed in the form of a 'detached console' standing in the middle of the gallery floor, from where the organist could view the choir and orchestra on feast days. In theory, such a visual-mechanical-tonal plan would encourage idiomatic organ-music for two manuals (like the earlier north German toccatas), but in practice it did not, probably because the Hapsburg organist still thought of his two manuals as two more or less separate organs. His pedal also remained undeveloped, the compass alone making it virtually impossible to play an integrated contrapuntal bass-line; this was because it generally included some repeated notes, as at Maria Langegg in 1782 (Forer 1973, pp. 13–14):

```
    F#   G#
    D    E    Bb         c#   d#        F#   G#
C    F    G    A    B    c    d    e    F    G    A
```

The inconvenience of doubled sharps would not of itself make it impossible for an organist to play a contrapuntal pedal-part; but the shape as a whole obviously speaks more for the pedal being used for toccata pedal-points and for cadences.

According to the diary of John Evelyn (23 August 1641) such Dutch organs as that in Haarlem Bavokerk were not:

> . . . made any use of in Divine Service or so much as to assist them in their singing of Psalms (as I suppos'd) but onely for shew and to recreate the people before and after their Devotions, whilst the Burgomasters were walking and conferring about their affaires.

Thus by association such organs as Alkmaar were secular rather than liturgical, and while we may see them today as clear developments of the old Brabant organ—with a big *Hauptwerk*, limited pedal, big solo *Rückpositiv*, full-chorus *Oberwerk*—to the town councils who so often owned them they were magnificent creations rivalling those of town councils elsewhere. The magnificent west-end organ of Stralsund, for example, is typical of those Hanseatic instruments dominating the tall brick gothic churches and their ambulatory spaces, and in the process raising the contribution of organ music in and out of the liturgy to heights it has scarcely ever equalled since. Stralsund is a completely enclosed wooden casket, immensely high but scarcely $4\frac{1}{2}'$ deep, standing free from the tower space behind and resonating (through its position and its materials) in an acoustic liveliness typical of such structures and such churches. Not until 1910 were congregational hymns in this church—and presumably churches of this kind elsewhere—accompanied by the organ; before that, the organist played only preludes and interludes, using the *Hw* as a slow, strong, rich but gentle manual based on 16′ tone, the *Ow* for flutes and brash Dutch reeds, the *Rp* for lively sounds, often with regals. It is as if the *Hw* were the ecclesiastical manual, the *Rp* the worldly, the *Ow* the orchestral. The array of flutes at different pitches provides an immense number of simple combinations—the purpose of such arrays—and obviously the pedal can play all conceivable types of *cantus firmus*, from bass *fortissimo* to soprano *dolce*.

The rivalry between town councils must have been a major factor behind the building of the new Haarlem organ (1735–8) by Christian Müller, a German who was evidently thought fit to make an instrument that would compare favourably with the recent organ by the Schnitger sons in Zwolle (1718–21), with the same builders' remake of the Alkmaar organ (1723–6), with the German Christian Vater's new organ in Amsterdam Oude Kerk (1724–6) and with the southerner Jean Moreau's new instrument at Gouda (1733–6). This series of fine organs is puzzling in so far as their musical repertory and purpose were so limited; but there is no doubt about the paramount German influence on Dutch organ-building from that period until Cavaillé-Coll spread the French gospel more than a century later. The Germans imported big pedal departments and, it seems, a heavy unseductive voicing by then fashionable in Westphalia and regions to the north; but later tastes have seen these fine organs as lacking German brilliance in the flue stops (hence Marcussen's addition of the now discredited mixtures at Haarlem in 1961) and French nobility in the reeds. One may wonder too whether the German influence on Dutch organs did not also lead to poor case-design, often rather shapeless (e.g. Amsterdam Oude Kerk) when compared with the fine classical lines and sense of proportion in the best of the old Dutch cases (Alkmaar, Leiden, Amsterdam Westerkerk).

Although, like most of the organs referred to here, that at Weingarten (see Plate 27) is not in as reliable a condition as is often maintained, its stoplist does serve as a useful example of a Highest Common Factor: it is a large organ summing up the ideas in the minds of organists and organ-builders in an important part of Europe over a long period (Bärnwick 1948):

WEINGARTEN, Benediktinerabtei
J. Gabler, 1737–50

Hauptwerk		Rohrflöte	8
C–c^{III}		*Oktave	4
Prinzipal	16	*Superoktave	2
Prinzipal (narrow)	8	*Hohlflöte	2

K

Piffaro	V–VII	Rohrflöte	4
Sesquialtera	IX–VIII	Querflöte (wood)	4
Mixtur	XXI–XX	*Flauto traverso	4
Zimbel	XII	Flageolet	2
Trompete	8	Piffaro	VI–V
		Cornet (narrow)	XI–VIII

Oberwerk
C–c'''

		Vox humana	8
		Hautboy	4
*Bourdon (part wood)	16	Carillon (bells, f–c''')	
Prinzipal	8		
Coppel	8	*Pedal*	
*Violoncello	8	C–g (*sic*)	
Salizional	8	*main chests*	
Hohlflöte (wood)	8	Contrabass (open)	32
Unda maris (wood)	8	Subbass	32
Mixtur	IX–XII	Oktave (wood)	16
†Oktave douce (bass)	4	*Violon	16
(treble)	8	Mixtur	V–VI
†Viola douce*	8	Bombarde	16
†Nasat	2⅔	Posaune (wood)	16
†Zimbel	II	Carillon (bells, C–g at 2')	

Unterwerk
C–c'''

‡*La Force*

north Rp chest

Bourdon (wood)	16	Quintatön	16
Prinzipal (part wood)	8	Superoktave	8
Quintatön	8	Flûte douce	8
Flöte (wood, conical)	8	Violoncello	8
Viola douce	8	Hohlflöte	4
Oktave (conical)	4	Cornet	XI–X
*Hohlflöte	4	Sesquialtera	VII–VI
Piffaro douce	II	Trompete	8
Superoktave (conical)	2	Fagott	8
Mixtur	V–VI		
Cornet (narrow)	VI–V	* Doubled ranks for all or part of
Hautboy	8	the compass
Tremulant		† Stops placed in a high Echo chest

Rückpositiv (south case)
C–c'''

Prinzipal doux	8
Flûte douce	8
Quintatön	8
Violoncello	8

† Stops placed in a high Echo chest (*Kronpositiv*) and played by *Ow* keys

‡ *La Force*, special register sounding 48 pipes of the C major triad at 4'

WP, now 70 mm

Pitch, now a¹ = 440 Hz

From the first, the Weingarten organ was meant to be exceptional, with its mechanism built around the west-end windows, its big mixtures, bells, stops of exotic materials (cherrywood, ivory), flutes of wood turned on a lathe, doubled ranks, undulating stops, string stops, faraway effects, soft thunder, pretty but emaciated reeds. But until the organ is restored to the kind of tone now heard in some of the renovated Swiss instruments of that period, it is pure guesswork as to how thin the reeds and other stops are really meant to be and whether or not the organist really had been reduced to a mere giver-out of wafting musical colours. These colours could once have been heard even more clearly in Gabler's little quire organ at the other end of the minster, for this was little more than a collection of 8′ and 4′ ranks showing what the traditional east-end quire organ of a large church had become during the rococo period (see also Plate 28). Some writers have described the large Weingarten organ as rococco-gothic or gothic-baroque, chiefly because of the big mixtures, but in its effect as a whole the organ rather gives the impression of a large grotto organ not unlike those in the Tivoli-emulating gardens of southern Europe; obviously there is no rough manual-balance of the kind for which Chair organs had then been built for two or more hundred years. Yet the technological skill behind an organ whose vast sprawling case holds only eight *non*-speaking pipes cannot be questioned, and Gabler's detached console alone is worth admiration. The influence of Weingarten was immense and indeed in some areas has never been eradicated; writers often admired it even when they had not heard it (Hawkins, 1776; Bedos, 1766–78), and its shadow over the large factory organs of the 1830s, and even over the compromise Organ Reform instruments still being built in southern Germany, is there to be seen by any patient analyst.

The compromise organ, however, is not the invention of the twentieth century. Southern Germany saw several interesting attempts at combining the French and south German elements when K. J. Riepp incorporated both in the two quire organs of Ottobeuren in 1757–66. Most major organs in both the large parish and the conventual churches of Bavaria, Württemberg and several cantons of Switzerland mingled organ cultures; the larger Ottobeuren organ was a pure amalgam made possible by its builder's personal experience both in eastern France and southern Germany (Williams 1966, p. 82):

OTTOBEUREN, Benediktinerabtei
K. J. Riepp, 1757–66

Hauptwerk
C–d'''
†Prinzipal | 8
Coppel | 16
†Flauto | 8
Coppel | 8
Viola da gamba | 8
†Salizett | 8
†Prestant | 4
Flöte | 4
Quinte (flute) | 2⅔
Waldflöte | 2
Tierce | 1⅗
Cornet (from c') | V
Mixtur | IV
Zimbel | IV–VI
Trompete | 8
Clairon | 4

Rückpositiv
C–d''', halving at f♯/g
†Prinzipal (treble) | 16
Coppel | 8
†Flauto | 8
Oktave | 4
Flöte | 4
*Viola da gamba | 4
*Nasard | 2⅔
*Quarte | 2
*Tierce | 1⅗
*Quinte | 1⅓
*Fourniture | V–VI
*Trompete | 8
*Krummhorn | 8
*Vox humana | 8
*Clairon | 4

Récit
C–d'''
Cornet (g–d''') | V

Echo
C–d''', halving at e/f
‡Coppel* | 8
‡Flöte* | 4
‡Quinte (bass) | 2⅔
‡Quarte (bass) | 2
Larigot (treble) | II (12.15)
‡Tierce (bass) | 1⅗
Tierce (treble) | II (17.22)
Oboe | 8

Pedal
C–c'
†Prinzipal | 16
Coppel | 16
Oktave | 8
Viola da gamba | 8
Quinte | 5⅓
Flöte | 4
Mixtur | III
Bombarde | 16
Trompete | 8
Trompete | 4

Rp/Hw
Tremulant forte for *Hw*
Tremulant forte for *Rp, Réc,
Echo*
Tremulant dolce for *Hw*
Tremulant dolce for *Rp, Réc,
Echo*

* Halved
‡ Serve as the bass for *Récit* Cornet
   and playable from both manuals
   (two pallets)
† Provide pipes for the case-fronts

WP, now 80 mm

All the classical French registrations are possible on this organ, despite its somewhat altered tone; so are the German registrations, such as the Viola combinations given by Samber (see p. 145), and the new solo music such as galant sonatas requiring *basso continuo* from the pedal.

Composite schemes as thorough-going as Ottobeuren were curiously rare in the eighteenth century. Usually, even adjacent areas—such as Saxony/Bohemia, Veneto/Carinthia, Flanders/Brabant—had very different types of organs, as if the builders of one area or religious denomination were totally opposed to the ideas of their neighbours. Although the organs of some of the religious orders, particularly the Augustinian and Cistercian, had elements that crossed the frontiers of central Europe, there was no great unifying style. More often it was local traditions that most influenced the builder of a new organ even when he was a foreigner. A good example is the fine Austrian organ at Herzogenburg, built in 1747–52 by a Westphalian, Johann Henke, who must have known very different organs but who was more influenced by Klosterneuburg; he 'modernized' the Klosterneuburg scheme by dividing the cases in typically Austrian manner and by giving the instrument a tonal and visual character that summed up, perhaps better than a native builder could have done, the regional style of Lower Austria. This very provincialism may have been the moving force behind some of the good late organs (Amorbach, 1774–82; Rot-an-der-Rot, 1793) that resisted the emasculating effect of fashion extremes, and kept rich choruses and classical contrasts.

The large organs of the late eighteenth century, from Seville to Königsberg, Naples to Stockholm, kept their regional styles through all the influence their builders may have been subject to. Thus the once famous organ of the Michaeliskirche, Hamburg, built by J. G. Hildebrandt (son of Silbermann's pupil and J. S. Bach's colleague Zacharias Hildebrandt) had 70 stops and three manuals incorporating elements from Saxony (Cornet, Unda maris, Chalumeau), following contemporary fashion (more difference-tone stops such as low Quints; but no Chair Organ) and yet remaining true to Hamburg in one vital respect: it was more complete and comprehensive than an organ anywhere else in Europe was likely to have been. The stoplist was long (Dähnert 1962, pp. 141 f, 207 f):

HAMBURG, Michaeliskirche
J. G. Hildebrandt, 1762–7

Hauptwerk		Quintadena (metal)	16
C–f'''		*Oktave (tin)	8
Prinzipal (tin)	16	Gedackt (metal)	8

Gemshorn (tin)	8	*Prinzipal (tin)	8
Viola da gamba (tin)	8	Spitzflöte (metal)	8
Quinte (tin)	5⅓	Quintatön (metal)	8
Oktave (tin)	4	Unda maris (treble, tin)	8
Gemshorn (metal)	4	Oktave (tin)	4
Nasat (metal)	2⅔	Spitzflöte (metal)	4
Oktave (tin)	2	Quinte (tin)	2⅔
Sesquialtera (tin)	II	Oktave (tin)	2
Mixtur (tin)	VIII (2′)	Rauschpfeife (tin)	II
Scharf (tin)	V (1⅓′)	Zimbel (tin)	V (1⅓′)
Cornet (treble, tin)	V	Echo Cornet (treble, tin)	V
Trompete (tin)	16	*Trompete (tin)	8
Trompete (tin)	8	Vox humana (tin)	8

Brustwerk
C–f'''

Rohrflöte (metal)	16
*Prinzipal (tin)	8
Flauto traverso (metal)	8
Gedackt (metal)	8
Rohrflöte (metal)	8
Oktave (tin)	4
Rohrflöte (metal)	4
Nasat (metal)	2⅔
Oktave (tin)	2
Tierce (tin)	1⅗
Quinte (tin)	1⅓
Sifflöte (tin)	1
Rauschpfeife (tin)	II–III
Zimbel (tin)	V
Chalumeau (tin)	8

Pedal
C–d'

Prinzipal (tin)	32
Prinzipal (tin)	16
Subbass (stopped)	32
Subbass (stopped)	16
Rohrquinte (metal)	10⅔
Oktave (tin)	8
Quinte (tin)	5⅓
Oktave (tin)	4
Mixtur (tin)	X (2⅔)
Posaune (tin)	32
Posaune (tin)	16
Fagott (tin)	16
Trompete (tin)	8
Trompete (tin)	4

Oberwerk
C–f'''

Bourdon (metal)	16

Tremulant for *Hw* (tremblant fort)
Schwebung for *Ow* (tremblant doux)
Zimbelstern

* Doubled ranks for all or part of the compass

Four Ventils
Hw/P
Manual shove-couplers
Swell for three stops (last three of *Ow*?), according to Burney 1773, p. 220
Pitch, *Kammerton* (a' = 415 Hz?)
10 bellows (four for pedal)

The case was heavy, massive, very much like many of the nineteenth century and so against the taste of such travellers as Burney who nevertheless heard in the sound a noble power 'more striking by its force and the richness of the harmony, than by a clear and distinct melody' (Burney 1773, p. 220), by which he meant that there were no preponderance of solo stops in the French–English manner and not much of a Swell department. Nor was Burney untypical of his period; theorists like Hess and Knecht encouraged particular imitations of string instruments and of the new woodwind instruments of the time, allowing organists to think that they could imitate the orchestra, not least in its rowdier aspects. The less reputable side to organ-playing in the late eighteenth century is represented by G. J. Vogler (Browning's 'Abt Vogler'), a travelling virtuoso whose pictorial improvisations proved irresistible to popular audiences from London to Vienna and Stockholm and who inveigled many an abbot or conventual head into letting him rebuild the organ according to the latest acoustical notions. Vogler's Simplification System was a method of building or rebuilding organs without difficult tracker design (presumably by using splayed trackers for one straight bass-to-treble chest) and without the bigger pipes which could be, in theory at least, replaced by smaller pipes planned in a harmonic series. Far more important to the development of the organ, but one more difficult to describe or understand exactly, was the impasse brought about by the sheer technical mastery of the late baroque organ. Where could it go next? Quite apart from the reorientation resulting from political and religious changes in the period 1790–1830, the organ seems to have been pushed as far as it could go: one thinks of the mechanical ingenuity of Weingarten, the myriad tonal palette of St. Florian or Oliwa, the reeds of Saint-Maximin or Toledo, the massive choruses of Hamburg or Rostock, the high wind pressures at Poitiers and elsewhere. By 1800, a total rethinking of the organ was necessary, though whether it was Europe's preoccupation with other events at this period that prevented such rethinking from taking place for another 40 years or so would be beyond the scope of any book to conjecture.

Bibliography

BÄRNWICK, F., *Die grosse Orgel im Münster zu Weingarten in Württemberg* (Kassel, 4th edn., 1948)

BEDOS DE CELLES, F., *L'Art du facteur d'orgues*, 4 vols. (Paris, 1766–78)

BURNEY, C., *The Present State of Music in Germany, the Netherlands and the United Provinces* (London, 1773; edited by P. Scholes, London, 1959)

DÄHNERT, U., *Der Orgel- und Instrumentenbauer Zacharias Hildebrandt* (Leipzig, 1962)

FORER, A., *Orgeln in Oesterreich* (Vienna/Munich, 1973)

HAWKINS, J., *A General History of the Science and Practice of Music* (London, 1776)

HESS, J., *Luister van het Orgel* (Gouda, 1772)

HRADETZKY, G., 'Organ-Building in Austria', *ISO Information*, 10 (1973), 691–720

KNECHT, J. H., *Vollständige Orgelschule* (Leipzig, 1795)

NĚMEC, V., *Pražské Varhany* (Prague, 1944)

PROST, D. W., 'Die Stellwagen-Orgel in St. Marien, Stralsund', *The Organ Yearbook*, 6 (1975), 137–45

SAMBER, J. B., *Manuductio ad organum*, 2 vols. (Salzburg, 1704–7)

VOGT, P. MAURITIUS, *Conclave thesauri magnae artis musicae* (Prague, 1719)

WILLIAMS, P., *The European Organ 1450–1850* (London, 1966)

19 The Background to Organs in 1800

The chief differences between an average organ of 1790 and one of 1840, wherever it was, were that the later organ was bigger and that its builder had probably attempted a few colour stops of his own invention (Clarabellas in England, overblowing flutes in Italy, fancy free reeds in Baltic countries, etc.), very likely introduced or enlarged the Swellbox, and generally roughened the tone even when on paper the stoplist itself looked highly traditional (e.g. the *Rückpositiv* at Utrecht Cathedral in 1826–31—see Plate 38). Pedal 16' tone, for example, was throughout Europe as crude in comparison with that of Schnitger or Silbermann as Rossini's use of the double bass was crude in comparison with Purcell's or Couperin's use of the violone: it was there simply for strong foundational tone. There were still national characteristics to the fore, however. Colour stops were as unfamiliar to the Scandinavian builders as Swellboxes were to the Dutch or full pedals to the English. In other countries, notably France, Spain, Austria, Bavaria, Prussia, Saxony, Bohemia and Poland, major happenings outside music not only pushed organ-building into the stage wings but gave builders new opportunities to rethink and replan when Europe settled down in the 1820s.

In addition to political events, several church movements had the effect of dampening the ardour of late baroque organ-builders. In Austria, the reforms of church music instigated by Josef II during the 1780s encouraged not only Freemasonry and other cults but led to a simplification of church services. Simple organs very different from the large monastic extravaganzas of St. Florian (1770) and Heiligenkreuz (1802) suddenly became usual. In countries occupied by the marauding French, only a few organs were destroyed; more destruction was to be found in France itself, where in the main regions an anti-clericalism and a reorientated economy meant total hibernation for the French organ immediately after the Poitiers instrument was completed. After the worst period 1789–92, the Revolutionaries used many churches for humanistic-patriotic purposes, finding the organs only too useful for those purposes. In southern Germany and Hapsburg countries it was the dissolution of the monasteries, particularly after the concerted attempt of 1803, that most affected organ traditions. Almost overnight, the most glamorous setting and the richest clients were denied to builders. In Spain and Portugal, no sooner had Napoleon's soldiers gone and, as in France, a myopic reaction set in, than the church found its funds reappropriated in the so-called *desamortización* of 1830. Scandinavia produced some advanced ideas in this interregnum period, not so much in Denmark (where a *Brustwerk* was made for the organ of St. Anders, Copenhagen as late as 1898) but in Sweden, where cultural ties with catholic or central Germany often resulted in an organ that owed more to Silbermann's successors than to Schnitger or the Hanseatic *Werk-prinzip* builders. In addition to these factors, however, the organ of 1800 was also subject to ideas of a more directly musical kind, and it would be difficult to understand the nineteenth-century organ without recognizing their influence.

One of these ideas was the theory of resultant tones, known to the better thinkers since at least Shakespeare's period and widely familiar since Tartini's (1692–1770). G. J. Vogler travelled through Europe in the 1780s and 1790s trying to prove that $16' + 10\frac{2}{3}' + 6\frac{2}{5}' = 32'$ and playing an instrument of his own design (the *orchestrion*, a one-man band with one of the many greekified names current at the time). Low quints had been found in Bohemia and Silesia since the seventeenth century, and it would not be necessary to discuss Vogler at all were it not that writers of this century have often credited him with notions improved upon by the key German builders of the next generation, chiefly Moser, Sauer and above all Walcker.

A second musical influence was the growing conviction that the organ was indeed a kind of one-man orchestra, an assumption betrayed in the writings of most authors by at least 1790, from London to Leipzig, Seville to Gouda. Obviously, organ manuals have always differed from each other in one respect or another, but the inference that one manual corresponded to the strings of the orchestra, another to the brass and a third to the woodwind was essentially nineteenth-century in origin. Similarly, although seventeenth-century theorists usually remarked that the organ was a compendium of all instruments, and although organ transcriptions of instrumental or vocal music are as old as the solo repertory itself, there is an important change of direction in nineteenth-century ideas of organs: the orchestra itself had become much more standardized, its instruments were gradually being improved technologically—i.e. the natural idiosyncrasies of old instruments, intelligently made use of by composers, were being ironed out—and its music was more and more composed exclusively for it, in styles and forms suitable for it alone. Moreover, orchestral tone was heavier in 1800 than in 1600, and any organ-imitation of it would therefore be farther removed from natural organ-tone. Thus it is that such views as those uttered by Cavaillé-Coll in 1846 (see also Plate 41) should be seen specifically in connection with the orchestra of his day, an orchestra formulated by Berlioz. The organist Danjou had written to Cavaillé-Coll as follows (Delosme 1977, p. 75):

La seule tendance qu'ait bien clairement manifestée, M. Cavaillé, c'est celle de perfectionner le mécanisme, d'accroître la puissance générale de l'instrument, et de donner à ses jeux le timbre et le caractère des instruments de l'orchestre dont ils portent le nom
the only tendency very clearly manifested is that of perfecting the mechanism, increasing the general power of the instrument, and giving to its stops the timbre and character of the orchestral instruments whose name they bear

to which the builder had replied:

C'est bien là, Monsieur, le but des mes efforts et de mes recherches; vous en avez parfaitement *compris le sens* . . .
the goal of my efforts and researches is certainly there; you have understood the direction of it perfectly

A third influence was what are called 'congregational needs': a new organ of 1820 in a new parish church was built chiefly for the sake of accompanying the congregation in its hymns. For this, 8′ stops were thought most suitable. In general, no doubt, mutations and mixtures were less well made in 1820 than in 1720, and in any case mixtures are difficult to justify in theory—they seem to contradict certain musical laws. But the better theorists like Wilke (1839) argued with those who thought that builders made them in order to increase the number of stops, and pointed out their traditional uses. Some of the dislike of mutations and mixtures must have been due to the all-too-common Tierce rank found in chorus mixtures of the period, from London to Vienna. Such chorus mixtures had been made by some of the best of the old builders—for example, Joachim Wagner in the 1730s—but obviously the rank was open to careless workmanship. The English Tierce-mixture, miscalled Sesquialtera, had already become the basic chorus-mixture during Renatus Harris's period, but precisely how Harris voiced it is not yet known, since no Harris organ has ever been properly restored. By 1800, the average Tierce-mixture produced neither true Cornet-tone nor as a chorus mixture would it suit counterpoint. So the result of such mixtures was to persuade the more advanced builders that they need not make them, which in turn resulted in such stoplists as the following (Erici 1965, p. 94):

KARLSKRONA, Trefaldighetskyrkan
P. Z. Strand, 1827

Hw	16.16.8.8.8.8.4.4.2.8
Ow	8.8.8.4.4.8
Ped	16.8.8.4.16

Mixture-less organs had occasionally been experimented with earlier (if not by F.-H. Cliquot, as once claimed) but the Karlskrona organ was more typical of wider movements of its time, throughout Europe and throughout the whole century.

A fourth influence on organs of the early nineteenth century was surprisingly insidious: the increasingly wider repertory of music available to the organist meant a dilution of national or regional styles. Such English firms as Boosey imported a vast amount of German organ-music from Leipzig and elsewhere, giving the organist cheap editions of competently written but irrelevant and outmoded organ-music. Even when seen at its best, namely the international revival of J. S. Bach, this tendency to widen the repertory meant that organists in England, France, Spain and Italy so often found their instruments inadequate, and imported music was thus responsible for persuading organists to have their instruments rebuilt. On the one hand, the Bach revival never led to a resurrection of the subtlety and charm of a Silbermann organ, but on the other neither did it leave local traditions intact in other countries. In effect, it reduced the value of national organ-types—the Bach revival is the biggest single reason why there are no Renatus Harris organs left—and did not replace them with real Bach organs. An even more curious result of the Bach revival was that it left organists in various countries convinced that their own organs were ideal for J. S. Bach, just as he was ideal for their organs. To this day countless English organists think it pure oversight that Bach never asked for a Swell organ.

Bibliography

DELOSME, R., 'L'Orgue français de transition, première moitié du XIXe siècle', *L'Orgue français: Double numéro de la Revue musicale*, 295–6 (1977), 57–82
ERICI, E., *Orgelinventarium över Bevarade äldre Kyrkorglar i Sverige* (Stockholm, 1965)
MOSER, H. J., *Orgelromantik* (Ludwigsburg, 1961)
TARTINI, G., *Trattato di Musica* (Padua, 1754)
WILKE, J., *Über die Wichtigkeit und Unentbehrlichkeit der Orgelmixturen* (Berlin, 1839)
WILLIAMS, P., *The European Organ 1450–1850* (London, 1966), 90–4

20 Aspects of Nineteenth-century Organ Technology

By the end of the nineteenth century, as can be seen in such works as Audsley's treatise of 1905, the organ-builder had a vast array of chest types, action, bellows, pipework, case designs and gadgets to choose from. The cheapest, least experienced builder had many books to help him make an instrument, and the sheer amount of work available amongst the thousands of churches built during the nineteenth century brought forward labour-saving designs and quick techniques.

Although in detail the whole century is only now gradually being adequately documented and understood—such recent studies as Uwe Pape's on the nineteenth-century German builder Furtwängler (1800–67) are a sign of things to come—the general outlines are clear. The big international exhibitions spread fashions quickly; builders travelled more to view developments elsewhere; some of them published essays or formed alliances with composers or theorists and built farther afield than had been usual; publicity or fame often induced them to introduce strange stops—Schulze's wooden cylindrical pipes and triangular cross-section pipes at Doncaster in 1862 are only two of hundreds of such examples. That some 'improvements' or 'inventions' were in fact much older—e.g. pipes with two mouths were already known in seventeenth-century Poland (Gołos 1978)—does not detract from the re-conceived attitudes towards them in the nineteenth. Any organ in any part of Europe was subject to several influences: changing taste (string stops, etc.), theoretical notions (harmonic stops), quick factory methods (standard pipe-scales), foreign influences (Swellboxes in France, etc.), new ideas on case design (quasi-Grecian, quasi-romanesque, quasi-gothic, perhaps made of some new material like cast iron). A generation later still the compendium of international influences would be yet wider, and the huge organs produced in the factories of Walcker, Sauer, Willis, Cavaillé-Coll, Rieger and others went all over the world, particularly in the colonial cities administered by the countries native to each of these firms.

Developments in central Germany influenced French and English builders in the 1840s not only because the book market meant that Wolfram (1815), Seidel (1843) and Töpfer (1833, 1843, 1855) were more easily available than Praetorius had been two hundred years earlier, but because the French and English organ at that period was open to new, foreign ideas. Töpfer gave full details of pipe scales, wind chambers, pallets, bellows, action; his treatise was more up to date and therefore prophetic than Bedos's which, though available again in Hamel's *Nouveau Manuel* of 1849, described an essentially obsolete organ. Töpfer's pipe scale, the so-called Normal Scale or Diapason Norm (*Normmensur*) was a calculated model, not empirical or subject to local conditions of acoustic or tradition, but something easily copied by the builders of cheap, quickly made organs. In itself, the scale was not revolutionary since it resembled that hit upon by builders many decades before and satisfying such worthy contemporaries as J. F. Schulze; but in its very claim to be a 'norm' it offered builders easy solutions at the drawing-board stage, which in turn lowered standards all round. Töpfer's calculation was that the area of the cross-section of a Principal pipe was $\sqrt{8}$ times the area of that of a pipe an octave higher; this resulted in a scaling in which the 17th inclusive pipe halved the diameter, i.e. a pipe was twice as wide as one producing eight whole tones above. This has been the case in many an organ before Töpfer, and other theorists had worked on G. A. Sorge's logarithmic calculations made in the middle of the previous century (Bleyle 1975). Töpfer seems to have reasoned that if pipes retained their just proportion, the ratio would be $\sqrt{16} : 1$; if the diameter were constant, however, it would be $\sqrt{1} : 1$; and therefore a mean was $\sqrt{8} : 1$. Such simple constants were convenient at the workbench, as were Töpfer's other formulae for calculating wind consumption and cut-up. Meanwhile, improved bellows, aided by the reservoirs then becoming more and more common, gave copious and constant wind, encouraging builders to seek overblowing registers and to experiment with higher pressures. Such developments were quite as important as constant pipe-scales, and Töpfer has perhaps had too much laid at his door for his simple $\sqrt{8} : 1$ formula.

As in other periods, many of the early nineteenth-century experiments were short-lived. Free reeds were developed in Baltic areas during the later eighteenth century and became popular in central Germany, though not often elsewhere, from about 1780 to 1850. They offered the first radically different type of organ pipe since flues and reeds had been perfected. Instead of a shallot or orifice in the reed against which the tongue beats, a thick oblong plate of brass (smaller than the corresponding reed of a reed pipe) is perforated with a narrow opening through which vibrates the close-fitting brass tongue. It swings freely (hence the name 'free reed'), has a pitch (without the resonator being necessary), and can be blown louder or softer without the pitch changing. When made by German builders about 1825 or French about 1850, free reeds had resonators of various types giving different tone-colours and contributing legitimate organ tone. Some stops, however, had one resonating chamber for all the notes of a rank, thus taking less room on the chest, less time at the factory and less part in the musical potential of the organ. It was such pipeless free reeds that led to the various kinds of harmonium. Schulze introduced them into his Doncaster organ, but England had no real equivalent of the 32′ free reeds at Wismar (1831) and elsewhere.

New materials, such as cast-iron organ cases and zinc pipes (Hohen-ofen, 1818), were soon seen as cheap and nasty alternatives; but complicated actions were also made for some bigger organs, especially those with double pedalboards. At the Paulskirche, Frankfurt (1827–33), E. F. Walcker gave all three manuals and both pedalboards different wind pressures, scattering a large pedal department as follows (Anon 1833):

Ped I (lower)   32.32.16.16.16.10$\frac{2}{3}$.8.8.6$\frac{2}{5}$.5$\frac{1}{3}$.4.16.8.4.2
Ped II (upper)   16.16.8.8.4.2.16

Buchholz's solo manual at Kronstadt Cathedral in 1839 confirmed an old German tendency towards such colour departments:

16.8.8.8.8.8.4

and on paper at least, was curiously reminiscent of the Weingarten quire organ.

Octave couplers and detached consoles never lost their popularity once they had won it in the 1840s, and one could expect either in an organ from London to Milan, Paris to Berlin. In England, ingenuity was often devoted to improving the Swellbox, usually with a view to giving the closed Swell a true *pianissimo* effect (Hodges of Bristol, organs *c.* 1825). In Germany at that period, J. Wilke listed the various devices for obtaining a crescendo–diminuendo effect on organs: triple touch (operating couplers or bringing on more stops as the key fell), increased wind pressure (for free reeds), lowered wind pressure (Vogler's net-curtain in the wind trunk), roof swells (devices for raising the lid of echo-boxes), door swells (doors in the front of boxes, opened by footlever), jalousie swells (the English horizontal shutters). Most Swellboxes remained simple: horizontal shutters replacing the sash-cord front-boards of the eighteenth century were operated by a wooden or metal footlever hanging to the right of the pedal keys, which had to be notched into position if the box were to remain open. With such pedals, a continual swelling of the sound was not very practical. Only now and then were other devices applied, such as Bryceson's hydraulic system of *c.* 1865 in which water was pumped along a lead pipe from pedal to Swell, harnessed to open the shutters.

Perhaps an ingenious builder would appear with an idea not widely adopted in that period but of great significance later. One such example is Jürgen Marcussen whose little organ of 1819 at SIESEBY, near Kappeln (Schleswig—see Plate 37) had three prophetic features: tuning slides (threaded and screwed to the pipe-tops), a form of box bellows (see p. 90) and an extension system. This last was the most remarkable: double pallets enabled one chest of pipes to supply stops at different octave-pitches for two manuals and pedal (Prip 1977):

Pedal		*Hauptwerk*		*Oberwerk*	
C–d¹		C–d¹¹¹		C–d¹¹¹	
		Bordun	16	Gedackt	8
		Principal	8		
Subbass	16	Gedackt	8	Flöte	4
Principal* (C–A)	8	Octave* (C–d)	4	Octave	2
		Quinte	2⅔	Quinte	1⅓
Octave	4	Octave	2	Octave	1
		Mixtur	III		
Posaune	16	Trompete†	8		

* Case-front
† Divided
Ow/Hw
Zimbelstern
Sperrventil
Hw Principal C–B stopped pipes

The extension organ was obviously complicated to make when chest and action were conventional; but Sieseby, though isolated, indicates the ingenuity being exercised in so many parts of Europe during a period which modern organ histories have simplified.

The stoplists of organs before about 1840 show compromises in the tonal design corresponding to the partly developed structural advances. Schulze, for example, built organs in which two out of three (or three out of four) manuals would be conventional and classical, while one further manual would show the way styles were to develop. At HALBERSTADT CATHEDRAL in 1837–8 he kept classical choruses and even the old Zimbelstern; but the fourth manual was something very different (Baake *c.* 1846):

Echo
C–f¹¹¹
Lieblich Gedackt (wood)   16
Lieblich Gedackt (wood)   8

Terpodion (tin)	8
Flauto traverso (turned wood)	8
Harmonika (wood)	8
Prinzipal	4
Flauto traverso (turned wood)	4
Physharmonika (free reed, zinc)	8

Such Echo Organs were a luxury, but many an up-to-date organ by 1850 had a Solo manual, even before the English Swell reached its true Victorian character by means of Henry Willis's 16′ reed, bright Mixture and traditional Diapason chorus (*c.* 1855). In Germany, Swells of the remote *Echowerk* type remained more popular and indeed still lurk behind the specification of many a recent German organ of four manuals.

Of the several new types of organ chest invented during the nineteenth century, the most important—though rejected by Cavaillé-Coll, Willis and other great builders—was the *Kegellade* or cone chest, perfected by E. F. Walcker and patented by him in 1842. In principle, the *Kegellade* is a ventil-chest with cone-shaped ventils, bulky but theoretically able to avoid the mechanical faults to which the sliderchest was liable, and in practice requiring less exact workmanship. In such a chest, all the pipes belonging to one rank are mounted on one channel running the length of the chest; wind is admitted to this channel when the stop-knob

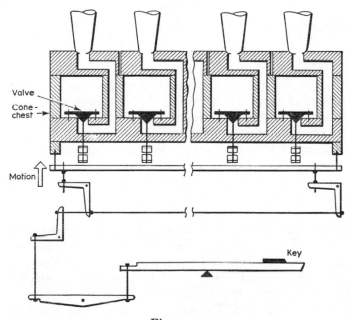

Figure 12

is drawn. There are no lateral channels or grooves in such so-called 'barless chests'. Each key operates a series of cone-shaped valves, one for each stop; thus, however many stops are required by the organist, all the valves move, producing a soft, dull 'accompaniment'. The valves need not be cone-shaped; they may even be replaced by little discs operated by small pneumatic motors (the so-called 'bellows chest'). Another barless chest or *Registerkanzellenlade* is the membrane-chest, associated with simple pneumatic or even electric actions and once the inspiration for many German and American patents. In such a chest, air pressure in the chest below the channel (to which it is constantly supplied) pushes a membrane up against the mouth of a conduit leading to each pipe foot, thus preventing wind contained within the channel from reaching the mouth of the conduit and hence the pipe. The depressed key releases the pressure from below the channel, so that the membrane is pushed down from the end of the conduit by the wind destined for the pipe foot itself. Yet another kind of chest is that in which the membrane on its rising and falling moves a cone-shaped pallet of conventional *Kegellade* kind.

For any such chest, as for the various high-pressure or varied-pressure chests found in the more advanced organs of the 1830s, constant, reliable and copious wind supply was indispensable. Before gas, water or electricity was applied to the task of supplying organs with wind, builders worked more with trying to improve conventional bellows by giving them reservoirs. Feeder bellows expel air under pressure to a receiver or reservoir, which then delivers the wind to the trunks at a constant and required pressure. For stability, reservoirs, which look like square bellows, often had 'inverted ribs', i.e. lower ribs closing inwards, upper ribs closing outwards. In England, this idea is said to date from 1762 and to be the invention of one Cummings. Some reservoirs were merely a second diagonal single-fold bellows into which the first or feeder bellows sent the wind (Snetzler, from about 1740); but by 1825 or so, horizontal reservoirs were more usual. In central and eastern Europe, other bellows-types were improved during the nineteenth century: box bellows (see p. 90) made by Marcussen in the period around 1820, and cylindrical bellows working on the same principle and known to smiths and metal-workers of the previous century before Ladegast applied them to organs in about 1840.

During the nineteenth century, the energy required to cock the bellows was raised by various means, for example by water under pressure or, later still, by electric motors. By the end of the century it was found that wind could be supplied directly to the reservoir by electric motors incorporating a rotating fan, and most organs old and new are now fed with wind by this method. The constant pressure given by such motors is therefore strictly a datable phenomenon. For organs before the end of the nineteenth century such pressure is an anachronism and cannot satisfy a sensitive restorer of today; for organs of its period, however, the rotating fan is part of the understood equipment and one allowing many of the effects characteristic of what is called the late romantic organ. Within the airtight chamber of the blower more than one fan can rotate along the same spindle, each successive fan increasing the pressure as it receives and passes on the wind, which can therefore be tapped off at any stage and conducted to a reservoir at a pressure required for special reeds or high-pressure flue stops.

Walcker is a good example of an immensely successful firm with a systematic mode of production and hence a large share in the market during the organ-boom in the middle of the nineteenth century, not least in the U.S.A. Machine-tools provided pipe metal of great precision and uniformity, doing away with all the capricious elements in pipe manufacture; Töpfer drew tools such as metal-planers, while Walcker made and sold them. From Ludwigsburg, where the firm moved in 1820, Walcker surveyed a large and important part of central Europe, supplying hundreds of compromise organs—with free reeds but still with mechanical action, sometimes with two pedalboards but always at first with sliderchests, perhaps with as many as 70 stops but with only the traditional couplers. As late as 1849 (Ulm Minster) and 1857 (Boston Music Hall, U.S.A.), the larger Walcker organs were still compromises, leaving more modern designs to be produced by smaller builders open to other influences, such as Gottschalg's organ in Cologne Cathedral: Gottschalg was more likely to have been affected by the Cavaillé-Coll organs in the Paris exhibitions than was Walcker. Before then, however, the French scene itself had been more confused, with minor builders such as the Englishman John Abbey doing successful work over large areas (Rheims to Caen) and introducing English reservoirs, Venetian Swells and refined English voicing of the Greene type. Farther east, Daublaine & Callinet came under Walcker's influence, aping his free reeds and double pedalboards.

Higher pressures were applied to reeds in England by the late 1830s, the first well-known example being Hill's Tuba mirabilis at Birmingham Town Hall (1840). But although by 1855 Hopkins could write that such stops were then made by nearly all English organ-builders, no real technical details are yet available of these high-pressure reeds and they have never been adequately described. Treble pipes of the reed stops were also often put on higher pressure ('increased the weight in the treble by an inch' is Hopkins's phrase), a technique perhaps picked up from Cavaillé-Coll's organ at Saint-Denis and perhaps from yet earlier French organs. For centuries, French builders had appreciated that reed-trebles needed 'boosting' if the splendid basses were not to peter out above g¹ or so; hence, presumably, the taste for the Cornet and its predecessors. Thus Cavaillé-Coll's overblowing double-length flue- and reed-pipes were new only in character, not in principle. The overblowing Flûte harmonique or Trompette harmonique is made for big, round tone and always requires copious wind, unlike the soft overblowing flutes of seventeenth-century Germany or the scratchy overblowing viola-stops of late eighteenth-century Italy. Cavaillé-Coll and others helped the node to form in such flue-pipes by piercing them with a small hole rather less than halfway along from the mouth, its exact position having some bearing on the overtone content of the sound. Reed and flue harmonic stops show how the 1840s desired smooth reeds that stay in tune and smooth flues that have no initial 'chiff' (the effect produced by a puff of wind articulating the start of each note). Full- or double-length resonators gave smoothness to reeds, while flues were made smooth by the paraphernalia of nicked languids, ears-and-beard and rollerboards aiding prompt speech at the mouth itself.

Other technical advances between 1825 and 1850 are those of the playing mechanism. Many nineteenth-century builders exercised great ingenuity in devising wooden rods, levers, battens and so on for accessories like the double Venetian Swell (Henry Willis, Gloucester Cathedral in 1847), stop combinations (Ladegast and Sauer in Germany, Roosevelt in U.S.A.), crescendo pedals (Haas) and various octave-couplers (Serassi in northern Italy). But many and more of such contrivances could be much more easily planned and executed by means of the Barker Lever or mechanical-pneumatic action. Figure 13 illustrates the principles of this celebrated invention. When a key is played, wind from the main bellows is admitted through a pallet-like valve to inflate small bellows (one for each key) which in moving open travel just far enough to pull a tracker connected with the main pallet in the pipe chest or pallet-box. On release, the exhaust valve at the top allows the small bellows to deflate immediately. In this way, average finger pressure on the key brings into operation enough wind power to operate pallets at some distance from the player, for the tracker can be relayed by rollerboards in the usual way. This would be particularly useful for the large-scaled pipes placed on separate chests or for the high-pressure chests on which were placed reeds of the new kind. The pneumatic unit or 'Barker lever' lies near the keyboards, at a point where the tracker normally rises vertically from the key shafts; a manual coupling system can also so work that the Barker lever draws other manuals' actions.

C. S. Barker had done engineering work on cylinders and compressed air and offered some kind of key apparatus—presumably of the kind described above—for the new organs of York Minster in 1833, Birmingham Town Hall in 1834–5 and, in France, to Cavaillé-Coll himself in 1837. This was a year or two after other builders, such as Booth of Wakefield and Hamilton of Edinburgh (whose model still exists in the

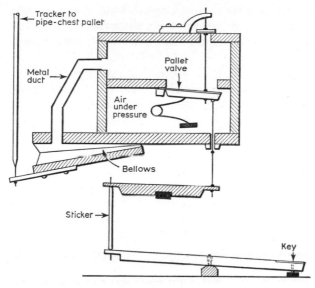

Figure 13

Royal Scottish Museum, Edinburgh), had made such actions. Barker's French patent was taken out in 1839 and he applied his action to the organ then being constructed by Cavaillé-Coll at Saint-Denis; according to his notes, quoted by Hopkins, the high-pressure stops of Saint-Denis were unplayable without his key action. By 1851, Willis also applied the Barker lever to the sliders themselves and to such accessories as thumb pistons. But it was probably in France that the first fully pneumatic action was made, in which all the backfalls, squares, rollers and other elements in a tracker action were replaced by one pneumatic tube from key to pallet.

'Pressure-pneumatic action' was that in which wind was admitted along the tube when the key was depressed, travelling to operate a further motor which opened the pallet. 'Exhaust-pneumatic action', the more popular of the two, was one in which the depressed key opened a pallet at the key end of the tube in which wind was already held, thus drawing that wind away from the pipe-pallet and so opening it. A tubular-pneumatic action is first accredited to P.-A. Moitessier in 1845 and was later modified with a partly mechanical action (Fermis, 1866) and improved by such major builders as Willis (St. Paul's Cathedral, 1872—see also Plate 43). By about 1889, Walcker too used this so-called tubular-pneumatic action in his cone chests, but on the whole the action never proved very popular outside England and some circles of organ-building in the U.S.A. A disadvantage was that the action became sluggish when the keys were far from the chests.

As for the chests, French and English builders preferred sliderchests to barless chests, often so making the pallets that they held some secondary mechanism allowing them to be opened without undue key pressure (Willis patent of 1861).

Throughout much of the nineteenth century electric actions were devised in England (Wilkinson 1826, Gauntlett 1852, Goundry 1863), France (Du Moncel, Barker, Stein & Fils) and elsewhere (Hope-Jones, organ in Taunton, Massachusetts, 1893). Only by the end of the century were electric actions so perfected as to admit of a general description. That shown in Fig. 14 is the 'electro-pneumatic action' in which an electro-magnet is activated when the key is depressed and its circuit completed. The armature acts as a valve, rising to the magnet and thus allowing the wind to escape from a pneumatic relay (previously filled with wind from the chest) which in turn collapses, opening the port below the main pneumatic motor and thus allowing its wind to escape. On collapsing, the main pneumatic motor pulls down the pallet. When the finger key is released, the electrical circuit is broken, the magnet drops the armature valve and wind re-enters the small pneumatic motor, a spring closes the port under the main pneumatic motor which then inflates and pushes up the pallet. The 'direct electric action' has its magnet operating the pallet direct, but a great deal of electric current is required even when the pallet is small; it is a system convenient for individual pipes, rather than whole ranks or chests of them, and has never become popular outside the world of American unit-chest organs (see p. 184), even though presumably it was such an action that attracted

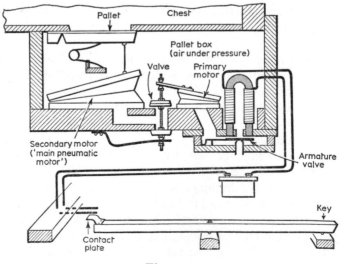

Figure 14

such organists as Gauntlett in the early days of electrical technology. One electro-pneumatic action is accredited to Peschard (*c.* 1860) who took out a joint patent with Barker in 1868 and who in turn licensed Bryceson to build such an action at the Theatre Royal, Drury Lane in 1868. According to Hopkins, an electrification (no doubt temporary) of the organ in Gloucester Cathedral for the Three Choirs' Festival of 1868 made it possible for the keyboards to be located nearer the conductor, i.e. on the nave floor away from the pipes of the screen organ— this can be seen as an updated version of the 'long movements' of the west-end gallery organ used in the 1784 Commemoration of Handel in Westminster Abbey. Other electric actions were devised, and by the 1890s Willis in England, Roosevelt in the U.S.A., Merklin in France and Walcker in Germany were all regularly producing reliable electric actions and in some cases electrically operated stops (Bryceson patent 1868). Many systems, especially in the U.S.A., were patented during the 1890s, to be later described by Audsley and Ellerhorst. However, electrical means of controlling Swell shutters or stop-combinations belong to the twentieth century. Only in the 1920s did Willis turn exclusively to electro-pneumatic action (instead of tubular pneumatic), and it should not be forgotten that most church and cathedral organs were far slower to incorporate technological advance than the big concert-hall organs.

Bibliography

Anon, 'Kurze Beschreibung', *Allgemeine musikalische Zeitung*, 35 (1833), 679 f
AUDSLEY, G. A., *The Art of Organ Building* (New York and London, 1905)
BAAKE, F., *Beschreibung der grossen Orgel der Marienkirche zu Wismar, sowie der grossen Orgeln des Domes und der St. Martinikirche zu Halberstadt* (Halberstadt, *c.* 1846)
BLEYLE, C. O., 'Georg Andreas Sorge: an 18th-Century Proponent of Logarithmic Scaling', *The Organ Yearbook*, 6 (1975), 53–63
ELLERHORST, W., *Handbuch der Orgelkunde* (Einsiedeln, 1936)
GOŁOS, J., 'Some Rare Technical Features Found in the Historic Organs of Poland', *The Organ Yearbook*, 10 (1979)
HAMEL, P. J., *Nouveau Manuel complet du facteur d'orgues* (Paris, 1849)
HOPKINS, E. J. and RIMBAULT, E. F., *The Organ, its History and Construction* (London, 1855, 3rd edn., 1877)
PAPE, U., 'Philipp Furtwängler (1800–1867), Orgelbauer in Elze bei Hanover', *ISO Information*, 11 (1974), 777–98; also *Acta organologica*, 8 (1974), 121–97
PRIP, S., 'Marcussen-Orglet fra Sieseby Kirke', *Orglet*, I/1977, 5–16
SEIDEL, J. J., *Die Orgel und ihr Bau* (Breslau, 1843)
SUMNER, W. L., *The Organ, its Evolution, Principles of Construction and Use* (London, 1952, 4th edn., 1973)

TÖPFER, J. G., *Die Orgelkunst* (Weimar, 1833)

TÖPFER, J. G., *Lehrbuch der Orgelbaukunst*, 4 vols. (Weimar, 1855)

WHITWORTH, R., *The Electric Organ* (London, 1930)

WILKE, J. and KAUFMANN, F., 'Über die Crescendo und Diminuendo-Züge an Orgeln', *Allgemeine musikalische Zeitung*, 25 (1823), 113 f

WOLFRAM, J. C., *Anleitung zur Kenntniss, Beurtheilung und Erhaltung der Orgeln* (Gotha, 1815)

21 Some Important Organs of the Nineteenth Century

In Germany, such organs as Walcker's for the Paulskirche, Frankfurt and Schulze's for Halberstadt Cathedral (to both of which reference has already been made) were very influential in their particular brand of classicism. It was not unusual for Walcker to give his Great Organs a 32' rank, and the powerful, booming pedal was a direct descendant of those eighteenth-century pedals built to carry big *plena* around the church rather than to present organists with rich choice of *cantus firmus* stops. Other German builders, in particular Schulze and Ladegast, seem to have preferred brighter sounds and always included large-scale mixtures, giving the *plenum* a force not new to central Germany. The reason for Schulze's influence in England was no doubt that his large Diapasons—perhaps ultimately derived from Silbermann's—appealed to traditional English taste for Diapason-tone and found admirers for some decades after his imported organ was heard in the Great Exhibition of 1851. Also, Schulze's little colour-stop, the narrow-scaled Lieblich Gedakt, was to be found in virtually every English organ over the following 100 years, though it too may have only extended a taste already fostered in England (e.g. Father Smith's Nason flutes). The high standard of workmanship and the sheer mass of good solid pipework at 8' pitch in a Schulze organ was seen as a sure sign of musical quality. Any casual glance into Sauer's organ for St. Thomas, Leipzig, for example, would have given the observer a strong impression of worthiness, of quality-worth-the-money, vastly superior to the array of little baroque ranks piled up inside a Silbermann or Schnitger. In a Cavaillé-Coll organ, the materials and craftmanship were similarly impressive; so were the spaciousness, the complicated actions, the careful planning of chest-levels within the amorphous case (see Plate 41), all aiding the resonance of the organ. The published drawings of the various elevations, tiers and cross-sections of the Cavaillé-Coll organ in Saint-Sulpice, Paris, are witness to one of the great engineering feats of the nineteenth century, as illustrative of its period's technology as Ctesibius's hydraulicon had been.

Without doubt, the great epoch-marking organ of the nineteenth century was that at Saint-Denis Abbey, near PARIS. Unfortunately, few technical details have ever been published and a full examination and description will have to await its restoration. The 'gothick' casework had already been designed when several builders tendered for the organ contract. This was a problem Cavaillé-Coll became resigned to, for at Saint-Sulpice, Chalgrin's case was of 'unusual size and awkward shape' and the voicing techniques had to be 'modified in order to compensate for the acoustical hurdles imposed by Chalgrin' (Eschbach 1978), hurdles imposed by the fact that so many pipes had to speak only indirectly into the church. At Saint-Denis, Cavaillé-Coll tendered two plans, and the stoplists of 1833 and 1841 respectively show the great changes overtaking organ-building during the crucial 1830s. In 1833, the five manuals were those of the classical models and included Cornets, mutations, the traditional reeds (with some free reeds) and certain theatrical effects liked by the Berlioz generation (drums, *chapeau chinois*, etc.). But in the 1841 plan, flutes and mutations were reduced in number, overblowing stops were now included, further string stops gave a new stridency, the free reeds were discarded, Barker's pneumatic lever made possible a more complicated layout of the chests, and the wind-raising was improved by being made more copious and at higher pressure for certain chests. Though undeniably founded on Dom Bedos's scheme for a large 32′ organ—even the pedal FF compass is probably to be seen as an antique feature (*ravalement*) extended for yet greater effect of sound if not of logic—the organ of Saint-Denis represented a great stride along the romantic road (Sumner 1946):

GO(II)   32.16.16.8.8.8.8*.4.4*.2⅔.2.IV.IV.IV.IV.V.8*.8*.8.4*
Pos   16.8.8.8.4.4*.2⅔.2.2*.1⅗.IV.IV.8*.8.8.8.4*.Trem
Récit   8.8*.4*.2⅔.2*.8*.8*.4*
Bombarde 16.8.8.4.2⅔.2.VII.16.8*.8*.4*.4*
Pédale   32.16.8.5⅓.4.16.16.8.8.8.4.4.

* Harmonic stops of double length, heavier wind

Compass, C–c¹–f¹¹¹ (pedal reeds from FF)
Pedal-coupler to all manuals; also IV/II, III/II, II/II, I/II couplers
Sub-octave coupler to all manuals
Récit in a Swellbox
GO could be 'prepared' (*GO* played only when II/II lever operated)

The *Bombarde* and pedal departments of Saint-Denis inspired hundreds of French and frenchified organs over the next century or so; scaling was wider than classical French and the voicing, with the increased wind pressure, stronger. (For examples of Cavaillé-Coll scalings see Eschbach 1978 and Lund 1976.) The Flûte harmonique, successor to the open Flûte 8′ drawn in the late classical *jeu de fonds* combinations, was probably used in the chorus, as were the string stops (with tuning slots at the pipe top) and Bourdons. Nicking of languids was generally severe, at least in the later organs of Cavaillé-Coll; this, added to the slots cut into even the smallest mixture pipes on many organs, helped to produce an even, smooth tone of the kind aimed at by such contemporary woodwind-makers as Boehm. However, at Saint-Sulpice, not all mixtures were slotted, and the nicking was empirical rather than doctrinaire, varying in its severity from stop to stop and from one section of a rank to another (Eschbach 1978). Cavaillé-Coll's spectrum or repertory of pipe forms was not strikingly wide, and in his organs neither conical nor narrow-scaled stopped pipes were very important. More crucial to his conception were the divisions into chests: foundation stops (*jeux de fonds*) of one manual placed on one chest, its reeds and perhaps flute mutations (*jeux de combinaison*) placed on another. Each chest could have its own wind pressure and each was usually controlled by a valve that admitted wind only when required, thus making it possible for the organist to 'prepare' a registration which sounded only when needed. In every instrument, the *Grand Orgue* was emphasized, dominant. Although the pneumatic action was somewhat cumbersome in the space it took, the feeders and reservoirs were also generous and well engineered; soundboards had ample size for their boldly treated pipework. But Cavaillé-Coll never favoured electric actions or general crescendo gadgets of any kind.

Serassi held in Italy a position similar to Cavaillé-Coll's in France. His place in the line of organ-builders firmly bound to traditional practices enabled him to use the new technologies to develop such traditions and to produce compromise organs that extended the old potentials and styles. Serassi organs are like those of Venice in the late eighteenth century, only larger and now larded with gadgets to aid registration. His Swells were much bigger than those of Callido but in conception neither new in themselves nor able to match the English and French Swells of 1850. The main manual would control some 20 stops, including 16' or even 32' Principale—another old Italian tradition—as well as flutes and violas of 8' or 4'. Many *plenum* stops were divided but the higher ranks were collected into mixture stops of northern kind, at least in theory. One or more subsidiary manuals, with six to ten divided stops, provided echo effects; compass was long (frequently from CC), pedals had six to eight stops, and there were many accessories, both purely mechanical (couplers including super- and sub-octave, composition pedals) and sounding (drum, bells, thunder, *chapeau chinois*).

In England and the U.S.A. (see Plate 42), the growing awareness of foreign organs and music—a cosmopolitanism denied to French, Spanish and Italian organists—coincided with good economic conditions to produce a new attitude towards organs, particularly those for the new town halls. During the 1820s, the Swell finally overtook the Choir as the chief second manual; indeed, in so far as the Chair Organ itself was virtually unknown between 1710 and 1810, the Choir Organ had already seriously declined or at least become moribund. Pedals, however, came to be regarded as normal, even if they usually contained no more than a rank or two of large-scaled wooden pipes. GG-compass was still popular in the 1830s, as was organ music of little if any close association with the church (Handel's organ concertos, Bach's *Well-tempered Clavier*). Much of the development of the British organ before Henry Willis's famous instrument for the Great Exhibition of 1851 has been attributed to the collaboration between H. J. Gauntlett the composer and William Hill the organ-builder (Clutton and Niland 1963). In about 1833, Gauntlett visited Haarlem (see Plate 24), apparently on the suggestion of Samuel Wesley—who presumably knew of it either from Burney's account in his *Travels* or directly from Vincent Novello, who had played organs abroad. There are various indications from the schemes with which Gauntlett was later associated that he had Haarlem ultimately in mind. Of the dozen or so organs built by Hill under Gauntlett's guidance —details of which are necessarily vague—that at the Great George Street Chapel, Liverpool (1841) was of particular importance. Gauntlett, like Hopkins, knew enough German organ music to see that C-compass was the most useful for both manuals and pedals, unlike S. S. Wesley who had Willis retain GG-compass for his early masterpiece in St. George's Hall, Liverpool. A similar reasoning lay behind Gauntlett's scheme for pedal departments (Hopkins 1877, pp. 525, 478–9):

LIVERPOOL, Great George Street Chapel W. Hill (advised by Gauntlett), 1841		LONDON, Christ Church, Newgate St. W. Hill (advised by Gauntlett), 1835	
Open Diapason	16	Open Diapason	16
Bourdon	16	Open Wood	16
Principal	8	Montre (open, metal)	16
Fifteenth	4	Bourdon	16
Sesquialtera ($3\frac{1}{5}'$)	V	Principal	8
Trombone	16	Fifteenth	4
C–d^1		Tierce Mixture	V
		Larigot Mixture	V
		Contra Posaune	16
		Posaune	8
		One octave for flute ranks	
		Four notes only for reeds	

Gauntlett's ideas, both at Christ Church and elsewhere, often remained unexecuted and purely theoretical (it is unlikely, for example, that he approved the limited pedal reeds); but such departments were supposed to be made to continental scaling and not according to traditional scales, i.e. those large open wood pedal scales described later by Hopkins as over twice too large. The limited compass obviously betrays imperfect ideas on somebody's part, and the Christ Church pedal received its conventional two and a half octaves only in 1867.

In his tour of European organ-builders, Cavaillé-Coll visited Hill's workshop in 1844 and the two builders' reciprocal influence deserves closer study. Stop names in French, German and Italian suggest either Gauntlett or Hill to have had paper-knowledge of organs in several countries, and there is no doubt that at least until 1871 (when he built the organ for the new Albert Hall in London) Henry Willis himself was closely influenced by Cavaillé-Coll. To what extent and exactly how has also not yet been examined in detail; but it can certainly be conjectured that without Saint-Sulpice, the Albert Hall organ would have been very different. As to Hill, his Liverpool organ was a compromise between old English and new European styles, with a 20-stop Swell (including 16' reed—what did Willis learn from this organ?), a little choir organ of flutes and the traditional Cremona reed, a high-pressure Tuba (played from the Swell keys), six couplers, five composition pedals and a complete compass of C–d¹–f'''. This last alone has a striking modernity about it. Hill also designed a pallet that slid open and admitted high-pressure wind to the pipe above without the touch-resistance being increased. Willis's organ for St. George's Hall, Liverpool (1855) helped to establish the modern British organ with less compromise. After the rebuilding in 1867, a few antique features still persisted (chiefly the compass), but in its comprehensiveness and colour spectrum it obviously offered a model for bigger organs throughout the ever-expanding British Empire (Hopkins 1877, pp. 525–7):

LIVERPOOL, St. George's Hall
H. Willis, reconstructed 1867 (advised by W. T. Best)

GO   16.8.8.8.8.8.8.5⅓.4.4.4.4.3⅓.2⅔.2.2.II.V.IV.16.8.8.8.4.4
Ch   16.8.8.8.8.8.8.4.4.4.2⅔.2.2.IV.8.8.8.4
Sw   16.8.8.8.8.8.4.4.4.2⅔.2.2.2.II.V.16.16.8.8.8.8.8.8.4.4.Trem
Solo   16.8.8.4.2.16.8.8.8.8.4.8*.8*.8*.4*
Ped   32.32.16.16.16.8.8.5⅓.4.V.IV.32.16.16.8.4

* Heavy wind (15″ to 20″)

Compass, GG–a'', pedal C–f''

Ten couplers (including sub-octave *Sw/Gt*, super-octave *Sw/Gt*)
42 pneumatic pistons (stop combinations)
2 bellows blown by steam engine (8 hp), with 14 reservoirs
W/P, from 32″ to 20″
Pneumatic lever for each manual, two for pedal
Unequal temperament of 1855 not changed to equal

Such instruments encouraged the age-old regard for large organs as an
end in themselves, useful for transcriptions of orchestral and vocal music
(which itself was performed on a big scale, with large forces) but none-
theless organs carefully planned as engineering projects incorporating the
latest details—in this case stop-jambs (presumably a reaction to Cavaillé-
Coll's tiers of stop-knobs), pneumatic thumb-pistons (placing 'the
varied tone-character of the immense instrument at the immediate
disposal of the player', according to Hopkins), concave and radiating
pedalboard (perfected by Willis soon after 1851 and already known in the
U.S.A. by 1857; Ochse 1975, p. 126), Barker levers to each department,
various wind pressure, new ways of raising the wind, pneumatic couplers
and one or other kind of Swell pedal. The contents of the Swell had by
now certainly achieved maturity; compare Liverpool with Saint-Denis
in 1841 (p. 172). In general, the Swell typified several attitudes; Willis
himself said of the double-Venetian-front Swell at Gloucester Cathedral
(1847) that its 'pianissimo was simply astounding', though neither he nor
anyone else ever explained why he thought this a worthy aim. In 1857
Willis had patented a crescendo pedal in which a footlever rotated a
cylinder that activated pneumatic motors at the end of the sliders. It was
in such ways that Willis took tendencies to their logical ends. Similarly, in
certain three-manual organs such as the Sheldonian Theatre, Oxford
(1877) he dispensed entirely with the traditional Choir organ and
replaced it with a Solo, while even at Gloucester thirty years earlier the
Swell was almost three times as large as the Choir organ.

The stoplists published by Seidel, Hamilton, Hopkins, van 't Kruijs
and others show how each major firm by the middle of the nineteenth
century had its own characteristics and tried to create individual organs.
Some had characteristic stops, such as Hill's Octave Clarion 2′ or Cavaillé-
Coll's Septime; some had customary features of construction, such as the
general Swell in the American organs of the Hook family; most had their
own patented action or chests or wind-raising device, particularly the
big German firms. Secular organs in Europe, the U.S.A. and the various
Empires often showed more advanced forms than church or cathedral
organs. It was one of Hill's secular organs in London (The Panopticon,
1853) that first had pneumatically operated sliders, as well as higher
pressure for treble flue pipes and a reversible crescendo pedal that

operated the stop-knobs themselves. Already in 1844, the town hall organ of Worcester had had pneumatic levers and a 32′ pedal. The solo organ, whether enclosed (Leeds, 1859) or not, also had its origins in the town hall organ. A comparison between two celebrated organs, such as Willis's for St. Paul's Cathedral, London and Hill's for Melbourne Town Hall, Australia, shows the differences between ecclesiastical and secular ideals: one would expect the secular organ to have a bigger Solo manual, a smaller Choir, perhaps bigger compass and certainly a larger array of unusual sound effects. It was for a secular building that one of the most remarkable organs of the 1860s was built: by 1863 Walcker had completed for the Music Hall in Boston, Mass. a vast organ of over 80 stops, no doubt only a 'monument to America's cultural inferiority' (Ochse 1975, p. 200) but, considered from a wider spectrum, certainly an organ of ill-defined aim, much more ambiguous and therefore old-fashioned in its Solo manual than a comparable English organ (Hopkins 1877, pp. 447 Boston, 538 Leeds):

BOSTON, Music Hall Walcker, 1857–63		LEEDS, Town Hall Gray & Davidson, 1857–9	
Bourdon	16	Bourdon	8
Gambenprinzipal	8	*Concert Flute	8
Aeoline	8	*Piccolo	4
*Concert Flute (from c)	8	*Ottavina	2
Corno Basetto	8	Clarinet	8
†Vox humana	8	Oboe	8
Gemshorn	4	Cor anglais (free)	8
Piffaro (4.2)	II	Tromba	8
Vox angelica (reed)	4	Ophicleide	8
Quinte	2⅔	7 mechanical couplers (giving	
Piccolo	2	e.g. 'Oboe & Bassoon in 8ves', 'Flute, Clarinet & Bassoon in double 8ves')	

* Overblowing
† Two ranks, one a reed; with its own Swellbox and Tremulant

Even the larger organs of churches and cathedrals often kept to severely classical lines, such as Ladegast's organ in Merseburg Cathedral (1853) for which Liszt wrote his BACH Prelude & Fugue and for which Ladegast employed both the late seventeenth-century organ-case already there and, one suspects, much of its tonal layout (Schwarz 1973, pp. 42–3):

Hw   32(from c).16.16.8.8.8.8.8.8.5⅓.4.4.4.2⅔.2.II.IV.IV.III–V.16.8
Ow   16.8.8.8.8.8.8.4.4.4.2⅔.2.1⅗.1.IV.8.8(Glockenspiel)
Rp   16.8.8.8.8.4.4.2.IV.II–V.8
Schwell 16.8.8.8.8.8.8.4.4.4.2⅔.2.II–IV.III.16
Ped   32.16.16.16.16.10⅔.8.8.8.6⅖.5⅓.4.4.4.IV.IV.32.16.16.8

The Merseburg *Rückpositiv*, still more or less intact, is one of the most interestingly reactionary products of the nineteenth century and could not possibly have been found in a town hall; but that the organ as a whole was a compromise is clear from the simple fact that it contains both a *Zimbelstern* and a Barker lever. Rather more typical was the smaller, sombre organ collecting together a group of highly differentiated stops (Metzler 1965, p. 42):

ETZELBACH
E. F. Schulze, 1869

I   16.8.8.8.4.III
II   8.8.8.4
Ped 16.16.8
II/I, I/P

For such organs was a good deal of German organ music composed between the periods of Schumann and Reger, organs with no particular splendour or colour. Even if the organ were bigger, the German builders often seem puzzled as to what the third or fourth manuals ought to be: they are not Cavaillé-Coll's Bombardes nor Henry Willis's Swells but merely alternative manuals relying on location or variety of voicing. Thus the organ of MAGDEBURG CATHEDRAL, built by the Reubke firm, was large, with five manuals, double pedals and no doubt many sounds close to the requirements of such composers as Julius Reubke; but the character delineation of the manuals is not sharply defined (Metzler 1965, pp. 45–6):

I   16.16.8.8.8.5⅓.4.4.4.2⅔.2.IV.VI.IV.16.8
II   16.8.8.8.8.8.8.4.4.2.II.V.III.8
III   16.8.8.8.8.8.8.4.4.4.2⅔.2.V.16
IV   16.8.8.8.8.8.8.4.4.4.2⅔.2.IV.8.8
V   8.8.8.4.2⅔.2.II–III
Ped I   32.32.16.16.16.10⅔.8.8.8.5⅓.4.2.V.IV.32.16.8.4
Ped II 16.8.8.5⅓.4.2.16
V, an echo department played from III keys

Walcker's organ of 1886 for the Stefansdom, Vienna, was less logically thought out, with a huge Great of 25 stops but only one stop in a Swell-box; nor was Walcker quick to make Barker lever action (Ulm Minster, 1857), much less a fully pneumatic action (1890). Stoplists themselves often show the builder to have had as standard an idea of his organs as Silbermann had in the previous century. Thus Sauer's two 60-stop organs in Leipzig (Peterskirche, 1885 and Thomaskirche, 1889) had almost identical specifications, both dominated by the heavy 8' ranks indispensable for the music and playing of Reger and Straube. Reger's registrations were based on an assumption that stops were changed for crescendo and diminuendo effects; 8' ranks were moved freely but a 4' stop aided the blend, particularly a wide 4' above a narrow 8'. An organ that cannot provide an accompaniment of

Gedackt 8' with Voix céleste 8' and Spitzflöte 4'

voiced and scaled on late nineteenth-century lines cannot provide the sounds required by Reger. But a General Crescendo is not necessary; free-combination pedals, which require good workmanship from the builder, are more useful, and certainly a large part of any new organ's cost in about 1900 must have gone on the accessories, which often number as many as the sounding stops themselves. Precision work of the highest standard was also necessary for the high-pressure reeds and large-mouth flues made by such firms as Weigle from 1890 onwards.

Although all nineteenth-century organs could now be said to deserve the status of historical monument, little musical sense can be made of the late-romantic instruments made about 1900 in all countries of the world, whatever the nationality of the builder; they all look like logical extensions of the Etzelbach stoplist above. Such organs are not so much 'romantic' as perversions of an organ-ideal inspiring builders from at least Gabler to at least Walcker. Even in their period they were found 'hard' (Schweitzer of the Weigle organ in Stuttgart Liederhalle; Schweitzer 1954, p. 61); and if there were not enough gadgets, they were criticized for making 'absolutely no attempt to place at the disposal of the *virtuoso* the ready means of producing complicated orchestral effects or of massing special tone colours' (Audsley of the same organ; Audsley 1905, p. 253). In short, they never satisfied anybody capable of discrimination.

As a final example of a true romantic organ related to a lively musical tradition, Cavaillé-Coll's organ for Saint-Vincent-de-Paul, PARIS, still keeps much of its original character (Hopkins 1877, pp. 342–2):

GO 16.16.8.8.8.4.4.2⅔.2.V.III.8.8.4
Pos 16.8.8.8.4.4.2.2.8.8
Réc 8.8.8.4.4.8.8.8

M

Péd 32.16.16.8.16.16.8.4
8 couplers
14 composition pedals
'Pneumatic lever attachment' (Barker lever)
Compass, C–c^{1}–f^{III}

A similar organ was played by César Franck at Sainte-Clotilde, Paris, from 1859 to 1890; the very quality of Cavaillé-Coll's materials and voicing, particularly of the reeds, would have given Franck a more musical instrument than most German organists would have had at their disposal. Registrations at Sainte-Clotilde or Saint-Vincent followed traditional ideas of *plein jeu, grand jeu, fonds d'orgue* and so on for which the several *pédales de combinaison* were thought necessary by organists now used to the idea of constantly changing the timbre. The fact that French builders remained faithful to sliderchests both in practice and in theory (Guédon 1903) suggests that they remained faithful to certain traditionalisms. Nevertheless, obviously a great change had taken place in the organs of all countries during the nineteenth century; even the monumental instruments of a few decades earlier were so often rebuilt in order to keep abreast of developments. Seventy-two years after their first organ in the classical Paulskirche, FRANKFURT (1827), Walcker's rebuilt it and in the process showed some of those changes that had come about in the design of each and every department of major organs. The great Organ can be taken as an example (Metzler 1965, pp. 55, 119):

1827		Quinte	$2\frac{2}{3}$
Untersatz	32	Oktave	2
Prinzipal	16	Waldflöte	2
Flauto major	16	Terz (treble)	$1\frac{3}{5}$
Viola di Gamba	16	Oktav	1
Oktave	8	Cornet ($10\frac{2}{3}'$)	V
Flöte	8	Mixtur ($2'$)	V
Gemshorn	8	Scharf ($1'$)	IV
Viola di Gamba	8	Tuba	16
Quinte	$5\frac{1}{3}$	Trompete	8
Oktave	4		
Hohlpfeife	4		
Fugara	4	Mechanical action	
Terz	$3\frac{1}{5}$	Sliderchest	

1899		Kleingedackt	4
Prinzipal	16	Oktave	2
Flauto major	16	Flautino	2
Prinzipal	8	Cornet (8′)	III–V
Gross-Oktave	8	Mixtur (4′)	VI
Tibia	8	Fagott	16
Jubalflöte	8	Trompete	8
Gedackt	8	Cor anglais	8
Gemshorn	8	Clairon	4
Viola di Gamba	8		
Quintatön	8		
Oktave	4	Cone chest	
Hohlflöte	4	Pneumatic action	

Bibliography

AUDSLEY, G. A., *The Art of Organ-Building* (New York and London, 1905)

CLUTTON, C. and NILAND, A., *The British Organ* (London, 1963)

ESCHBACH, J. E., 'Some Details of Voicing Techniques at Saint-Sulpice, Paris', *The Organ Yearbook*, 9 (1978), 11–50

GUÉDON, J., *Nouveau Manuel complet du facteur d'orgues* (Paris, 1903)

HAMILTON, J. A., *Catechism of the Organ* (London, 1842, 4th edn., 1865)

HOPKINS, E. J. and RIMBAULT, E. F., *The Organ, its History and Construction* (London, 1855, 3rd edn., 1877)

VAN 'T KRUIJS, M. H., *Verzameling van Disposities der Verschillende Orgels in Nederland* (Rotterdam, 1885)

LUND, C., 'Opmåling af Jesuskirkens Orgel', *Orglet*, 3/1976, 19–28

METZLER, W., *Romantischer Orgelbau in Deutschland* (Ludwigsburg, [1965])

OCHSE, O., *The History of the Organ in the United States* (Bloomington, Ill. and London, 1975)

SCHWARZ, P., *Studien zur Orgelmusik Franz Liszts* (Munich, 1973)

SCHWEITZER, A., *Aus meinem Leben und Denken* (Frankfurt, 1954)

SEIDEL, J. J., *Die Orgel und ihr Bau* (Breslau, 1843)

SUMNER, W. L., 'Aristide Cavaillé-Coll and the Organ of St. Denis Abbey', *The Organ*, 26 (1946), 22 f

SUMNER, W. L., *The Organ, its Evolution, Principles of Construction and Use* (London, 1952, 4th edn., 1973)

22 Contributions to the Nadir of 1890–1930

To most musicians, and even by now to many organists, the ripe 'late romantic' organ of 1900 produces an unpleasing sound even when it is playing music written at the time for it. Whether it was that builders cared less about the musical use of their instruments or whether the music itself is poorer than that composed two centuries earlier is impossible to say. Certainly technical ingenuity outran musical demands, or at least reduced their importance.

Apart from electronic pseudo-organs, it is generally agreed today that the worst organs ever made by a careful, professional builder were those of Robert Hope-Jones. Alas, not a single organ of Hope-Jones survives in anything like authentic form, so enlightened have later organists become and so limited a life had the various component parts. The stoplists of such organs push forward the trends briefly described in the previous section of this book; they discard all ranks above a wide 2' flute and result in such schemes as the following (Fanselau 1973, pp. 48–9):

WORCESTER, Cathedral
R. Hope-Jones, 1896

GO   16.8.8.8.8.8.4.4.2.16.8
Sw   16.8.8.8.8.8.4.4.2.16.8.8.8.8.4
Ch   16.8.8.8.8.8.4.2.8.8
Solo 8.4.16.8.8.8.
Ped 64.32.32.16.16.16.16.8.8.32.16.16.8
25 couplers
Compass, C–f¹–c¹¹¹¹
Electric action

By 1921, the Worcester electric action was useless; but the stoplist itself, with its many diaphones described below, was a monument to the style of the period. The tone was characterized by a smoothing-out of acoustic 'interest', as shown in some recently made sound-graphs (Fanselau 1973, pp. 52–69), and by a royal indifference to blend in general. Hope-Jones built few organs himself and had limited commercial success in Britain and the U.S.A.; but his influence was wide and represents very clearly the state reached by some organs shortly before the various reform movements of the twentieth century were felt. German and French historians who ignore him miss one of the great formative influences of the period; his lecture of 1910 on the auditorium organ of Ocean Grove, New Jersey (1907) showed his aim to be to produce an organ 'avowedly designed for amusing a large section of the public' (Ochse 1975, pp. 335–7).

During the quarter century from 1889 to 1914, Hope-Jones made two particular contributions, typical of his period and in both instances pushing the organ to a kind of limit. These were, firstly, electric key-action (with stop-switches for registration, 'double touch' for the keys and accessories), and secondly, a new kind of pipework (large harmonic Trombas, very narrow Trumpets, heavy-pressure Diapasons with leathered lips to reduce brilliance, very narrow string stops, and very wide scales throughout). His diaphone or valvular reed of 1893 was a new invention. In it he adopted an old observation of the physicists, namely that any device admitting puffs of wind into a tube will create a sound if the frequency rises to audibility. Wind admitted through the bore sets the thin 'vibrator' into motion, whereupon the disc attached to its free end sends a regular series of puffs of wind into the resonator, i.e. the pipe standing above. As wind is increased, the sound rises in volume but not in pitch. Though no doubt more effective as a foghorn—the diaphonic flute consisting of 'a small aluminium piston' could 'produce a sweet musical note that could be heard twenty miles away', Hope-Jones claimed in his 1910 lecture—the diaphone indicates the kind of tone accepted and even desired by players at the turn of the century. Wor-

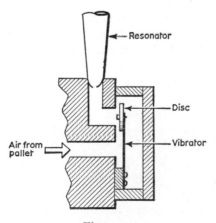

Figure 15

cester Cathedral had some half dozen, and by designing various resonators Hope-Jones was able to vary the timbre sufficiently as to call
some diaphones 'reeds' and others 'flutes', as were the other builders
of the period such as Weigle who experimented with these radically new
sound-producers. Hope-Jones's key-actions are said to have been too
finely detailed for organs, but the period saw much experimentation with
electricity, not least for the borrowing of stops from one department to
another which, though still frowned upon by Audsley in 1905, led to
several well-known devices in the early twentieth-century organ. Two
of these, the 'unit chest' and the 'extension organ' are referred to below.
In effect, Hope-Jones laid the way for such extraordinary creations as the
140-stop organ of 1904 for the St. Louis Exposition; the Kufstein organ
in the Tirol (Walcker 1926–7, 10″-pressure organ on top of a tower
played by a console over 100 yards away); the stadium organ in Chicago
(Bartola 1929) in which 44 ranks of pipes and various percussion traps
produced an organ of six manuals hanging in chambers above an auditorium of 25,000 people and played by a movable console of 884 stop-
knobs; and the Atlantic City Convention Hall organ of 1929–32, with its
seven manuals of 1439 stops (some of them reeds on 100″ wind) taking
in all or any tonal or structural devices that electrical organ-technology
had been able to devise at that period. Clearly, the cinema pipe-organ
of the 1920s required—or was itself a manifestation of—a combination
of this technology and this aesthetic; without either, the Wurlitzer organ
would have been impossible. But even in the more respectable organs
of the up-to-date concert halls of that period the extension system and
the crude voicing that seem by nature to go with it proved popular. In the
John Compton organ in Wolverhampton Civic Hall (1938), for example,
50 ranks in two front-less chambers (both with Swell shutters) held in the
roof above the stage produce an organ of four manuals, over 80 stops and
60 registration aids of one kind or another, as well as an electronic
department and a complete electric action throughout. Indeed, such an
organ lay as much under the influence of the Chicago organ of 1929
(see above) as Gauntlett had been under the influence of Haarlem.

Electricity was used to replace the key-to-pallet action, to operate
stop mechanisms and accessories, to drive a motor for raising the wind,
and to replace older chest-types. Some sophisticated gadgets, such as
Willis's 'infinite speed and gradation Swell' (in which the amount the
pedal is pressed down from its neutral position is a measure of the speed
at which the shutters open), date only from the 1930s, and in 1905
Audsley was still bemoaning 'the tentative state of that branch of organ
construction at this time' with respect to designing electro-pneumatic
actions. Nevertheless, pure electric actions were advanced enough at that
time for E. M. Skinner to use one at St. Bartholomew, New York in order
to connect two organs, at opposite ends of the church, to one console, a

feat paralleled and even exceeded by Hope-Jones's experiments in Birkenhead at the end of the century, when he put the pipes inside the church and the console in the churchyard. More radical still was the use of electricity to connect any key of an organ to any pipe in it: each pipe could be given its own little chest or 'unit' to stand on, and such 'unit chests' can be used for any number of ranks in an organ. In practice, the unit construction was associated with the 'unit organ', an instrument resulting from Hope-Jones's notion of redesigning the Great, Choir, Swell and Solo divisions into Foundation, Woodwind, String, Brass and Percussion departments, each enclosed in a (cement) Swellbox and each available on any keyboard at various pitches. Each keyboard could then have its own combinations independent of the others and is thus reduced to a kind of registration device: a manual for each 'prepared stop-combination'. There is a sickening logic behind this conception—a furthering of the old 'extension' practice in which a 2' pipe could be c' of a nominal 8' stop, c of a 4' stop, F of a $2\frac{2}{3}$' stop and so on. The rank of pipes in such a system could be extended to give a complete compass at all pitch levels, and electricity would make it all only too feasible.

That the idea is basically foreign to organ tone and to the old notion of how organ sound is built up is obvious enough from the Wolverhampton organ where, for example, one Diapason rank gives the following stops

pedal 16', $10\frac{2}{3}$', $5\frac{1}{3}$'
GO 16', 8', 4' and 2'

It must have often been so in the sixteenth century that a Quinte $2\frac{2}{3}$' rank was made to the same scale as and voiced virtually identical to the Principal 4'; but open-foot voicing produces a more natural and blending sound than the Wolverhampton rank, which was in any case extended to no fewer than six pitch levels. Besides, scaling and voicing two different ranks in much the same way is no logical justification for using the same rank at two different pitches. Nor can extended ranks produce as much power and variety as the sheer number of stop-knobs promises to the player. So builders felt the need to compensate by coarsening yet further the tone of the pipes concerned: the pressures were raised, languids sharply angled, upper lips leathered (i.e. thin leather strips were glued around the edge of the lip), scaling made extreme in either direction, often with double languids (two sides of a square pipe given a mouth), reed tongues 'weighted' to produce yet stronger foundation tone, cheaper metal alloys used (zinc and iron at Hope-Jones's organ in Worcester Cathedral), and particularly in the pedals some kind of diaphone rank providing a lot of power, with resonator tubes of large diameter. New chests, in particular the Pitman chest (E. M. Skinner), were devised in which the finger key and the stop-knob had equal access to the pallet below each pipe, which therefore sounded only when both were put into operation. Such systems are witness to a fine technology: 'the fact that the average American electric action is so reliable and quick, especially with the technically unsurpassed Pitman chests . . . may be part of the reason that the present return to tracker action is happening somewhat slowly' (Noack 1976, p. 6).

Many of the techniques listed above, for example the weighting of reed tongues with brass or lead, have very uncertain origins and only their application to an extreme can be blamed on the builders of 1900. Of these extremes, the Wurlitzer theatre organ of the 1920s—named after the Wurlitzer organ company of New York State, organ-builders since 1910 and purchasers of several Hope-Jones patents—represents the true nadir: an instrument peculiar to itself, containing relatively few ranks, but these voiced to one or other extreme, 'extended' to provide many stops available at every pitch in every department, and reducing *ad absurdum* the principle of 'floating chests' (chests playable by more than one manual). With its percussion effects, its high-pressure pipework enclosed in one or two grille-fronted chambers, its movable console containing nothing but electric switches (though disguised as keyboards), its flat acoustic, vulgar repertory and loathsome sound, the cinema organ can be seen not only as keeping the ideas of a Hope-Jones but bringing to fruition the kind of organ sub-culture once popularized by Abt Vogler.

Why an organ of 1900 sounds different from an organ of 1700 can be answered by tracing such technical details as those outlined in these pages; but the reason for the gradual change is much more difficult to state simply. It was not the desire for intense tone as such that led to the difference: sixteenth-century voicing must also have been often taken to the limit, though on lower wind pressures. It was not the new kinds of pipe: every period invented new, colourful stops that were by nature merely peripheral to the true *organo pleno*. It was not the use itself of pneumatic or electric actions which, though insensitive to the player and therefore discouraging to the voicer, were perfected only for practical reasons, not for aesthetic. It was not the desire to imitate the orchestra as such, for organs in 1500 had tried to do that as thoroughly as those in 1900. It was not the dull, dark, sombre setting in the nineteenth-century church itself that obliged organ-builders to forget charm and prettiness of sound, for they had already forgotten them before the dark 'gothick' revival. Besides, the most advanced organs of 1900 were those in concert halls, not in 'gothick' churches. It was not that organists became indifferent to music of other kinds; on the contrary, an average organist of 1900 knew much more of how contemporary symphonies or chamber works sounded than did his predecessor of 1700. It was not that organ technology became its own *raison d'être*, so skilful that one forgot the music:

no distant high-pressure reed impressed a listener of 1900 more thoroughly than did the intricate moving statues of the Strasbourg Minster organ in 1500. Only by comparing for himself the sound produced by a good pipe made by Silbermann and one made by Wurlitzer can the musician begin to define what, if anything, went wrong during the nineteenth century and led to the absurdity of the 1920s.

It should not be forgotten that technical matters are still vague. For example, more scaling figures are available for the organs of Gottfried Silbermann than for those of Sauer, far more for the Clicquots than for Cavaillé-Coll. Virtually no such details of English organs have ever been published or become known outside a few builders' workshops. But whatever the scaling, voicing or materials, why was it that the sound produced by the new arrays of 8′ stops was so solid or so loud or so hard or so jejune or so emaciated? It need not have been. It seems that characteristics run together: electric action (slow, remote, invariable, insensitive, unreliable, unpleasant to the touch) played from a detached console (i.e. keyboards detaching the player from his sound production) leading to chests of poor-toned pipes (manufactured more easily than before and voiced by those with less specialized ears) located behind a mere case-façade (not integrated into one resonating whole) and all so constructed in order for the organist to play music written either for another instrument (orchestral or vocal) or for another culture (popular styles, background music, pictorial effects). None of these features belongs exclusively to the organ of 1900 and all had their origins at different points over the previous centuries.

Bibliography

AUDSLEY, C. A., *The Art of Organ-Building* (New York and London, 1905)
FANSELAU, R., *Die Orgel im Werk Edward Elgars* (Göttingen, 1973)
NOACK, F., 'Trends in American Organ-Building in 1976', *ISO Information*, 15 (1976), 5–10
OCHSE, O., *The History of the Organ in the United States* (Bloomington, Ill. and London, 1975)
WHITWORTH, R., *The Electric Organ* (London, 1930)

23 Early Indications of an Organ Revival

'Organ Revival' or 'Organ Reform Movement' are English equivalents of the term *Orgelbewegung* coined in about 1930 as a simplified form of Gurlitt's phrase *Orgel-Erneuerungsbewegung*, said to have been used at the 1926 Freiburg 'Conference for German Organ-art' and the title of an essay published by Gurlitt in 1929. That conference, and the movement as a whole, was concerned with 'reviving' some of the 'historical principles' behind each organ type over the centuries, because by then the 'true purpose and nature' of the organ had 'declined' and therefore required 'regeneration'. Although such terms are still frequently used, they were not so baldly stated at the 1926 conference, nor in Germany itself have they always led to a full appreciation of true 'historical principles', either in the building of new organs or the restoring of old. Holland, Denmark and Switzerland have seen more consistently good work over the last 40 years.

A key word in the 1926 Conference title was 'German', for that period in Germany saw many political–cultural movements geared, consciously or unconsciously, towards clarifying and ultimately glorifying the achievements of a country still seeking unified identity. The *Orgelbewegung* was only one of several in music alone—folk music, school music, youth music, church music, individual composers—and like all 'movements', it was based on common assumptions (Eggebrecht 1967, pp. 9 f). These were, firstly, a simple reaction to the previous period: a natural moving away from whatever it was that the organ of 1900 stood for. Secondly, key issues were simplified: Schweitzer's 'best and sole' standard for an organ was its suitability for playing J. S. Bach which, personal tastes apart, can hardly be maintained as a logical starting-point. Moreover, glorifying Bach became itself justification for a further over-simplification: the 'Bach organ' became synonymous with the 'baroque organ', and to this day only limited success has been achieved in understanding what exactly is the right organ for the *Orgelbüchlein* or for the mature Preludes and Fugues or for *Clavierübung III*. It certainly had little to do with the baroque ideas tentatively approached by some of Schweitzer's organ-builder colleagues in Alsace in what has been called the 'Alsatian Organ Reform', precursor of the *Orgelbewegung*. Thirdly, the tendency was towards standardization: Schweitzer's views given at the Vienna Congress of the International Musicological Society in 1909 and at the Freiberg Organ Conference of 1927 naturally enough equated *tonschön* ('beautiful in tone') with *alt* ('old'), but it was an equation that led to the lazy uniformity of countless neo-baroque organs built in Germany during the last 40 years.

Early written works influencing the Organ Revival were Schweitzer's book *J. S. Bach* and the pamphlet *Deutsche und Französische Orgelbaukunst*, both still of importance in Germany, not least in East Germany where the only available theorist of the *Orgelbewegung* to this day is Schweitzer himself. The first of these publications must have had a negative effect since it perpetrated the idea of Bach as a kind of romantic, by implication requiring an organ to match; but the second was more down to earth and therefore beneficial. Schweitzer himself had a precursor in Alsace in the person of Emil Rupp, for whom Walcker, ever an inventive and eager firm, built a 'reformed organ' at St. Paul, Strasbourg in 1907. Rupp and Schweitzer, however, were only part of a general current flowing towards greater historical awareness: a current showing itself in, for example, Guilmant's series of editions of old French organ-music, begun in 1901 with the title *Archives des maîtres de l'orgue* and far outstripping most other editions of the time, including Karl Straube's volumes of old German organ-music (1904). In England, at least a generation earlier, Charles Salaman, Carl Engel and A. J. Hipkins had already begun to exhibit and even to play harpsichords again in public, creating a climate not only suitable for basic musical research—A. J. Ellis's articles of 1880 on the pitch of organs and other instruments are still not sufficiently valued outside Britain—but one in which such craftsmen as Dolmetsch could reconstruct old instruments. As in France, however, renewed interest in the harpsichord did not lead directly to enlightened ideas in organ-building, but it did lead to some kind of historical awareness admirably summed up by Dolmetsch in 1915 (pp. 436–7):

> The makers of 1815 worked much on the same principles as those of 1615. . . . The church organs in addition had that power based on sweetness which constitutes majesty. The change came on, and for the sake of louder tone, pressure of wind was doubled and trebled. The same pressure acting on the valves which let the wind into the pipes made them too heavy for the fingers to move through the keys. A machine was then invented which did the work at second hand. . . . So the music of the organ dragged on after the player's fingers as best it could. Personal touch, which did so much for phrasing and expression, was destroyed. . . . Modern compositions are intended for this machine, and all is well with them; but it is a revelation to hear Handel's or Bach's music on a well-preserved old organ.

Dolmetsch never used the term 'baroque organ' and the phrase was only later taken from German art-historians to refer to a type of organ more ideal than real. As important as the sound-ideals behind such views is their insistence on good direct key-action, and it is a strange peculiarity of many *Orgelbewegung* organs that they play from non-mechanical actions; and even where they are mechanical, their stoplist rather than their action has taken the builder's chief priority. Dolmetsch implied here that a good mechanical action was the only way; so did, for example Jean Huré in 1923 and Christhard Mahrenholz in 1938. By then, Mahrenholz was also able to insist on sliderchests. Important too was the gradual realization that organ cases themselves were not merely frontal embellishments but an integral part of the total resonating structure. One particular aspect of this was the growing conviction that the *Rückpositiv* ought to be reintroduced (e.g. Supper, 1934)—though again, this had the effect of oversimplifying the issues, since after all some of the best organs ever made had no *Rückpositiv*.

Unfortunately, in England practice did not follow Dolmetsch's theory, and the ideas of such advisers as Thomas Casson and George Dixon merely kept the English organ of the early twentieth century from becoming worse than it was. As with so many English and German writers of the period 1900–1950 and beyond, their emphasis on stoplists was not radical enough to lead to a genuine rethinking of the organ; English amateurism may at times have led to less unmusical instruments than those inspired by some theoreticians and musicologists in Germany but in the long run has proved more blocking to progress. In France, factions still govern organ-building and any new organ could be one of several totally opposed kinds, depending on who the builder and adviser were. Thus in France and England, almost all organists have only a compromise organ of mixed and dubious lineage, at best going back to Cavaillé-Coll in the one and William Hill in the other, and perhaps faintly tinted with the influence of some outsider such as Hope-Jones or D. A. Flentrop, as the case may be. In both countries, most organists have still to learn that it needs more than a low-pressure Nasard or two to create a 'baroque organ' and one 'suitable for the music of all periods'. And throughout the world, there are still only a handful of builders who have yet understood that they have only a tiny margin to work in if they are to voice pipes to their truest beauty of tone.

Bibliography

CASSON, T., *Reform in Organ-Building* (London, 1888)
DIXON, G., 'The Tonal Structure of the Organ', *The Organ*, 1 (1921–2), 129 f, 215 f

DOLMETSCH, A., *The Interpretation of the Music of the XVII and XVIII Centuries* (London, [1915])

EGGEBRECHT, H. H., *Die Orgelbewegung* (Stuttgart, 1967)

ELLIS, A. J., *see* MENDEL

GURLITT, W. (ed.), *Bericht über die Freiburger Tagung für deutsche Orgelkunst* (Augsburg, 1926)

GURLITT, W., 'Zur gegenwärtigen Orgel-Erneuerungsbewegung in Deutschland', *Musik und Kirche*, 1 (1929), 15–27

HURÉ, J., *L'Esthétique de l'orgue* (Paris, 1923)

MAHRENHOLZ, C. (ed.), *Bericht über die dritte Tagung für deutsche Orgelkunst in Freiberg/Sa* (Kassel, 1928)

MAHRENHOLZ, C., 'Fünfzehn Jahre Orgelbewegung, Rückblick und Ausblick', *Musik und Kirche*, 10 (1938), 8–28

MENDEL, A. (ed.), *Studies in the History of Musical Pitch* (Amsterdam, 1968); includes Ellis's papers from the *Journal of the Royal Society of Arts*, March and April, 1880

SCHWEITZER, A., *Deutsche und französische Orgelbaukunst* (Leipzig, 1906, 2nd edn., 1927)

SCHWEITZER, A., *J. S. Bach, le musicien-poète* (Leipzig, 1905)

SUPPER, W., *Architekt und Orgelbau* (Würzburg, 1934)

TAGLIAVINI, L. F., 'Mezzo secolo di storia organaria', *L'organo*, 1.i (1960), 70–80

24 The 'Orgelbewegung' and its Aftermath in Germany

With the collaboration of Wilibald Gurlitt, professor of music in the University of Freiburg, Oscar Walcker designed and built a remarkable organ at FREIBURG in 1921: this was the so-called Praetorius-Orgel, an instrument often claimed today to have ushered in a new period and approach to organ-building. Inaugurated by Karl Straube, the Praetorius organ was the first avowed attempt at reconstructing the tonal character of an old organ, in this case not from the flesh but from the spirit of a model described by Praetorius in his *De organographia*. After the organ was destroyed in 1944, a second Praetorius-Orgel was built in 1954–5, showing the development in German thinking over those thirty or so years. In 1921, the first organ had no proper casework, the stoplist was 'improved' on Praetorius's original, the pipes were placed not on a sliderchest but a 'stop channel-chest' and the action was electro-pneumatic; in 1954, Gurlitt was still the adviser but Walcker's successor Walcker-Mayer also collaborated with acoustic and technical experts (E. K. Rössler, W. Lottermoser), kept his stoplist closer to Praetorius (*Syntagma musicum* II, p. 191, first specification), took details from extant pipework by Praetorius's friend Esaias Compenius, and followed a stricter *Werkprinzip* structure, with mechanical action, sliderchest and meantone tuning:

Rückpositiv		Dolcan ('strong')	8
Principal	4	Bauerflötlein	1
Quintadena	8	Singend Cornet	2
Hohlflöte	4		
Nachthorn (wood)	4	*Oberwerk*	
Blockflöte	2	Principal	8
Oktave	2	Gedackt	8
Quinta	$1\frac{1}{3}$	Oktave	4
Zimbel		Gemshorn	4
Schalmei	8	Gedackt (wood)	4
		Nasat	$2\frac{2}{3}$
Pedal		Scharfquinta	*4
Untersatz (open wood)	16	Superoktave	2
Posaune (Sordun)	16	Mixtur (2')	III

Brustpositiv		Zimbel	II
Krummhorn (wood)	8	Sifflöte	I
Quintetz	$1\frac{1}{3}$		

Tremulants in *Ow* and *Rp*, 'each to be usable separately'
Couplers, *Rp/Ow*, *Bw/Ow*, *Rp/Ped* (only?)
8 'good steady bellows'

* *Sic* in Praetorius ($1\frac{1}{3}'$)

Were a third Praetorius organ to be built thirty years later again, one would expect enlightenment to have developed far enough for a sensitive builder to know more clearly how Compenius voiced, to be able to determine more precisely such details as the scaling and materials, and to appreciate the need for a casework to copy closely those of the early seventeenth century. Already in 1969, Walcker-Mayer improved on his firm's record in antiquarian organ-building by making a new copy of the Roman organ of Aquincum according to his reasoned hypotheses.

Not least because Schweitzer himself favoured the organs of Cavaillé-Coll, regarding them as 'the ideal so far as tone is concerned' (Phelps 1967, p. 4), the French influence on early reformist ideas were strong. After Rupp and Walcker visited the workshop of Mutin, Cavaillé-Coll's successor, a few organs were built with the express purpose of combining the musical capabilities of both German and French organs: a somewhat simplistic aim but one not foolish in view of the attempts to do the same thing two centuries earlier by G. Silbermann and K. J. Riepp. But it was an aim not likely to further the cause, since neither old German nor old French ideas were properly understood. Nevertheless, one such organ at St. Reinold, Dortmund (Walcker, over 100 stops), inaugurated in 1909 by Schweitzer, attracted the attention of Reger, for whose music a festival was held in that city in 1910 and whose immensely popular organ-playing drew attention to organs as serious instruments. This alone helped to create a good climate for the Organ Reform, though Reger himself was said never to be able to get enough 8' tone on whatever organ he happened to be playing (Högner 1968, p. 1155). In theory, the dual nature of Reger's mature style—polyphonic yet homophonic—would gain much from the 'Alsatian Reform' organ, and to this day one can often see it claimed that the German organ is good for polyphony, the French for homophony. This is the kind of simplistic generalization that led to, and still does lead to, the German eclectic organ. Such giant organs as those in Dortmund or in Passau Cathedral (Steinmeyer, 1930, 208 stops, 'the world's biggest church organ' of its time) were giant in order to provide the organist with a 'German romantic organ', a 'French organ' and a 'baroque organ' lumped in one. As usual, the more northerly firms such as Kemper and Ott remained closer to classical tradition, but elsewhere the influence of Steinmeyer was great, not least in the so-called restoration of all the famous south German baroque organs. Only during the last decade or so has the ineradicable non-logic of eclecticism emerged, and then only here and there.

Returning to a fully committed *Werkprinzip* was bound to be slow. The much lauded organ by Furtwängler & Hammer in the Marienkirche, GÖTTINGEN (1925), was another compromise with pneumatic action; but its stoplist and pipescales (prepared by Mahrenholz and alerting all experts to this important factor) suggested the way things could develop (Mahrenholz 1926):

Hw	16.8.8.8.4.4.2.V.V.8
Rp	8.8.8.4.4.2.2.III.II.16.8
Ow	8.8.8.4.4.2$\frac{2}{3}$.2.1.III.16.8.4
Ped	16.16.10$\frac{2}{3}$.8.8.8.4.2.IV.32.16.2.16.8.4

Such an instrument is sometimes called the 'Hindemith organ'—Paul Hindemith had been one of those taking part in the 1926 Freiburg/Breisgau Conference—and was itself a mean between extremes. Meanwhile it was becoming clearer that new groundwork on the fundamentals of organ-building was necessary, at least amongst the ever-influential theoreticians and 'organ experts' called in whenever a new German organ was projected. Papers were written and published on such technical matters relating to organs as acoustics (*Akustische Zeitschrift* 1936, *Archiv für Musikforschung* 1939), sliderchests and their effect on organ tone (H. H. Jahnn 1931), pallets (*Zeitschrift für Instrumentenbau* 1933), casework (Supper 1934) and scaling (Mahrenholz 1938). In Italy, questions concerning old organs and their character had never entirely disappeared from the journals (e.g. *Musica sacra* 1901–3), and even large electric organs like that in the Pontificio Istituto di Musica Sacra, Rome (Mascioni, 1933) had never quite shaken off traditional features and had rather 'rediscovered the value of a few classical timbres and combinations' (Tagliavini 1960, p. 82). In France, however, intensive historical research, witnessed by the archival essays and books of documents published by Raugel (1927 etc.) and by Dufourcq (1934 etc.), had very unfortunate results in that many old organs came to light, were then modernized in the course of the next few decades and are now represented by only a handful of instruments snatched from the grasp of advisers and experts. The eclectic ideals of such advisers are those behind the eclectic-romantic organs for which Messiaen and his earlier contemporaries composed.

In Germany, old organs were not always so badly treated, though here too there have been dreadful mistakes made in restorations. For the musician during the first stages of the *Orgelbewegung*, the position of surviving organs was difficult. Important as the Lübeck Totentanzorgel was to such writers as H. H. Jahnn (*Kongressbericht*, Leipzig 1925) or the Silbermann in Freiberg Cathedral to E. Flade (*Tagung*, Freiberg/ Sachsen 1927), such organs were obviously unsuitable for the whole repertory. Günther Ramin could explain in his notes how he played the Pastorale of Bach on the Freiberg Cathedral organ (*Tagung*, Freiberg 1927, p. 211), but what was an organist to make of Silbermann's pedal-compass, so short that even the *Orgelbüchlein* could not be played on it without ingenious juggling? It requires a sophisticated historical instinct to see that 'ingenious juggling' can teach the player much about Bach's notation; this is a subject still not sufficiently researched. Nor was progress helped at the beginning by theoreticians claiming without adequate evidence that such devices as barless chests are by nature 'bad'; the result is merely to polarize opinion. It is also probably true that an organ of 1700 is more versatile than one of 1900; but such generalizations are not exactly scientific. Nevertheless, the beauty of Freiberg was unquestioned, and the publication in facsimile of the treatises by Schlick, Antegnati, Praetorius, Werckmeister, Mattheson, the *Dresdner Handschrift*, Adlung and Dom Bedos—all before World War II—must have heightened interest in the old organs that did survive. True knowledge of them has come only slowly. While the best opinion would not now agree with Klotz's claim that 'it is the large Schnitger organ that best corresponds to the demands made by J. S. Bach's music' (Klotz 1934), we still hardly begin to understand the sound aimed at by Schnitger, and only now are major organs of this kind (Stade, Groningen A-Kerk) being restored to standards comparable to those of the best harpsichord-restorers.

While almost all 'old' organs north of a line from the Adriatic to the Bay of Biscay are untrustworthy as historical instruments, a higher standard of restoration has begun to prevail in some quarters from the late 1960s. Each step in the no-compromise restoration process has had to be slowly won—the reconstitution of the original stoplist and compass, the keyboards, mechanism and console furniture, the reversal to the original pitch and temperament, the making of missing pipes on the scale and style of the old, the establishment of voicing styles. During the 1960s it was recognized that steady wind-supply was an anachronism; at Évora Cathedral, the restorer D. A. Flentrop and the adviser M. A. Vente noted that 'the narrow channels and the low wind-pressure . . . prevent the supply of wind having that stability considered desirable for a modern instrument' (1970, p. 10). The restoration by Jürgen Ahrend of the Innsbruck Hofkirche organ in the early 1970s matched the standards achieved by Metzler in restorations at Muri (Switzerland), Nieuw

N

Scheemda (Netherlands) and elsewhere: the original wind trunk was preserved, the wind pressure ascertained and the voicing patterns established; the original short compass was restored (though the keys belonged to the eighteenth century and were replaced only more recently); the original pitch, casework, chests and action were restored; and the tuning is unequal. New mixture ranks had to be made; but as with Ahrend's more recent and even more remarkable restoration of the Schnitger at Stade (1975), the creation of missing parts of an old organ is now a fine science. Although history speaks against perfection being achieved in 1978 or any other particular year, the good restorers of today have standards beyond the imagination of the early Organ Reformers; future development will be concerned even more closely with establishing and distinguishing between the various voicing styles of different periods and countries.

To a great extent, the making of new organs has followed along similar lines, reflecting the best builders' dual rôle as builder and restorer. In Germany as a whole after World War II, the organ at its more enlightened developed faster at the hands of the many new and small firms, particularly as they were encouraged by the newly appointed organ-advisers for each of the regions in the country. From the early 1950s, Beckerath of Hamburg and the two Schuke firms of Berlin (West, East) produced organs of less compromise quasi-baroque tone and stoplists, with mechanical actions perhaps not always as sensitive as those old organs which they had restored and been influenced by (Beckerath by Schnitger, Alexander Schuke by Wagner). Beckerath was also one of the first firms to take such quasi-baroque organs of north Germany to the U.S.A. (see Plate 47) and even Britain: a trend encouraged by the formative *Archiv* gramophone records and the performances of J. S. Bach by Helmut Walcha on the quasi-Schnitgers of Cappel and Alkmaar. More recently, Ahrend and his former partner Brunzema (pupils of Paul Ott) continued the trend towards strong-toned organs, omitting most mutations and relying on highly coloured flue and reed stops, made of hammered metal and voiced on strong, pre-baroque lines thought to have been usual in northern Europe. Old organs restored by Ahrend (e.g. the seventeenth-century instrument at Westerhusen) have a natural, unforced, powerful, telling, breathy tone quite different from the sweet waftings and pretty mutation colours admired on the baroque organs of the eighteenth century. The little organ at Westerhusen (restored 1955), like the big positive at Nieuw Scheemda (Schnitger, restored Metzler) or that in the Halle Marktkirche (seventeenth century, restored Schuke), offers a revelation of the kind of sound known to a seventeenth-century organist. To the reader, the stoplist of an organ built by firms actively engaged in uncompromising restorations may often seem nondescript:

BREMEN-OBERNEULAND
Ahrend & Brunzema, 1966

Hw	16.8.8.4.4.2.Mixtur.8
Rp	8.4.4.2.1⅓.II.Scharf.8
Ped	16.8.4.16.8.2

But the sound is far from nondescript and has made a great contribution to our understanding of historic organ-tone.

While the number of small, non-compromising organ firms in Germany is yearly growing, there is still a very large number of anonymously-toned quasi-baroque organs being made. Swells, either as enclosed *Oberwerke* or enclosed *Brustwerke*, are still popular and are necessary, it is said, for French music. Only in the last few years have a few inventive organ cases been designed. For thirty years after the war, German builders relied on simple geometric shapes repetitive and careless in detail, sometimes conforming with the surroundings in an imaginative way (Karl Schuke's design of 1962 for the Berlin Gedächtniskirche—see Plate 46), but only rarely aspiring to a genuinely interesting shape, sinuous and restless (Beckerath's design for the Marktkirche, Hanover). Perhaps old cases will have a growing influence on new designs—for example, the old Perpignan case suggesting certain lines in the Marcussen –Andersen organ in Linz Cathedral, 1968. While the standard German practice of making mechanical action throughout an organ may lead to such bizarre *tours de force* as the new six-manual organ by Karl Schuke in South Korea, on the whole it has done nothing but good. It is surely correct that 'the most recent organ-music . . . with stationary and variously moving tone-clusters can only be played on mechanical organs . . . . The cluster technique shows complex flutter beats and not the sound-components of harmonics; its overall sound is neither tempered nor harmonic. Such foreign sound-colours and untempered tunings can be performed only through the increased playing-possibilities of mechanical action' (Holtz 1972, p. 45). While several of these statements deserve a controlled experiment to test their validity, the general tenet must be true, given the kind of pipe-voicing associated with a sensitive tracker action. It is also characteristic of the influence old organs have on modern that not only is a rigidly steady wind supply now seen as anachronistic before the second third of the nineteenth century but that unequal temperaments too can provide 'a useful alternative . . . in the case of new organs. The pronounced key-characteristics and lively chromaticity of the Kirnberger temperament represent a gain for a modern instrument' (Rensch 1974, p. 53).

Bibliography

DUFOURCQ, N., *Documents inédits relatifs à l'orgue français* (Paris, 1934–5)
HOLTZ, J., [Notes on Frauenfeld], *ISO Information*, 8 (1972), 45
HÖGNER, F., 'Max Reger und die deutsche Orgelbewegung', *Ars organi*, 32 (1968), 1153–8
JAHNN, H. H., *Der Einfluss der Schleifwindlade auf die Tonbildung der Orgel* (Hamburg, 1931)
KLOTZ, H., *Über die Orgelkunst der Gotik, der Renaissance und des Barock* (Kassel, 1934)
MAHRENHOLZ, C., *Die neue Orgel in der St. Marienkirche zu Göttingen* (Göttingen and Augsburg, 1926)
MAHRENHOLZ, C., *Die Berechnung der Orgelpfeifenmensuren vom Mittelalter bis zur Mitte des 19. Jahrhunderts* (Kassel, 1938; Eng. trans., Oxford, 1975)
PHELPS, L., *A Short History of the Organ Revival* (St. Louis, 1967)
RAUGEL, F., *Les Grandes Orgues des églises de Paris et du Département de la Seine* (Paris, 1927)
RENSCH, R., 'The Kirnberger Temperament and its Effects on Organ Sound', *ISO Information*, 12 (1974), 45–54
SUPPER, W., *Architekt und Orgelbau* (Würzburg, 1934)
TAGLIAVINI, L. F., 'Mezzo secolo di storia organaria', *L'organo*, 1.i (1960), 70–80
VENTE, M. A. and FLENTROP, D. A., 'The Renaissance Organ of Evora Cathedral', *The Organ Yearbook*, 1 (1970), 5–19

The Organ Revival in Scandinavia, Holland, the U.S.A., England, France and Italy

Builders in Scandinavia and to some extent in the Netherlands had never sunk quite so low as those elsewhere, and most locally-built organs—as distinct from the big instruments occasionally imported from France and Germany—were in less dire need of reform. The enlightened organs built in these countries during the 1940s could be regarded as survival rather than revival instruments: the traditions had never quite died. On the whole, the Swedish organ had become more decadent than the Danish during the nadir period of 1890–1930, but in the stoplists themselves mutation ranks had never quite disappeared. Naturally, German barless chests of various types were found in Scandinavia. Theodor Frobenius, a German-born builder settling in Copenhagen and giving his name to one of the best firms, had indeed made the 'first and for a long time only Danish electric action' in only about 1915 (Friis 1959, p. 12), not to mention 'gothick' cases as nasty as any in nineteenth-century Germany or France (e.g. at Tønsberg, 1923).

Though unsatisfactory by present-day standards, the Frobenius 'restorations' of the old organs of Roskilde and Aarhus Cathedrals in the 1920s helped to alert the better thinkers to the crucial issues. By 1940, Marcussen's new quire organ in the startling Grundtvigskirke, COPEN-HAGEN (see Plate 45), provided the world with one of its first radically re-thought, classical organs (Kriek and Zandt 1964, p. 75):

Hovedvaerk		*Rygpositiv*	
C–f^{111}		C–f^{111}	
Principal (case-front)	8	Gedakt	8
Nathorn	8	Principal (case-front)	4
Oktav	4	Rørfløjte	4
Quint	2⅔	Quintatøn	2
Oktav	2	Scharf	II
Mixtur	IV	Krumhorn	8
		Pedal	
		C–d^{1}	
Sliderchests		Subbass	16
Mechanical key and stop-action		Bordun (from *Hw*)	8
Hw and *Ped*, same chest		Oktav (from *Hw*)	4
Case-design by K. Klint		Dulcian	16

By the late 1930s the firm of Marcussen, headed since 1920 by Sybrand Zachariassen and developed by P. G. Andersen (whose history of the organ, though simplistic, has proved useful to the Revival), was producing almost nothing but mechanical action, useful when it came to restore old organs (Sorø Cathedral, 1942). In the same year as the Grundtvigskirke organ, Frobenius had added a *Rückpositiv* and Zimbelsterne to the early sixteenth-century organ of St. Peter, Malmö (now in Malmö Museum—see Plate 44), showing not only that builders were recognizing the *Werkprinzip* as a method of enlarging organs but that they were, perhaps unintentionally, beginning to follow in the old builders' footsteps. By 1944, the new organ of Jaegersborg, near Copenhagen, had three uncompromising *Werkprinzip* manuals complete with Trumpet *en chamade*. Moreover, builders contributed to theoretical studies: Walter Frobenius's paper on end-correction (1947) is the most important work by an organ-builder in such fields since the lectures of Cavaillé-Coll, while already by 1937 Sybrand Zachariassen was making studies of pipe scales in northern Europe (Oussoren 1972, p. 46).

Smaller organs were important to the true development of the instrument since in them builders could more easily discard compromise, as is still the case today. By 1950, Flentrop had given his characteristic voicing to the 17-stop organ at Loenen a/d Vecht, having only a year or two earlier still been engaged in larger instruments with Swells (Driebergen, Bussum). But the Driebergen Conference of 1950 called attention to the need for the rethinking of the Dutch organ (Kriek and Zandt 1964, pp. 25–6), and by 1951 Flentrop was creating the perfect classical organ at DOETINCHEM, with its formative Great, Chair and two Pedal towers (Kriek and Zandt 1964, pp. 84–5):

Hoofdwerk		*Rugwerk*		*Borstwerk*	
*Prestant	8	*Prestant	4	Prestant	2
Quintadeen	16	Holpijp	8	Eikenfluit (oak)	8
Roerfluit	8	Quintadeen	8	Fluit	4
Octaaf	4	Roerfluit	4	Gemshoorn	2
Ged. Fluit	4	Octaaf	2	Octaaf	1
Nasard	$2\frac{2}{3}$	Quint	$1\frac{1}{3}$	Cymbel ($\frac{1}{3}'$)	II
Octaaf	2	Scherp (1')	IV	Regaal	4
Mixtur ($\frac{1}{3}'$)	V–VI	Sesquialter	II		
Trompet	8	(treble)			
		Dulciaan	8		

Pedal

*Prestant	16
Octaaf	8
Octaaf	4
Nachthoorn	2
Mixtur (2')	IV
Bazuin	16
Schalmei	4

Rp/Hw, Bw/Hw
Hw/Ped, Rp/Ped
Case-design by J. G. A. Heineman
* Pipes in the case-front

Even making a 4' regal stop was something notable for the time. The classical case of Doetinchem can certainly be seen as an improvement on the freer non-classical cases of Marcussen–Andersen (e.g. Utrecht Nikolaikerk, 1957), whose geometric designs incorporate important oblique lines and whimsically shaped flats of a kind unknown to the old builders but much regarded throughout Europe during the last two decades. Nevertheless, other classical features of Doetinchem became the norm: open-toe voicing, mechanical action, encased (but not enclosed) departments and in general an attempt to respond to the natural acoustic of the church. These ideas were understood as fundamental by the younger builders. Such instruments went far beyond the theories of the *Orgelbewegung*, and it is a mistake to regard them as mere baroque pastiche.

In the U.S.A. meanwhile, a compound cultural heritage had led to a complex situation as far as Organ Reform was concerned. In some cities, Boston in particular, small organs were still being made in the 1920s with mechanical action. But the indirect German influences on Walter Holtkamp resulted in his contract for an unencased *Rückpositiv* to be added to the 1922 Skinner organ in the Cleveland Museum of Art as early as 1933:

$$8.4.2\tfrac{2}{3}.2.1.1\tfrac{3}{5}.1\tfrac{1}{3}.4.\text{III}$$

Such a department must have seemed startlingly new, and was again the result of collaboration between builder and musician, in this case Melville Smith: its sliderchest was in advance of the Freiburg Praetorius Organ, even though its multiple valve-system was doomed once purer ideas took root after the war. In the same period as the Holtkamp positive, G. D. Harrison, an Englishman working for the Aeolian–Skinner Organ Co. in the 1930s, had a great influence on the development of voicing and tone-production; the low pressure he tried out in the organ at Groton, contracted for in 1935, must have opened organists' minds to new ideas, as must the stoplist for his 1934 organ in Westminster Choir College Chapel, N.J., with its three manuals including a Choir Organ of:

16.8.8.4.4.2⅔.2.1⅗.III.8

These organs were the earliest 'new' organs in the U.S.A.—'baroque organ-experimental', as Harrison called that of 1936–7 in the Germanic Museum, Harvard (Fesperman 1975, p. 44)—and were somewhat removed from the north-German ideal lurking behind *Orgelbewegung* theories. Cavaillé-Coll and Silbermann were much admired, at least on paper, and the resulting warmth of tone compensated for the crude reeds and compound stops. But the German influence can also be seen in the 1939 Harrison design for WESTMINSTER COLLEGE: a 'Praetorius Organ' installed with advice from Carl Weinrich (*ibid.* p. 59):

Hauptwerk		*Positiv*		*Pedal*	
Gedackt	8	Quintadena	8	Bourdon	16
Spitzflöte	4	Rohrflöte	4	Gedacktpommer	8
Principal	2	Nachthorn	2	Koppelflöte	4
Scharf	III	Sifflöte	1	Krummhorn	8
Krummhorn	8	Nasard	2⅔	Krummhorn	4
		Terz	1⅗		

In several American organ-schools, from the neo-baroque ideals of 1935 to the eclecticism of 1960, there has often been a liking for the un-encased organ: the organ of naked ranks of pipes sitting on a chest and perched on a wall or in a gallery, very often played by non-mechanical actions. No doubt German influence from the early days of the *Orgelbewegung* was behind this taste. One important early example was the Holtkamp positive in Cleveland, another the 1937 Harrison–Skinner in the Germanic Museum, Harvard.

Soon after World War II, academic and musicological writers in the U.S.A. leant as heavily on old German treatises for matters relevant to organs as they did on German writings—and even German prose-style—in other musical spheres. Although this German influence eventually led to such writers as Bunjes attempting a more rational and sensible language of organ terms, it had one serious drawback: 'German' meant specifically 'West German'. Very influential indeed on the way organ-building has developed throughout the world since 1945 has been the relative in-accessibility of the East German organs, notably those of Silbermann himself. The whole direction of German and American organ-building shifted in the aftermath of Marshal Zhukov's visa-checkpoints in the east away from the instruments so carefully studied in the 1927 Freiberg Conference and on to the Schnitger schools in the north; this trend was abetted by the Walcha recordings for *Archiv* already referred to. Thus any European influence on American builders tended to become polarized: it was a question either of the moribund national schools of France and England or of the rather severe, impersonal styles of the West German builders.

Gradually European builders exported small organs to the U.S.A. (Rieger by 1952, Flentrop by 1954); in 1956 Flentrop made a significant address to the American Guild of Organists; and in 1956–7 Beckerath consolidated the trend by taking a large 44-stop organ of four manuals and simple geometric box-design to the Germanic capital of Cleveland (Trinity Lutheran Church—see Pape 1978). Naturally, the larger native firms such as Schlicker were influenced by such organs, and while Beckerath went on to build several equally important and formative organs in Canada (Montreal), native builders like the American Charles Fisk (Andover) and the Canadian Casavant Frères (Quebec) soon produced their own versions of the new styles. It was in 1961 that Fisk made for the Mount Calvary Church, Baltimore 'the first sizable mechanical action organ built in the United States in this century' (Fesperman 1975, pp. 75 f), with Fisk's wonderfully simple aim 'that old music be played right'. Shallow cases and classical design, sliderchests, low pressures ($1\frac{3}{4}''$ for manuals, $2\frac{3}{8}''$ for pedal), *mécanique suspendue* and a neo-baroque stoplist on two large manuals together produce an organ in which 'each of the classic essentials for an optimum design was treated as it might have been in the early eighteenth century' (*ibid.*)—in the words of the builder, 'typically American . . . naive, non-academic'. A further example of the new-old organs was Casavant's of 1963 for ACADIA UNIVERSITY, typical of the small instrument inspired by European Organ Reformers (Phelps 1967, p. 13):

Hw	$16.8.8.4.4.2.IV.8$
Bw	$8.4.2.1\frac{1}{3}.II.II.8$
Ped	$16.8.4.IV.16$

The Acadia case is elegant and classical, though obviously modern; such organs were far in advance of the big unencased instruments made by the larger firms (such as Möller's paired organs in the Church of the Immaculate Conception, Washington D.C., 1970), which rarely play with the geometric shapes as inventively as they could easily be made to.

In North America as a whole, Flentrop, Metzler, Ahrend, Frobenius, Janke and others have gone on to build important instruments of great beauty; up to 1976, five firms have each made more than 35 organs for the U.S.A. (Beckerath, Bosch, Flentrop, Rieger and Walcker—Pape 1977, p. 147). Recently, more specific stylistic influences have become apparent even in larger conventional instruments, such as the classical French elements in the stoplist and voicing at St. Thomas, New York (G. F. Adams, 1969) or the Italian department in the large electric organ of the First Congregational Church, Los Angeles (Schlicker, 1969). While it may be true that neither organ shows a complete understanding of its putative models, such attempts are important stepping-stones towards stricter historical copies—a trend so successfully followed by almost countless American harpsichord-makers of recent years. The young American organist feels obliged to hear old European organs, and the seasoned virtuosi naturally introduce elements or sounds they have heard in Europe when they come to advise on a new organ in the U.S.A. (e.g. Power Biggs and the 1958 Flentrop organ in the Busch-Reisinger Museum, Harvard). The result of these factors is a fitful and still sparse but at best a very lively organ-culture in the States (see Louder and Wolff's essay 'Future Trends' in Pape 1978), constantly aiming at historical truth which, if it is truth, cannot go out of date.

In Britain, the situation was one of more or less unbroken gloom until the last few years saw the emergence of small, young firms not always well-positioned financially but serving as hotbeds of enlightened ideas. It seems to be true that the Organ Revival in England 'really took root only with the opening of the organ in the Royal Festival Hall, London, in 1954' (Clutton 1963, p. 115), but even then the roots were thin, weedy and unprogenitive. Only in 1958–9 was the curtain on the classical organ lifted somewhat higher, with the two little organs built for the Finnish Seamen's Mission (Marcussen) and Danish Seamen's Chapel (Frobenius). At the Festival Hall in 1954, despite the thought put into it by the adviser (Ralph Downes) and builder (Harrison & Harrison), the quasi-comprehensive nature of the organ results in little more than an out-moded compromise organ characteristic of a period, still with us, in which eclecticism seems a possible and worthwhile aim. The Festival Hall's 103 stops provide German flutes, Anglo-German choruses, French reeds and other elements carefully calculated to allow many types of organ music. But the size of the organ, the sprawling, largely un-encased construction and electro-pneumatic action make it impossible for either player or listener to achieve true sympathy with any musical style other than the town-hall transcription, of which presumably it had hoped to sound the death knell. Nor did the Festival Hall organ have much direct influence on other new organs, although English organists did suddenly become aware of what a Quintadena or a Cornet was and hastened to have one when finance made it possible to rebuild their Willis or Walker. The cause of tracker action was also slow to find much support in Britain, at least in practice; Noel Mander's trackers of 1961 at St. Vedast, London, made use of new materials and seemed important in their time. Only ten years ago it was impossible to imagine a book being produced in which all the new British organs listed in it were, though small, nevertheless mechanical and encased in a classical construction (Rowntree and Brennan 1975).

The most that an English organ of 1960 could hope for was a touch of eclecticism, for example by combining an English Swell with a Positive manual and a large pedal of mixed European lineage (J. W. Walker, Italian Church, London, 1959). The 1969 organ by Grant, Degens & Bradbeer at New College, Oxford is 'primarily based on the North European School' but is also able to give a 'true performance of French classical organ-music' (Lumsden 1970, p. 84). Whether the recent organs in Britain by Frobenius, Rieger, Beckerath, Marcussen, Hradetzky, Metzler and Ahrend will lead to a lively national organ-culture or remain as isolated, foreign instruments cannot be said; some, particularly the Hradetzkys, could prove counter-productive. Perhaps organists will come to see that on the one hand they must accept a stylistic limit in their instrument and that on the other the older the sound aimed at by the builder, the more it will reach back to a period when there can not have been so much difference in basic sound between one European organ-type and another. In any case, the financial difficulties of the larger British firms over the last few years may well mean that a new English organ-school is about to emerge.

The French organ has developed on roughly similar lines to the English, the peculiar French term 'neo-classical' indicating not a classical organ but a frenchified composite or eclectic organ designed to play both de Grigny and Bach, both Franck and Messiaen. Most of the larger French churches have such an organ, many made by Gonzalez on the advice of N. Dufourcq. Closer imitations of older French styles have been more recently attempted, for example the partial Bedos copy (with low pitch) by J. G. Koenig at Sarre-Union in 1968, built into an old case (see also Plates 48, 49). In France as in England, 'restoration' of old organs has been almost universally disastrous; nor have French builders and their advisers yet shaken off the notions that resulted in, for example, the intact pedal department at Auch Cathedral (1693/1832) being rebuilt in 1959 from a classical specification of flutes 8' and 4' (C–e) with reeds 8' and 4' (FF–e) to an eclectic, international 16.16.8.8. 4.16.8.4. Few builders in France, as in England, have shown enlightened attitudes towards the subtle problems of historic style, although the views aired in the journal *Renaissance/Connoissance de l'Orgue* have helped to improve matters. Factions characterize the French scene even more than they do in other countries, and although a major restoration project such as Saint-Gervais, Paris can last for years, involving careful discussion on one hand and sour dispute on the other, the finished product is not certain to be free of compromise and temporized solutions.

In Italy the late 1960s saw a movement towards a version of the *Werkprinzip* organ, with typical Italian choruses and even Italian reeds of the early nineteenth-century kind. Indeed, Italy offers some curious examples of a strong, idiosyncratic organ-culture on which a few players and well-read organ advisers have attempted to graft quite foreign and frankly alien elements. The result, in the isolated examples such attempts are limited to, betray a strange eclecticism of which the *Grand' Organo* of S. Maria Assunta, MERANO (Formentelli, 1967–8) is typical (Krauss 1968):

diapasons	$8.4.2.1\frac{1}{3}.1.\frac{2}{3}.\frac{1}{2}.\frac{1}{3}.\frac{1}{4}$
flutes	$8.4.2\frac{2}{3}.2.1\frac{3}{5}$
reeds	$8.4.$

Larger three-manual organs such as the Chiesa dei Servi, Bologna (Tamburini) unite an Italian chorus, German and French mutations, Spanish Trumpet, Italian compass and *Werkprinzip* relationships between the manuals, the whole played by a mechanical action. *Rückpositiven* are also not unknown in recent Italian organs (Rovereto, for example), but even smaller organs have attempted to be comprehensive, like Zanin & Figlio's organ of 1968 in S. Severino, BOLOGNA:

Go	$8.4.2.1\frac{1}{3}.1.\text{IV}.8.2.\text{II}.8.8$
Pos	$8.4.2.1\frac{1}{3}.1.8.2\frac{2}{3}.8$
Ped	$16.8.8.4.16$

Bibliography

ANDERSEN, P. G., *Orgelbogen* (Copenhagen, 1956; Eng. trans., London, 1969)
CLUTTON, C. and NILAND, A., *The British Organ* (London, 1963)
COIGNET, J. L., 'Is the French Neo-Classical Organ a Failure?', *The Organ Yearbook*, 4 (1973), 52–66
FESPERMAN, J., *Two Essays in Organ Design* (Raleigh, 1975)
FRIIS, N., *Th. Frobenius & Co. 1909–1959* (Kongens Lyngby, 1959)
INGERSLEV, F. and FROBENIUS, W., *Some Measurements of the End-Corrections and Acoustic Spectra of Cylindrical Open Flue Organ Pipes* (Copenhagen, 1947)
JONGEPIER, J., *75 Jaar Flentrop Orgelbouw* (Zaandam, 1978)
KRAUSS, E., 'L'organo della chiesa parrochiale di Santa Maria Assunta in Merano', *L'organo*, 6.ii (1968), 245–8
KRIEK, P. H. and ZANDT, H. S. J., *Organum novum* (Sneek, 1964)
LUMSDEN, D., 'The New Organ of New College, Oxford', *The Organ Yearbook*, 1 (1970), 84–6
NOACK, F., 'Trends in American Organ-Building in 1976', *ISO Information*, 15 (1976), 5–10
OUSSOREN, H. L., 'Il contributo di Sybrand Zachariassen allo studio degli antichi sistemi di misura delle canne', *L'organo*, 10.i (1972), 29–48

PAPE, U., *The Tracker Organ Revival in America* (Berlin, [1978])

PAPE, U., 'Der mechanische Orgelbau in Amerika seit 1935, II', *Ars organi*, 53 (1977), 144–52

PHELPS, L., *A Short History of the Organ Revival* (St. Louis, 1967)

ROWNTREE, J. P. and BRENNAN, J. F., *The Classical Organ in Britain 1955–1974* (Oxford, 1975)

While compromise organs, eclectic designs, expensive rebuilds or other foolish instruments in our cathedrals will no doubt continue to deflect the true development of the organ, in three important respects knowledge has become refined beyond the anticipation of the Organ Reformers of the interwar years. These are: understanding the true nature and purpose of each particular organ-type; deducing more from fact than from conjecture what each composer of organ music requires; and restoring old organs without anachronism, or at least in so far as that is possible for an organ that may itself belong to different periods.

These three developments are related but are not particularly committed historically. They do not of themselves assume that 'old organs are best'; they do not favour any one period above another—most connoisseurs have their own favourites, though the time is surely not yet ripe for copying a pristine Hope-Jones unit-organ; and they recognize that even the eclectic organ is a historical phenomenon typical of its period. Development in organ-thinking will move during the next half-century towards more awareness of style, of the kinds of music required by each organ type and *vice-versa*, of the virtues and faults of each period or area, and of the need to accept these faults in the way that an oboe player anxious to understand e.g. Hotteterre's music will accept the 'faults' of a late seventeenth-century oboe. In the past lies the future of the organ, and so much of what has been done since 1945 has been geared to understanding that past. It is possible to imagine organs of a totally new type: organs beyond the dreams of Hope-Jones in which new pipe forms or myriad electronic sound-producers are operated by whatever means contemporary technology may suggest (computers, memory banks), 'organs' for which some schools of composition have already found appropriate musical language. But meanwhile, the influence of the past is daily growing, and with it comes a reaction to superficially conceived organs of the *Orgelbewegung* type, many of which have only the poorest mechanical action. In the words of one particular builder, 'we feel that the trackers of the last twenty years, with [in] other words the "screaming neo-baroque boxes", with their inflexible wind, low cut-ups, waste of tin and rattling metal actions are not serving the musical needs. Even an old 1880 tracker action [organ] is musically superior to those neo-baroque organs' (Fritz Noack in *ISO Information* 15).

Lines of development in Europe are evident in the work of a few builders whose specialized restoration of old organs of various periods is matched by a pronounced idea, in their new organs, of what makes beauty of sound. Organ restoration is still uneven; but there were a few interesting attempts made in this direction during the late 1960s, and each year brings greater hope in the handful of builders who accept as little compromise as possible. A good example is Metzler & Söhne, who have restored several baroque Swiss organs to the tone that conscientiously collected data suggest to have been that intended (Muri, 1962–72—see Plate 28). Often this sound is surprisingly strong, suggesting either that Metzler's taste for strong sound (particularly before about 1970) has influenced the thinking behind the restoration, or that a new approach, starting without preconceived notions, has resulted in a sound unexpected by those used only to the dubiously restored organs of southern Germany. Either way, advanced builders such as Metzler (see Plate 50), Ahrend, Fisk and Brombaugh (see Plate 51) are obviously related closely to the past—a position that it has taken time to reach. Thus at the Grossmünster, Zürich in 1959, Metzler made a conventional *Werkprinzip* case of modern geometric design (P. G. Andersen) and a conventional stoplist composite enough in its make-up (Swell, reeds *en chamade*, harmonic Trumpet, etc.) though naturally by then without a full palette of string and romantic flute stops. But in 1963, Bernhardt Edskes joined the firm, aiming to make new organs in the spirit of the old; and by 1969, St. Nikolas, Frauenfeld held fewer compromises. The third manual is a truer *Brustwerk*, the stoplist is thoroughly classical, and the large, shallow case of solid oak is more truly fitting in its context. The importance of this case to the sound cannot be overstressed: the whole organ shows (in the words of the builder) 'a logical arrangement deplored by adversaries as being merely historical yet [which] is modern in design and technologically advanced' (*ISO Information* 8). Such historically inspired organs have a wide spectrum of colours, including rarer stops like the Dolkan, Suavial, doubled case-front pipes (joined at the feet) and French reeds. Some firms, indeed, would not call their strong, unencumbered reeds 'French' but assume rather that the tone is time-honoured, historical and traditional, even 'normal' before the baroque builders refined them during the seventeenth century.

The tendency towards strict and very specific stylistic imitation is becoming increasingly marked, particularly for organs commissioned by universities for whom restrictions imposed by a liturgy, circumscribed finances and the individual taste of the organist concerned are not so severe as they are in the average church or cathedral. Thus French classical organs could be found influencing the design of a university organ of 1970 in Holland (see Plates 48, 49) or the U.S.A.; as the years pass, these designs will admit of less compromise. And in the later 1970s closer French copies are already being planned or made (Taizé, by Ahrend; Montreal McGill University, by Wolff; a Silbermann copy in Basel by Metzler). It may only be a question of a few years before a classical Italian organ of 1600 or an English Restoration organ of 1680 is made for such specialist clients. Already the influence of Schnitger has passed from general approval (1920, Hamburg Jakobikirche) to compromised restoration (1950s, Steinkirchen etc.), to fairly close copying (Scheveningen, 1973) and to truer restoration (Stade, 1975—see Plates 20, 21, 22). The last includes a faithful restoration of galleries, casework (anticipated by Ahrend's restoration of the 1615 Bremen Martinikirche, 1962), keyboards (with short octave), pipework, higher pressure and unequal temperament, the whole resulting in an organ of limited musical repertoire but unlimited musical instruction. It seems likely that by *c.* 1990 an organ will be built for a church in which builder and consultant have planned to copy exactly the Schnitger conception, including such details as original compass and pitch. The fine, recently published study of the Schnitger organ at Cappel (see list of references for section 12) should prove helpful and formative. Even in Britain, pretty copies of old organ cases (such as Bruggencate's neo-Schnitger at Haverfordwest, 1974) suggest that it is only time before the historical copy becomes an active force. For the moment, British builders may have to pass through the *Orgelbewegung* phases and are already producing very creditable north German instruments with fewer eclectic elements (Collins's organ of 1976 for Southampton University) and some promising 'restorations' (Mander at St. James, Clerkenwell). It will be some years before England sees a new-old organ of the kind built (not faultlessly) by Marc Garnier for Saint-Paul, Strasbourg (1976), with springchests for the 13 stops, *mécanique suspendue*, short octave, cuneiform bellows and an 'antique' console.

Meanwhile, organ-building is again in a changing state, and even the enlightened fraternity shows a very wide gap of attitude between its members—between, for example, the fine detail of the restorations under way in Groningen (A-kerk and Martinskerk) and the brashness of the big eclectic organ-reconstruction in Rotterdam Grote Kerke (Marcussen–Zachariassen), with its 86 stops scattered over a Dutch-German chorus, French mutations, quasi-Spanish Trumpets, Hanseatic pedals and much else. On the whole, progress is measured and moderate, since organists are reluctant to scan their instrument's history and prefer to find comfort in assumptions that have no historical basis whatever—such as that 'liturgical demands' make it necessary to have a Swellbox for Anglican chant. Or it could be that financial climate is critical. For although the 1972 organ made for the Baptist Church, Toledo, U.S.A.

by John Brombaugh, which for the first time followed certain characteristics of the sixteenth-century Dutch master Niehoff—type of case design, hammered lead pipes, short keys—was no more expensive than most 19-stop organs, the ideas opened up by such an instrument seem to be able to flower only in a luxurious economy. From the first, the plan for a Niehoff organ at Wellesley College, for example, suffered from financial problems.

At the same time, what appears to be a small detail in the restoration of an old organ may lead to a whole new way of thinking about organs. For example, short keys imply certain playing techniques which in turn will govern the design of a new keyboard if conditions allow the organist to specify some kind of historic copy. Or when Flentrop introduced flexible wind to the restored organ at Evora, he began a move that will have repercussions amongst all thinking builders (see Charles Fisk's essay 'The Organ's Breath of Life' in Pape 1978), both in new organs and in restorations of old. This may be especially true of organs made for ideal conditions in universities or other secular contexts, and the gap between the church and the non-church organ may increase. But whether for church or concert hall, cathedral or university, better organs will be by definition not only those of striking beauty (Toledo, Frauenfeld) but those whose voicing techniques suggest, in the words of J. Holtz concerning Frauenfeld (*ISO Information* 8), 'the breathing of a choir. The over-perfected and explosive speech of the neo-baroque organ of the fifties has completely disappeared. One can once again experience with this instrument that an organ is a large wind instrument.'

o

Glossary

Aulos (pl. *auloi*; 'pipe') was the most important of the Greek wind instruments and consisted of two slender cylindrical tubes diverging from a short barrel at the top of which was enclosed a reed, probably a double reed. The *aulos* was descended from Near Eastern pipes and was called *tibia* by the Romans.

Backfall is that part of a mechanical action—usually a strip of wood similar in thickness to the key but shaped deeper and stronger at its mid or pivotal point—that transfers the upward movement at the distal end of the key to a downward movement pulling down the tracker. See Fig. 10, p. 92.

Bourdon, a word complex both in history and in etymology denoting in the context of organs various kinds of stop: bass pipes in an early positive organ, latched on to produce a held tone (fifteenth century; cf. the name for the low strings of a hurdy-gurdy or the drones of the bagpipes); the large front or inside pipes, so named in some sixteenth-century contracts; the stopped pipes an octave below the main 8' rank (usual meaning, particularly in French organs); the basic pedal 16' rank in English organs since about 1820.

Brustwerk is the 'breast department' of a German organ, so called because its pipe chest, usually but not always with its own keyboard, is encased below the *Hauptwerk* (Great Organ) 'in the breast' of the organ. Many early *Brustwerke* contained only a regal or two, but even when flue stops were added the manual kept its character as a chamber organ or large 'regals'. Such chests were common during the seventeenth century, were too small for most tastes in the eighteenth and were revived in the twentieth. They are now often given the shutters of a Swell organ, a compromise that kills true *Brustwerk* character and fails to give it the character of a true Swell.

Castellated towers in the context of organ-design are those side-towers (see Pipe towers) shaped and decorated at the top to look like battlements on a medieval tower. This decorative detail may well have had deeper meaning: see the caption to Plate 1.

Chair organ is the English term for the little organ separate from the main organ and placed behind the player's stool or chair. The terms *chaire*, *chayre*, *cheire* etc. are known only from the seventeenth and eighteenth centuries, but throughout large parts of Europe over the previous two centuries various names had circulated for the same 'little organ': *positieff an die Stoel* (Delft, 1461), *positif de devant* (Rouen, 1524), *positiff en rück* (Schlick's *Spiegel*, 1511) and even *la cheyere* (Valenciennes, 1515). See also *Rückpositiv*.

Chorus is a term in modern parlance used to denote the basic ensemble in an organ: one speaks of 'flue chorus with or without mixtures' (meaning the 16.8.4.2⅔.2 diapason ranks) or the 'reed chorus' (meaning the group of 16', 8' or 4' reeds) as distinct from 'the flutes' or 'the mutations'.

Conduits are the little wind trunks, usually lead tubes, leading from a pipe chest to a pipe foot in those instances where the pipes stand some way away from the chest—for example, those in the case-front of the organ—and so require the wind to be conveyed specially for them.

Cornice is the horizontal moulding at the top of a structure, crowning it and projecting from it.

Cut-up is an organ-builder's term for the height of the mouth of a flue pipe considered as a fraction of its width. Thus a 'quarter cut-up' or a 'cut-up of 1 in 4' means that the rectangle of the mouth is four times as broad as it is high. The larger the cut-up, the duller the note produced by any given wind-pressure, but if the cut-up is beyond a certain height the note will jump to a harmonic.

Cymbale is a late medieval word presumably derived from (and alluding to the sound of?) Cymbalum (q.v.) and denoting a high chorus mixture separated off from the *Blockwerk*. The precise contents varied from period to period and country to country. Henri Arnaut de Zwolle's contained a third-sounding rank, while that of Gottfried Silbermann merely duplicated the top two or three ranks of the *Mixtur*. For the French classical period, *cymbalisée* denoted a mixture (q.v.) or *fourniture* (q.v.) that began with high ranks, broke back twice in each octave, and did so to the next rank in each case (12th to 8ve not 5th, 22nd to 19th not 15th etc.).

Cymbalum (pl. *cymbala*), a Vulgate version of the Greek *kymbala*, denotes the late Roman cymbals, which were metal plates with concave centres. By the eleventh century, the term was used for small bowl-shaped bells perhaps arranged in a tuned series and offering *exempla* of acoustic phenomena, i.e. the properties of struck solids as distinct from plucked strings or blown pipes.

Difference tone stops are those stops, known intuitively to all good organ-builders of all periods but specifically described and concocted during the late baroque, which contribute 'difference tones' to the total sound by making use of the observation that particularly at low pitches a pipe sounding a fifth above another will combine with it to give the illusion that there is a suboctave being generated. The equation $16' + 10\frac{2}{3}' = 32'$ was one to be much favoured at the irrational end of the Age of Reason. 'Resultant tone stops' or 'acoustic bass stops' are other names once in use.

Double touch is the name given by twentieth-century British builders to that action, necessarily indirect, which operates more stops when the key is fully depressed than when it is only half depressed. The key (or stop-knob) therefore operates as a mere switch, though now with two on-positions.

Ears-and-beard are constructions added to the mouths of organ-pipes. *Ears* are small metal plates soldered at the sides so that they project outwards and help to direct the windflow on to the languid or upper lip; they can also be used for fine tuning of stopped pipes, as in the best modern Gedackts with soldered caps. *Beards* (much more recent in origin) are little metal or wooden rods, one of which is fixed between the ears to act as a front baffle and so to stabilize the tone by hindering the formation of vortices at the mouth. Such beards therefore make it easier to keep a reliable pitch and timbre in narrow-scaled, string-toned stops.

End correction is that factor or quantity (the larger the wider the pipe) that has to be added to the length of an open pipe to calculate the pitch of the note it produces, an addition necessary because the wave of compression produced within a pipe swings out some distance beyond its end before it returns as a wave of rarefaction.

Entablature is that part of a classical structure immediately above the column and including architrave, frieze, cornice and any other moulding.

Finial is a term probably derived from 'final' to denote any ornament on top of a canopy, gable, pediment or, in organs, pipe tower, finishing it off and completing the profile.

Flue denotes the windway in an organ pipe, i.e. the narrow rectangular space through which the wind is allowed to pass from the foothole to the mouth and so become directed on to the upper lip. Hence 'flue stop' as distinct from 'reed stop', in which the pipe produces its sound by means of a beating reed.

Foothole denotes the hole at the bottom of the pipe foot through which the wind passes from chest or conduit to pipe-flue. Such theorists as Sorge (*c.* 1750) calculated the foothole to have the same area as the flue. In the history of organ-building, the foothole has been more than a structural detail, for on its size depends a great deal of the character of the tone produced by the pipe: the large foothole of 'open-toe voicing' requires relatively low wind and helps to produce the direct tone once characteristic of all organs before the late baroque builders (particularly in England) began to refine it, emaciate it or vary it according to different wind pressures.

Fourniture is probably derived from a late medieval term and denotes the basic French mixture *pour fournir le plein jeu* ('to furnish the full chorus'), according to the contract at Ste-Geneviève-des-Ardents, Paris, in 1549. The Parisian mixture of the late seventeenth century acquired a standard composition, its 8ve and 5th ranks breaking back at f and f¹ to an octave below in each case.

Impost-cornice is the horizontal moulding projecting from a structure (e.g. organ case) not at the top, as with a crowning cornice, but at the impost level, i.e. about halfway up at the level just below the pipe chest, at a point where any pillars holding up the pipe-chest storey would be meeting it.

Key-slider denotes that early kind of organ-action in which the key is itself the frontal end of a slider whose holes admit wind from channel or chest to pipe when aligned with the foot hole of the pipe. Such 'keys' therefore need to be pulled and pushed rather than pressed. See Fig. 3.

Languid is the name given the plate of metal fixed horizontally across the top of the foot of a metal flue organ pipe and leaving a long slit through which the wind passes (the 'flue'). Its front edge is bevelled.

Magrephah is the small ancient Hebrew instrument supposed to have been shaped like a rake or shovel, containing pipes (short and untuned?) sounded by bellows-driven wind and used as a signal in services held during the Talmudic period of the Temple. Nothing is certain about its construction, sound, precise purpose, origin or decline.

Mixture is that stop, or that family of stops, that is composed of several ranks of pipes at various 8ve and 5th pitches (and occasionally of 3rd and even other pitches) designed to produce the penetrating 'chorus' sound so familiar in most organs of most periods. The history of mixtures is the history of the organ itself, and the contents, voicing and scaling of the various kinds of mixture stop vary more—and challenge the builder more—than any other single stop.

Monochord was a device used in Greece from the sixth century B.C. onwards and described by Boethius (*c.* A.D. 500) as a device (rather than a musical instrument) for demonstrating musical intervals on a string stretched over a soundboard or box. From about the eleventh century, the mono-chord was given musical uses in various iconographical and literary sources, but essentially it remained a demonstration-instrument like the *cymbala* or the theorists' *organum*.

Mouth is the name given to the horizontal slit-like opening of an organ pipe above the foot and at the lower end of the tube which will carry the wavelength of the sound produced by wind passing up from the flue to strike the upper lip of the mouth.

Mutation is an English term of uncertain origin used during the nine-teenth century to denote single or multi-rank stops introducing pitches other than unisons, sub-octaves and super-octaves to the tonal spectrum, in particular 5ths, 3rds and their 8ves. In modern parlance, a mutation is a rank of flute-like tone, perhaps wide-scaled but in any case not intended for use in the chorus (q.v.), and based on e.g. the $2\frac{2}{3}'$, $1\frac{1}{3}'$ and $1\frac{3}{5}'$ pitches. In the French classical organ, *les mutations* were those ranks remaining when the flue and reed chorus-stops were discounted, and thus included the 2' flute; in the Spanish organ over several periods, the *mutaciones* were the several registrations or stop-combinations.

Open-toe voicing, see Foothole.

Organo pleno is an Italianate term used (like 'Allegro', 'Presto' etc.) by composers of various nationalities from at least *c.* 1700 to denote the full chorus, usually of flue stops only, required for certain kinds of music (toccatas in Italy, preludes and fugues in Germany, first Kyrie interlude in France etc.). Each historical organ school had its own kind or own kinds of *organo pleno*, but today the term is interpreted by the organist in his own way, like César Franck's *fff*.

Organum, other than being the Latin equivalent of Greek *organon*, denotes the earliest type of polyphonic music sung, particularly in

Benedictine churches, from the ninth century onwards. No one knows whether the term originated as some kind of allusion to the instrument (did the parallel 8ves and 5ths as sung resemble the sound of an organ, and was the weaving of lines around a plainsong in some way an analogy to organ-playing?) or whether *organare* (cf. *organisandi*) simply meant 'to organize' or assemble in due order etc. the new parts added to the old melodies.

Orgelbewegung (Ger. 'organ movement') was the name gradually assumed by some leading German theorists in the 1920s for their approach to the building of organs. See Chapter 23.

Pallet is that part of a mechanical action—a long piece of wood basically rectangular in plan and triangular in cross-section—that acts as a valve, closing and opening the long mortice running below part of the pipe-channel, above which stand all the pipes belonging to one key. The pallet is operated by a rod (tracker (q.v.) or sticker (q.v.)) connected directly or indirectly to the key; it should not be too large, too small, too stiff, too easy, too noisy or too flexible. See Figs. 5, 6, 7, 9 and 10.

Pilaster is a rectangular column, particularly one set into a wall; in practice therefore, a partial column (or deep vertical moulding made to look like a partial column) protruding from a flat surface.

Pipe-flats and *pipe towers* are the English names, probably of ancient origin, for the two chief means of distributing sets of organ pipes in the case-front: *flats* are the flat expanses or fields of pipes, often very small and in several levels or tiers; *towers* are the narrow groups of taller pipes, often set in a semicircular or triangular cross-section, and protruding from the main surface and generally framing the flats.

Pipe-shades are those decorative panels, usually carved and often gilded, set above the tops of pipes in pipe-flats and pipe towers (q.v.) and so filling in spaces left by the stepwise line produced by the tops of those pipes. Often baroque builders outside France, Italy and England also added such panels below and/or between the feet of the pipes.

Plenum is in modern parlance a synonym for *organo pleno* but in the history of the organ has been used in various forms to denote the chief flue mixture or the total flue chorus produced by that mixture: *plein jeu* in the French classical organ, *ripieno* in the Italian, *plé* in the Spanish renaissance organ, *lleno* in the Iberian baroque organ, etc.

Positif is the French equivalent of *positive* or *Positiv* and thus denotes either a small organ (chamber organ, table organ, portable organ) or that part or chest of a larger organ that has the character and function of a separate small organ, perhaps set into the gallery-front behind the player (*Rückpositiv, positiv de dos*), or placed high above the main chest (*récit, écho,* Swell), or enclosed deep inside the main case (*écho, eco*), etc.

Principal always denotes one or more of the basic ranks of the organs (i.e. the fundamental open metal pipes) but has had various detailed meanings in different organ-cultures: in England from at least the sixteenth century, a single 4' rank the 8ve above the basic Diapason; in sixteenth-century Netherlands, the full chorus of the Great Organ produced by drawing the mixtures, case-pipes, sub- and super-octaves; in most but not all parts of Germany and Italy from at least *c.* 1600, the stop provided by the main case-pipes (i.e. 16' or 8' or 4' Diapason); in France, Spain and Scandinavia, generally replaced by other terms ('Montre', 'Flautado', 'Prestant' etc.).

Pull-blinds are those roller-blinds of fabric placed at the top and just inside the case-front of some Italian organs of the sixteenth to nineteenth centuries, which can be pulled down to cover the pipes of a case-front—a cheaper and, in cramped sites, more convenient alternative to wings (q.v.).

Putto (pl. *putti*) is the child's figure, in particular the cupid-like angel-boy, decorating structures of the baroque periods. On organs of the eighteenth century, from the lower reaches of the Danube to the coast of the North Sea, *putti* were often carved playing instruments 'contained' within an organ (violins, flutes, cellos, horns and eventually clarinets).

Quire is a modern convenience term, though ancient in origin, to distinguish that part of a church in which the choir and priests celebrate the liturgy from the choir itself, i.e. a band of singers performing there.

Reed strictly denotes that part of a reed-pipe that holds the brass tongue vibrating in the wind held within the boot of the pipe. A 'reed' is common parlance for 'reed stop'; see also Flue.

Regals is a term still of unknown origin (but probably German) denoting either a small keyboard instrument producing its sound from a set of beating reeds provided with little resonators (known from *c.* 1475) or a family of organ-stops built in the same way (i.e. without the longer resonators of the true reed stops) and placed in a larger organ, where by *c.* 1500 they might have a name describing their sound (e.g. Vox humana).

Roller is that part of a mechanical action—usually a cylindrical or eight-sided wooden rod—that transfers motion from one vertical plane to another. Thus it conveys the pressure and release transmitted (via a tracker) from a key situated vertically under one end of it to a tracker rising from its other end to the appropriate part of the pipe chest. See Figs. 9 and 10.

Roller-arm is that part of a mechanical action (most frequently a short batten of wood) connecting the roller (q.v.) to the tracker (q.v.). See Fig. 10.

Rollerboard is that part of a mechanical action, usually a flat rectangular board of wood with its unused corners sawn off, on to which the set of rollers (q.v.) is fixed by means of the bearing shafts at their ends rotating in a short block of wood glued to the rollerboard. See Fig. 9.

Roundel denotes a disc, medallion or other round decorative motif ornamenting an otherwise flat or plain surface between other architectural elements, e.g. in a spandrel.

Rückpositiv (Ger. 'back positive') is a term analogous to others in Scandinavia and the Netherlands to denote the little organ placed at the organist's back and built into the front of the gallery. During the sixteenth century various names circulated for it: *den stoel* or *im Stuhl* were common, perhaps indicating 'in the stool' (i.e. at the organist's chair), although it is also possible that *im Stuhl* meant 'at the foot' or 'in the lower storey' of the main organ. However large and whatever its tone and function, the *Rückpositiv* was always meant as a contrast to the *Hauptwerk* or main organ, which in parts of Germany and the Netherlands may well have been used far less often during the liturgy or the public recitals. It is still the most important of all secondary manuals in so far as (a) the classical repertories require it, and (b) its mechanical and acoustic properties are not easily imitable.

Scale is a technical term denoting the comparative sizes, in particular the diameters, of pipes. One speaks of a rank 'having a narrow scale', meaning that its diameters throughout are smaller than the usual Principal scales.

Splayed trackers are those that spread out fan-wise up from the key-ends to the chest above without the help of a rollerboard, splaying or rollers being necessary because the chest will always be wider than the keyboard since most pipes take up more room than a finger-key.

Sticker, see Tracker.

O

Tester is the canopy or little roof cantilevered out over a pulpit or other structure from which the sound of the speaker is reflected down to the listeners.

Tonos (pl. *tonoi*) is a particular distribution of tones and semitones over the kithara's octave e–e¹ to correspond to each of the Greek *harmoniai* or modes, each of which strictly speaking began on its own note.

Tracker is that part of a mechanical action—usually a thin strip of pine or similar wood—conveying the movement from key to pallet by *pulling* (Dutch *trekken*) down the pallet above when the finger key presses the key and by pulling up the key action when the pallet-spring is allowed to draw it back. A sticker on the contrary *pushes* the pallet open and therefore needs to be made heavier and stronger, like a rod or stick; pallets in such cases are located below the keys, e.g. those of a Chair Organ (q.v.).

Tribune denotes the platform or raised floor for the magistrate's chair in the apse of a Roman basilica, hence that part reserved for bishop or emperor in Carolingian times and hence any raised structure from which pronouncements or ceremonial contributions are made, e.g. pulpit or organ gallery.

Triforium denotes that tier-level above the main arches of quire or nave in a medieval cathedral that is no mere flat decorative arcade but a recessed gallery in which people may stand, the floor being placed on the vaulting arches of the aisles.

Trundle is that part of a mechanical action (usually a strong rod of wood) that by rotating transmits the movement of the stop-knob at the console to the slider end on a higher horizontal plane.

Wings or doors hinged to the side were usual for the full-size organs of many (or most?) areas of Europe before the end of the seventeenth century. Written sources suggest that their purpose was to protect the organ when not in use particularly during Advent and Lent, though from what is not certain—smoke, sun, dust, birds, bats, temperature changes? But at least part of the purpose must have been the visual effect (i.e. a decorative element in a piece of expensive equipment open to iconographical significance) and the acoustical advantage of having directional reflectors placed so near the source of sound.

Index of Subjects

Bold figures refer to plates and their captions

Index of Persons

Index of Organs

Bold figures refer to plates and their captions

PLATES

1. The 'world's oldest playing organ' on the west wall of the cathedral of
Notre-Dame, Valère sur Sion (Switzerland). Neither date nor provenance is
certain: *c.* 1380 is often claimed, but the style of the painted doors (now
replaced by copies) suggests *c.* 1435. Perhaps it was originally the organ for
nave, transept or quire of a larger church, such as the Abondance Abbey, Savoy.
The rear pedal-pipes belong to the eighteenth century, the present location
on the west wall to the seventeenth.

As a whole, the shape is very like the organ in mitre-form drawn by Henri
Arnaut de Zwolle and serves as an example of a basic medieval organ design
from which such fanciful shapes as Scheemda (see Plate 6) were conscious
developments. Although the Sion design is often compared to an altar, with its
painted wings or doors (which may not even belong to the original organ), it in
fact reflects two more formative desires of the builders: firstly, to show the
structural outline of an organ (narrow base with key-trackers behind the panels
leading up to a wider chest, supported by curved side pieces, the whole with a
vertical emphasis); and secondly, to convey certain graphic symbolisms (the
castellated towers suggesting the fortified town, the Heavenly Jerusalem, the
civitas dei of St. Augustine) See p. 50.

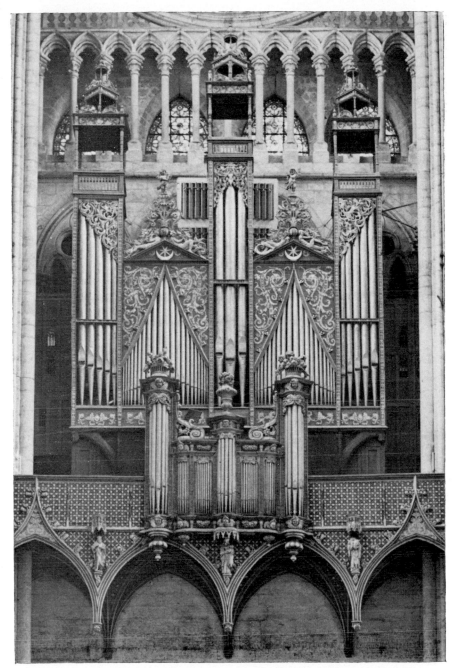

2. The west-end organ in *Amiens Cathedral* (France). Often dated to *c.* 1425, the main organ probably achieved this particular shape only during the sixteenth century (1549 rebuilt): early sketches of the original organ show it to have been plainer. The *Positif* belongs to 1623 and shows the simple design embellished with heavy carving that was to be typical of the classical French organ. The gallery looks like early fifteenth-century work, but both the location of the organ (originally in a transept) and the high Swellbox belong to the post-Revolution period.

3. The quire organ in *Saragossa Cathedral* (Spain), usually dated 1443. Like
Sion and Amiens, this organ preserves the towers of a walled town; but it also
appears to have two chest-levels which almost certainly were not reflected in
the structure of the organ itself. Since the horizontal trumpets are more recent
additions, there is doubt about what if anything occupied the horizontal panel
between the two chest-levels; how far this and many other 'old' cases were
altered over the centuries is very uncertain. Nevertheless, the photograph is
clear in its illustration of the *coro* or quire of a Spanish church: an enclosure
within the building, self-contained and holding on one side or both sides a
high organ speaking in several directions.

4. The rear façade of the organ on the south side of the quire in *S. Petronio, Bologna* (Italy). Both the south and more famous north façades of this organ preserve the flat gothic shape and original timbers of the organ made in 1474–83 and encased within a baroque framework of stone between 1661 and 1675. Natural to this Italian gothic design were the three pipe towers (longest in the middle) and the two double-storey pipe-flats between them, the whole designed in one completely flat vertical plane. Brescian and Tuscan builders of the following periods kept this plan even when they turned to renaissance or mannerist details (see Plate 10). See also pp. 64, 70, 84–5.

5. The organ on the north wall of *S. Bernardino, Verona* (Italy). A fifteenth-century organ of uncertain history, the instrument shows some important and typical characteristics of pre-baroque design: the flat case hanging on the wall, the straight lines (in all three dimensions), the doors or wings (in this instance closed), the casket-like tribune and gallery front (on which, in other areas of Europe, a small Chair Organ might be hung), and the proximity of the altar (out of view immediately to the right).

6. The organ from *Scheemda, Hervormde Kerk* (Netherlands), now an empty
case in the Rijksmuseum, Amsterdam. Usually dated 1526, the organ is typical
of the many small organs of northern Europe at the period—conventional in
the winged shape, the narrow base and the division into three pipe towers and
two double-storey pipe-flats, but exceptional in the detail of its flamboyant
gothic decoration. Obviously the space between keyboard and main chest-level
could be usefully given over to a small chest or regals or *Brustwerk*.

7. The organ from *St. Nicholaas, Utrecht*, now in the Middelburg Koorkerk (Netherlands) where it was removed from the Rijksmuseum, Amsterdam, in 1956. The main case of 1479–80 was made by Pieter Gerritsz of Utrecht. Double pipes, soldered together at the feet, are a characteristic of Dutch organs in the earlier period and have been made again by the more advanced builders of today. The Chair Organ was added in 1580 and—a further characteristic of Dutch organs—follows a much more curvaceous profile than the main organ; its mannerist pediments and pinnacles are obviously an updated version of the medieval castellations and finials (see Plate 3). See also pp. 81–2.

8. The west-end organ of the *Jakobikirche Lübeck*: main case or *Hauptwerk*
from 1504, chair organ or *Rückpositiv* of 1637 (rebuilt from or in the position
of a *Rückpositiv* of 1572), pedal-towers of 1673. The total ensemble, including
galleries and position, was typical of the larger churches in the Hanseatic cities
from the sixteenth century onwards—cities along the coast from Antwerp to
Königsberg, Riga and beyond, their churches with high brick vaults allowing
large, dominating organs, whether before or after the Reformation. The flat
Hauptwerk, given scale by the variegated pipe-flats, still preserves something
of the Sion shape and detail in its gothic filigrees and castellations (see Plate 1),
while the clustering effect of the protruding *Rückpositiv* pipe-towers is much
more in the style of the sixteenth-century Dutch or Brabant chair organs. In
their lanterns, pendants and side-panels, the pedal-towers clearly belong to the
seventeenth century, having presumably made it necessary for their builder to
discard the gothic wings to the main case; their slim lines are still those of a
period before the total breakdown of proportion characterized so many baroque
organs. See p. 97ff.

9. The organ in the south transept of the *Cathedral of Le Mans* (France). The province (Maine) and period (1501–36) are represented here by an organ less ornate than the high mannerist cases of Normandy and elsewhere (see Plate 10), but one nevertheless owing much to wood-carvers and joiners. Presumably the Great Organ chest itself did not stretch right across the transept end-wall, and the casework held a more modest instrument than it seems to—a characteristic too of the early Spanish and Italian organ. Both in this appearance of size and in its location at the end of a transept, the organ at Le Mans is typical of a cathedral instrument of the period.

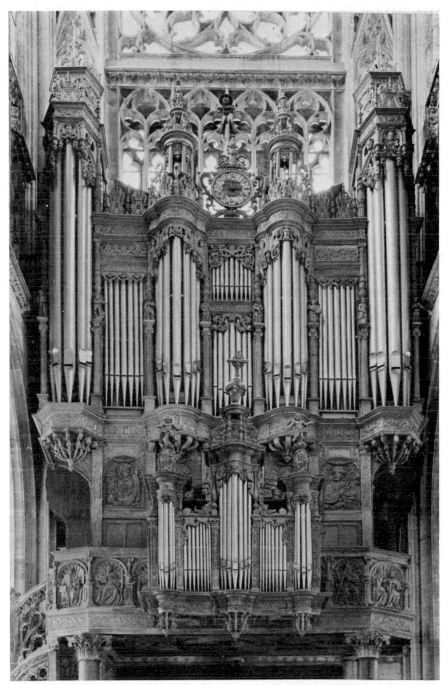

10. The free-standing organ and gallery at *Rouen, Saint-Maclou* (France). With the comparable great cases of Alençon and Caudebec-en-Caux, this instrument belongs to the years 1537–42 and shows a shape and a detail typical of mid-century Normandy. Pipe towers and pipe-flats are distributed in ever new and inventive patterns, the essential conventions behind which can still be seen in the overhanging sides and in the classical Chair Organ. See p. 86.

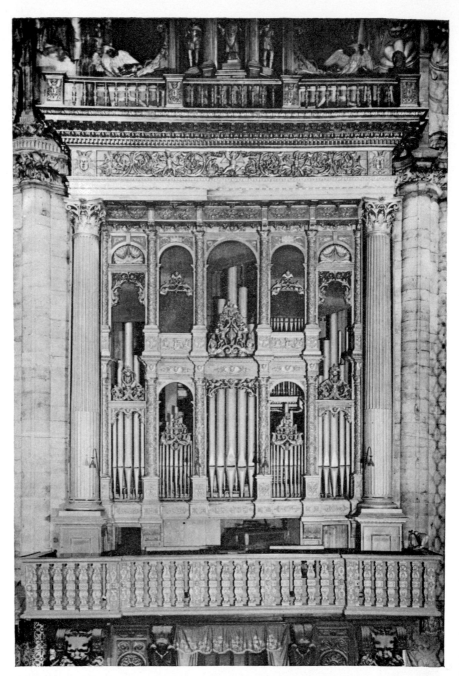

11. The south façade of the north organ in the quire of *Milan Cathedral* (Italy). This instrument, built in 1552 by G. G. Antegnati, was first placed against a wall near one of the side altars of the cathedral and had wings or doors painted in 1559 (the pull-blinds are a substitute). In 1578, the shape of the cathedral presbytery or quire was changed, and the Antegnati organ was placed there between pillars on the north side, matched by a new organ to the same design made for the south gallery by C. Valvassori. The Antegnati organ also received a rear façade. See pp. 83–5.

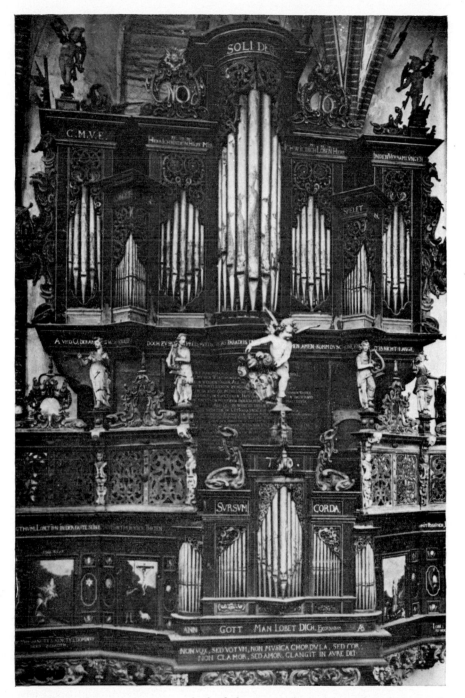

12. *Kloster Lüne*: an organ typical of the monastic or court chapels in north and central Germany during the seventeenth century. The ornate gallery and use of several media (statuary, painted panels, carving) would be exceptional for a parish church, but the overhanging sides of the main organ and the freer design of the Chair Organ could have been found in any kind of church.

13, 14. The original keyboards and case-front of the west-end organ in
Marienhafe (Germany). A classical north German or Frisian two-manual organ
of the period before and after Schnitger (in this instance, made in 1713 by
G. von Holy), Marienhafe is unusually well preserved (restored Ahrend &
Brunzema, 1970). The position of the stop-knobs, the recessed upper keyboard, the proximity of the *Rückpositiv* on the left, the type of pedalboard, the
spacious gallery, the west-end position, the overhanging sides to the Great
Organ and its miniature reflection in the Chair Organ are all typical of such
instruments. See pp. 101–3.

15. The west-end organ in the *Westerkerk, Amsterdam*. This church was built after the Reformation and hence had somewhat different priorities in design from most of the major Dutch churches in which stand the famous organs. The organ was placed against the end-wall of one of the arms of the church and forms with its gallery and pillared substructure a complete unit in principle more unified and striking than the usual gallery-with-organ. Behind the upper row of pillars (those visible in Plate 15) can be discerned the traditional curved structure rising between keyboards and chest. Further conventional details in the magnificent clock-like design of such seventeenth-century Dutch organs are the curvaceous Chair Organ, the triple storey of pipe-flats and the painted doors. See p. 147.

16. A detail of the keyboards and stop-levers of the west-end organ of *Kloster-neuburg Augustinian Abbey* (Austria), by J. G. Freundt (1636–42). The iron stop-levers sliding in grooves seem to have been popular on organs of central Europe, being (it seems) preferred by Arnolt Schlick and found both on large church organs and on small positives. In this instance they operate sliders but may well have originated as hand levers for springchests. See p. 142.

17. The west-end organ of *Auch Cathedral* (France), made in 1688–94 by J. de Joyeuse. The side towers holding the 16′ manual *Montre* still overhang the sides, as they continued to do during the French classical period; both large and small cases are of the kind to influence English builders, though the degree and amount of carved work was rarely found in England. Typical of the French organ are the single-storey pipe-flats and the rounded towers relieving the flat façades. Note that the subsidiary manuals (*Echo*, *Récit*) are not shown in the case design of such organs. See p. 104ff.

18. The transept or side chapel on the north side of *S. Domenico, Bologna* (Italy). Both the organ galleries and their position in the chapel are characteristic of the seventeenth-century Italian church, though in larger buildings the galleries would face down the nave. In fact, the left-hand organ case is a dummy and the music desk in the gallery front, if used at all, would be that from which to direct a small choir. The details of the organ design (one flat, pipes placed in mitre form, framework attached to the wall) could have been found throughout northern Italy in the eighteenth century.

19. The organ on the wall to the left of the altar in *S. Pietro in Vincolo, Rome*. The tripartite case-design was already typical of Roman organs in the sixteenth century, those of the seventeenth (as here) having a freer baroque shape and less classical ornamentation. See p. 126ff.

20, 21, 22. The case-front, keyboards and interior of the *Brustwerk* of the west-end organ in *St. Cosmae, Stade*, built in 1668–73 by B. Huss and his pupil Arp Schnitger. The pedal was separately contracted for in 1671. After both organ and gallery had been much rebuilt, the whole ensemble was restored to an authentic form in 1975 by Jürgen Ahrend: a landmark in the history of organ-restoration.

Schnitger's tendency to give a horizontal emphasis to his cases is already clear at Stade, where the Great Organ is joined by pipe-flats to both pedal towers: but note that the whole case is placed high under the ceiling. The keyboards, newly made by Ahrend, only partially protrude, though details of Huss's consoles are uncertain in this respect; either way, toe-pedalling would be the most feasible for an organist seated at such keyboards. The *Brustwerk* pipework from front to back is: Schalmei 4′ (Schnitger), double-conical Krummhorn 8′ (Schnitger), Scharf III (Huss, partly visible), 1′ and 1⅓′ (Paul Ott, 1948–9), Tertia 1⅗′ and Oktave 2′ (Huss) and three oak ranks (Huss): Blockflöte 4′ (open), Gedackt 8′ and Querflöte 8′ (open, but c¹–c¹¹¹ only). Note the oak chest and the pitch-letters written on paper at the front, near the reeds just inside the *Brustwerk* doors. See p. 101ff.

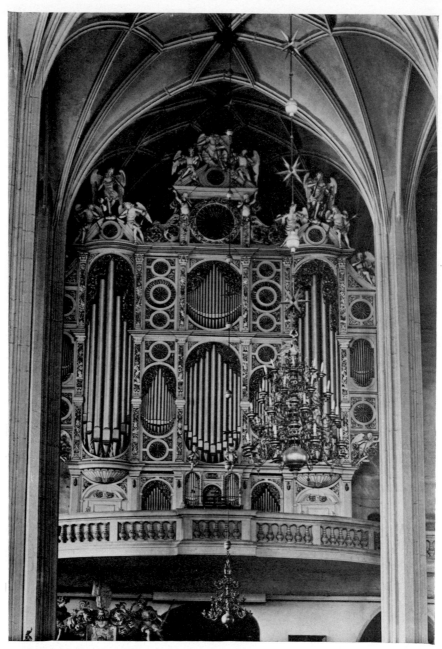

23. The west-end organ of *SS. Peter and Paul, Görlitz* (Germany), made in
1690–1703 by E. Casparini. For the large stone hall-church of Görlitz,
Casparini attempted an original and highly unusual design, with Italian
features (the roundels as at S. Giustina, Padua), central German features (the
vertical trumpets in the lowest storey as in Schütz's chapel at Dresden) and
various standard features (shallow case, rounded towers, three clear chest-
levels). Some of the details influenced later builders, such as the shape of the
pipe-flats. The roundels held the pipes of the pedal Mixture and were conducted off the pedal-chests. See p. 127.

24. The west-end organ of *Haarlem, Grote Kerk*, built in 1735–8 by C. Müller and engraved by J. C. Philips in 1763, three years before the child Mozart played it. The case, probably by J. van Logteren, has traditional Dutch features: the central round pipe-tower, the triple-storey pipe-flats, the *Oberwerk* case, the curved *Rückpositiv*, the independent gallery and substructure, making a total west-end ensemble not unlike certain Westphalian organs of the kind Müller knew and presumably aimed to introduce in a Dutch guise. Baroque, as opposed to classical, are the tower tops and coat-of-arms, the sunken pedal towers, the gallery decoration, the rhetorical statuary, the wooden side-consoles and the pyramidal shape to the whole; for a comparable classical shape, see Plate 15. See also p. 147.

25. The west-end organ in the village church of *Grosshartmannsdorf, near Dresden* (Germany), made in 1739–41 by Gottfried Silbermann. Typical of such organs are the general outlines of the case design (showing the manual chests on two levels), the rear of the case running into the wall and not free-standing, the sides not overhanging but running straight down, and the box-like unity of the whole (without Chair Organ or pedal towers). Since such features could be considered poor, compensation is given by the immediacy of sound in such churches: plaster walls and low ceilings, wooden galleries on three sides of the church, and a simple rectangular plan to the building. Any subtlety of voicing can therefore be heard clearly and directly. See pp. 114–15.

26. One of the ink-and-wash drawings for the organ in the *Hofkirche, Dresden*, begun in 1750–54 by G. Silbermann and completed after his death by J. G. Hildebrandt. (The white, gold and silver colouring has been reintroduced into the new case replacing that burnt by bombs in 1945.) The various 'poor' features listed in Plate 25 can also be found here; but the elegance of the whole produces a particularly fine example of baroque organ-art.

27. The keyboards of the west-end organ in the *Benedictine Abbey Church of Weingarten* (Germany), made by J. Gabler between 1737 and 1750. The ivory stop-knobs and labels, carving and veneering are clearly those of an exceptionally sumptuous organ; the console, being detached, gave the organist a view over both the gallery and the church as a whole, but inevitably led to a heavy action and to a remoteness of sound for the player himself. Of the keyboards themselves, the tall sharps may have been characteristic of Swabian organs, but the scored lines of the naturals and the long veneered strips between the manuals are more typical of harpsichord keyboards made by builders brought up in this or neighbouring areas of Europe, in particular Kirkman and Shudi. See p. 147ff.

28. One of the two quire organs of the *Abbey Church of Muri* (Switzerland), made in 1743–4 by V. F. Bossard (restored by Metzler, 1961–2). The single-manual instrument has a somewhat old-fashioned simplicity both in appearance and in sound; in such quire organs there was usually no attempt made to compete with the main west-end organ, and the player had at his disposal only a few choruses (from soft to loud) and a few colours on the one manual (including flutes, reeds, Gamba and Tierce). See p. 209.

29. The organ at the end of the quire in the church of *Tiradentes, Matriz*
(Brazil). Such eighteenth-century Spanish baroque organs are still often to be
found in Mexico and a few South American areas, usually derelict. At Tiradentes, there were probably once horizontal reeds protruding from one or
other moulding of the impost-cornice.

30. The west-end organ of the *Benedictine Abbey Church of Melk* (Austria), made in 1731–2 by G. Sonnholz. The divided cases held the *Hauptwerk* and pedal. These cases are still relatively classical at Melk, with overhanging sides and a more or less free-standing structure; in later designs they became more plastic, more freely moulded around the wind or across the corners, fixed against the walls, each unit asymmetrical in itself. The statuary is characteristically restless, as if the baroque *putti* and angels were taking part in the music. See p. 146.

31. House organ at *Newby Hall* (England), designed by Robert Adam in
c. 1775. The furniture aspect of such English chamber organs was that on
which most care was lavished; the instrument itself would be a conventional
single-manual usually without pedals and without much musical potential
beyond that given by a small-scaled chorus, a flute or two and (at most) a
tiny Swellbox.

32. The west-end organ of the *Marienkirche, Rostock* (Germany), made in 1766–70 by P. Schmidt. The monumental appearance of the whole, and the unpleasant detail of the pipe rows, swinging lines and heavy substructure, was no doubt a reflection of the widespread attempts at that period to make heavy, new designs both original and free from baroque frivolity. But this organ case, typically showing little if anything of the chest-levels or *Werke*, was built after the Prince's Gallery below (1749–51) and must have been designed as a kind of ceremonial superstructure to it. See p. 153.

33. Interior view of the small organ at *Avila* (Spain), made in *c.* 1780. The somewhat disorganized chest-levels are typical of an Iberian baroque organ: pipes in different groups scattered within the organ case, many speaking by means of conduits. Notice the damaged pipe tops, the profusion of conical pipes, the wide wooden pipes of the pedals, the rows of vertical reeds (rear centre), and the spaciousness of the whole. See pp. 122–4.

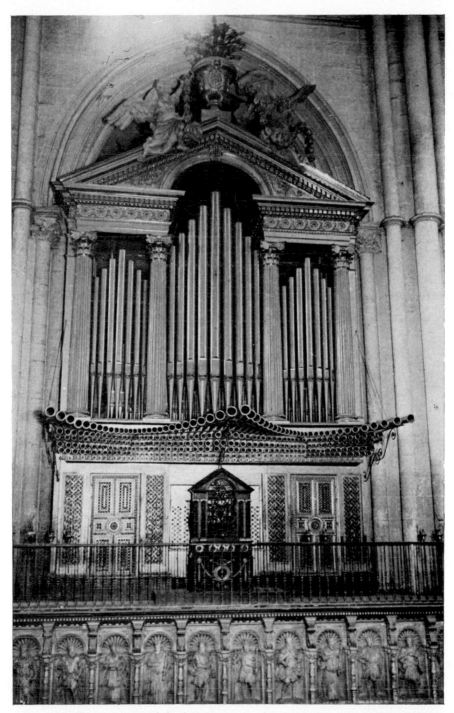

34, 35, 36. Three views of the late baroque quire organ on the Epistle (south)
side of *Toledo Cathedral* (Spain), made in 1796–7 by J. Verdalonga: the main
façade to the quire (with nine ranks of horizontal reeds and regals), the façade
to the side aisle, and the keyboards (with two rows of pedal-buttons and knee-
levers for changing stops). The classical restraint of the case design was no
continued

doubt a reaction to the older baroque cases of such organs; but it also resembles the pre-baroque organ made by members of the Netherlandish family Brebos at El Escorial in *c.* 1585. In effect, each of the façades had its own manual; but neither showed the presence of a large Swell department complete with reeds
continued

in a second Swellbox. The manuals are, from top to bottom: main façade organ, rear façade organ, Swell. No other Iberian organ had quite this arrangement, for each of the large instruments was unique. See pp. 122–5.

37. The organ of the village church of *Siesby* (Schleswig), made in 1819 by
J. Marcussen; view of the organ as it was before 1969. Though particularly
notable for its extension system (see p. 162), the organ was also entirely
typical of such small altar-organs in northern Europe, in which behind the
pious simplicity of the whole baroque elements in the details can still be
discerned: compare the side towers, the flats, the entablatures and the fretwork
above the pipes with Grosshartmannsdorf (Plate 25).

38. The 'west-end' organ in *Utrecht Cathedral* (Holland), made in 1826–31 by
Bätz & Co. Like some other large churches in northern Europe, Utrecht
Cathedral had had its original size reduced and shape altered by means of a
wall across one arm of the building; a neo-gothic organ was later built on to
this wall in the period when 'gothick' meant the application of unrealistic
gothic elements (such as the impossibly narrow case-pipes in the Chair Organ)
to classical shapes quite alien to the genuine gothic designs of the fifteenth
century, some of which were then found in or near Utrecht. The angled
gallery-front and large Chair Organ, however, show Bätz to have had no wish
to break with tradition. See p. 155.

39, 40. The west-end organ of the Unitarian Society, Newburyport, Massachusetts (built by Joseph Alley, 1834, much altered but finally rebuilt with tracker action by the Andover Organ Company, 1975) and the quire organ of Grace Episcopal Church, San Francisco (built by James Treat, 1894, to the designs of Henry Vaughan). Almost any pair of organs from almost any country in which Protestant churches were an active force during the nineteenth century would show a similar change of taste: from a simple, classically designed church in which the organ is placed free-standing in the west-end gallery to a neo-gothick aisled and/or cruciform church in which the organ crouches under one or more arches, very likely on or near floor-level and certainly near the altar by then contained in every church. Both kinds of organ needed actions other than mechanical only when they were scattered over a large area or when 'liturgical demands' new at the period required the organist to be removed from the chests. The respectively classical (or late baroque) and gothick details of the cases may be derived from older organs but are as likely to owe their origin to the books of designs common during the century. By these means, gothick details in particular were disseminated unfeelingly, grafted on by architects for their clients, to neither of whose cultures were such details natural or native.

41. The organ of *La Madeleine, Paris* (France), completed by Cavaillé-Coll in 1846. The unique classical shape of the church itself influenced the organ design in which such elements as the pillars and pilasters recall the organ case engraved in Kircher's *Musurgia universalis* (Rome, 1650). The detached console became customary for such organs, as did the massive façade giving little idea of the number or level of the chests within. Clearly such designs could be used for the new music halls and town halls.

42. The organ of *St. Luke's Hospital Chapel, New York City* (U.S.A.), made by G. Hutchings in 1896. This simple but interesting design must owe its details of carving and tall pipe-flats to French influence, but the total ensemble suggests an English college chapel organ of the same period, an organ for which one or other remote key-action would be necessary.

43. The organ on the north side of the quire of *Truro Cathedral* (England), made by H. Willis for the new gothic cathedral of J. L. Pearson (built over the period 1880–1910). The free pipework, without case but looking as though it has been arranged to have one put around it, is unusual in England; one of the neo-gothic re-creations by Pugin might have suited Pearson's Early English gothic copy more closely. Father Willis's idea of using the triforium gallery of an English cathedral as open chambers in which parts of the organ could be scattered at will and unified by some remote key-action became common in the late nineteenth and twentieth centuries and still shows little sign of being discarded. See p. 175ff.

44. The Malmö museum organ, once in *St. Peter, Malmö* (Sweden). The Great Organ has been dated *c.* 1490 and 1511; but the Chair Organ was added by Frobenius in 1941, signalling the new and more advanced ideals of organ restoration or renovation at that period. Such museum-organs gave a new meaning to the term 'secular organs', which had been associated with the more advanced ideas for some time, since they were not compelled by liturgical demands to a compromise electicism. The straight, simple lines were such as to be highly influential in the new neo-classical organs of the post-war years. See p. 200.

45. The quire organ of the *Grundtvigskirke, Copenhagen* (Denmark), made by Marcussen in 1940. The imaginative neo-gothic church was able to return to old ideals in which a quire organ placed near the altar could have a purely classical tonal design. Only the Scandinavian builders were producing such cases by 1945. See p. 199.

46. The west-end organ of the post-war octagonal church *Kaiser-Wilhelm-Gedächtniskirche in West Berlin*. The simple geometric plan of the church and its decorative motifs (each wall of glass a square divided into smaller squares) is suitably mirrored in the simple geometric elevation and details of the organ: a matching of organ and church rare for the last half century. The 64-stop instrument was built in 1962 by Karl Schuke and has four manuals (*Hw, Pos, Bw, Swell*). Comparably inventive designs in Scandinavia tend to be less straight-sided and square in detail, but in both *Orgelbewegung* traditions the spacious choir and orchestral gallery is usual. See p. 197.

47. The organ of *Pomona College, Claremont, California* (U.S.A.), made in 1972 by R. von Beckerath. Such designs are very typical of the late *Orgelbewegung* designs in Germany: simple box-like components with straight lines and a severe geometricism. The *Brustwerk*-Swell is also typical, being larger than a true *Brustwerk* but without the special reed and acoustical qualities of an English Victorian Swell. Such organs were made in their hundreds by many West German firms and sent to all parts of the world over the last quarter century; East German equivalents would be sent to a few cities in the socialist world, from Berlin to Novosibirsk. See p. 196ff.

48, 49. The eighteenth-century keyboards of the 'Couperin Organ' of *Saint-Gervais, Paris* (before 1922, when the pedals were replaced by a German pedal board) and those of the 'Couperin Organ' in the Free University of Amsterdam, completed in 1973 by J.-G. Koenig. The making again of French pedal boards is characteristic of the move towards greater historical authenticity in specialized new organs, as are the short finger-keys, the placing of stop-knobs and the overall design of such consoles set into the face of the organ (*claviers en fenêtre*). However, it should be noticed that the keyboards of the new organ overhang the pedals farther than do those of the old organ, thus facilitating an anachronistic *legato* playing. See pp. 209–10.

50. The organ of the *Reformed Church, Netstal* (Switzerland), built in 1964 by Metzler & Söhne. Historical elements in the *Werkprinzip* design are the classical arrangement of main organ, pedal towers and Chair Organ, the over-hanging sides of the main organ (with *Brustwerk* between), the lively cornice levels, the inverted pipes, and the lines of the pipe shades mirroring the lines of the pipe mouths. Less historical and more individualistically modern are the emphasis on straight lines (in all the planes), the design of the pipe shades and their covering of the pipe tops (compare Plate 16, for example), the folding doors of the *Brustwerk*, the pedal towers standing back from the gallery front, the simplistic lines of the Chair Organ and the absence of carving (particularly on the over-thin cornices and frames). See also p. 209.

51. John Brombaugh's Op. 16, a two-manual organ for *Grace Episcopal Church, Ellensburg, Washington*, 1974 (set up temporarily in Trinity Episcopal Cathedral, Cleveland, Ohio). The return to historical detail is more consistent than in Netstal (Plate 50), although its modernity is shown by such details as the polished panels or the long keyboards and hence the overall width. Despite such 'compromises', it is difficult to see how the essential principles of such designs—the structure allowing suspended action, the overhanging sides, the shallowness of the whole, the details of the façade arrangement—could ever be bettered, whatever the size of the organ.